The Crime of Nationalism

The Crime of Nationalism

BRITAIN, PALESTINE, AND
NATION-BUILDING ON THE FRINGE OF EMPIRE

Matthew Kraig Kelly

UNIVERSITY OF CALIFORNIA PRESS

University of California Press, one of the most distinguished university presses in the United States, enriches lives around the world by advancing scholarship in the humanities, social sciences, and natural sciences. Its activities are supported by the UC Press Foundation and by philanthropic contributions from individuals and institutions. For more information, visit www.ucpress.edu.

University of California Press
Oakland, California

Library of Congress Cataloging-in-Publication Data

Names: Kelly, Matthew Kraig, author.
Title: The crime of nationalism : Britain, Palestine, and nation-building on the fringe of empire / Matthew Kraig Kelly.
Description: Oakland, California : University of California Press, [2017] | Includes bibliographical references and index.
Identifiers: LCCN 2017016676 (print) | LCCN 2017019351 (ebook) | ISBN 9780520965256 (ebook) | ISBN 9780520291485 (cloth : alk. paper) | ISBN 9780520291492 (pbk. : alk. paper)
Subjects: LCSH: Palestine—History—Arab rebellion, 1936-1939. | Palestine—History—1917-1948. | Great Britain—Foreign relations—Palestine. | Palestine—Foreign relations—Great Britain. | Palestine—Politics and government—1917-1948. | Violence—Palestine—History.
Classification: LCC DS126 (ebook) | LCC DS126 .K39 2017 (print) | DDC 956.94/04—dc23
LC record available at https://lccn.loc.gov/2017016676

Manufactured in the United States of America

26 25 24 23 22 21 20 19 18 17
10 9 8 7 6 5 4 3 2 1

For my parents, Kraig and Dolores Kelly
In memory of David Batza

CONTENTS

ACKNOWLEDGMENTS

I cannot put into words my gratitude for the many people who made this book possible, but I will try. Above all, I want to thank my family. My wife, Tammie, traveled with me to England and to Israel during the research phase of the book. To help support me, she waited tables in London, and taught dance workshops all over England, Israel, the Netherlands and France. And she did it all without complaint. My parents, Kraig and Dolores Kelly, were unfailing in their support, both moral and material, through my years in graduate school and during the research and writing phases of the book. My uncle and dear friend, the great Dr. Gary Lynch, carefully read and commented on various drafts of the manuscript. He also saved this project from the scrapheap of books-to-be by stepping in with financial support on more than one occasion. More generally, "UG" has been a source of intellectual and spiritual inspiration to me for many years. I have to thank a number of friends who happen also to be first-rate scholars and therefore readers. These include my lifelong friend Tommy Givens, and two of my most cherished confidantes, Fredrik Meiton and Adam Talib. Tom offered invaluable advice early in the writing process, and has been a source of personal strength for as long as I have known him. Fred and Adam went well beyond the call of duty in closely vetting the manuscript and offering me indispensable historical, linguistic, and stylistic advice. The book would never have seen the light of day without the support of James Gelvin. I am profoundly thankful for his years of institutional, intellectual, and moral support. It is fitting that he gave me the book title. In addition to Gelvin's, I am fortunate to have received the learned input of the other three members of my dissertation committee, David N. Myers, Gabriel Piterberg, and Michael Mann. As important, my good friends Gaby Goldstein and Tony Peterson, as well as Nehad Khader,

Nadia Naqib, Lexi Newman, Maia Tabet, and Natasha Wheatley were all kind enough to offer many thoughtful comments on early drafts of the manuscript. Other fine scholars who took the time to correspond with me include Hillel Cohen, Kate Halls (a tremendous help), Joshua Landis, Benny Morris, Sami Moubayed, Jacob Norris, Rafi Stern, Stephen Wagner, and Alex Winder. I also benefitted from the research support of Mansour al-Sheikh, Walter Lorenz and Alya al-Marakby, all of whom helped get this project over the hump by being professional, punctual, and just good. Colin Mackie gave generously of his time to help me nail down certain opaque institutional developments in the Foreign Office in 1938. Ami Ayalon and Mustafa Kabha, too, offered me valuable research advice. The great Jason Pickersgill once again brought a project of mine to visual fruition by imagining what I would, but only he could. At the institutional level, I am indebted to the staffs of UCLA's History Department and Young Research Library, the National Archives and Imperial War Museum in London, the Middle East Centre at Oxford, the Central Zionist and Israel State Archives in Jerusalem, and the Haganah Archives in Tel Aviv. I am likewise indebted to the Library of Congress, Punch Ltd., and Getty Images. Finally, I would like to thank the University of California Press, and especially Niels Hooper and Bradley Depew, for believing in and supporting this project.

Introduction

ON 21 JUNE 1936, Muhammad Hajj Husayn Qaʿdan and Ahmad Muhammad Sulayman were traveling from their village of Dayr al-Ghusun southeast along the hilly terrain to Balʿa, near Tulkarm. The path of their journey ran through an area that the British, who then governed Palestine, regarded as a "trouble spot." The British dubbed the territory between Jenin, Nablus, and Tulkarm the "triangle of terror" in reference to its residents' habit of firing on police and soldiers. But the triangle was just one of several problem areas for the British. Across Palestine, His Majesty's security forces had been encountering armed resistance for the better part of June 1936, and the Arab population at large had, since April, been observing a strike against British policy in the country. While the two villagers likely sympathized with the strike and perhaps with the armed attacks, on 21 June, they went simply in search of water for their cattle. Nevertheless, when a British pilot monitoring the area caught sight of the men on the hills, he fired on them, prompting them to take shelter in a nearby cave. The pilot then radioed the pair's location to British soldiers in the vicinity, a number of whom shortly arrived on the scene. One of them, a Sergeant Sills, approached the mouth of the cave and fired into it without warning. The villagers—who, in keeping with custom, bore their own arms—fired back, fatally wounding Sills in the head and chest.[1]

The case of Muhammad Hajj Husayn Qaʿdan and Ahmad Muhammad Sulayman ultimately reached the supreme court of Palestine on appeal, after a lower court sentenced both men to death. The high court denied none of the details noted above, but nevertheless rejected the right of the two villagers to defend themselves. On the contrary, the court asserted: "Yet another point was raised [by the appellants' lawyer], namely that it was the natural reaction for the appellants to shoot back when fired upon. This astounding theory, which allows men to retaliate when either police or military are doing their duty, is unknown to me."[2] The court seemed to suggest that the British, by virtue of their constituting the state in Palestine, behaved legally by definition, and that those resisting them were therefore criminals by definition. Palestinian rebels did not reject this logic, but rather adapted it. Indeed, they took up arms in its name.

Not initially, though. The British had occupied Palestine since the end of the First World War, and their presence there had been met with a decade and a half campaign of Arab protest. British policy in Palestine centered on open-ended Jewish immigration and land purchases, with the stated goal of establishing a "Jewish National Home." Arab protest against this policy was mostly peaceful, though occasionally violent. In either case, it was ineffectual. And that failure fed the popular frustration that would boil over into open rebellion in mid-1936. The Palestinian Great Revolt lasted from 1936 to 1939. It is the temporal focus of this book.

As the cave anecdote suggests, the book has a thematic focus as well. It seeks to understand how violence is coded and construed, both by historical actors and by the historians thinking about those actors. When is violence visible, and when is it invisible? When does it emerge as the primary explanation for a given historical episode, and when does it appear incidental to that episode? As the book demonstrates, the answers to these questions lie in the interplay of the mutually constitutive discursive formations of "nation" and "crime." I use the term "crimino-national" to refer to this area of analytic focus.

In the age of nationalism, the nation names the criminal. In so doing, the nation claims for itself the prerogatives of violence, from incarceration to killing, while at the same time disinheriting the criminal of these prerogatives. Looked at from the other end, violent crime claims for itself rights normally associated with the nation-state: to control the bodies of others, up to and including the point of death. It is therefore imperative that the nation-state police the boundary between itself and the criminal, such that any criminal effort to dissolve that boundary is resoundingly repudiated. It is for this reason that coercion lies at the heart of so many definitions of the modern state, such as Ernest Gellner's, which characterizes the state as "that institution or set of institutions specifically concerned with the enforcement of order."[3] Before enforcing order, the state must name order, and conversely disorder. The state, acting in the name of the nation, cannot countenance any criminal enterprise claiming to represent not disorder, but an alternative order. And this is exactly what modern revolutionary movements, acting in the name of their own nations, have done. The Palestinian rebels are a case in point.

Although less so than other interwar insurgencies, the revolt of 1936–39 is well studied. It has given birth to a literature that offers a range of theoretical perspectives on both its origin and its outcome. One useful way of construing this theoretical spectrum is by reference to the archival materials on which studies of the revolt have drawn: the reports, correspondence, and memoirs of British officials in London and Jerusalem; those of the Jewish Agency and the Haganah; and the memoirs and diaries of Palestinian nationalists, to name the most salient sources. Some studies have taken on board one or another of the theoretical perspectives implicit in these materials, and have produced what we might think of as chronicles of the rebellion. Such chronicles—many of them eminently readable—rehearse a series of facts, highlighting watersheds such as the revolt's outbreak in April 1936, its cessation in October of that year, its recommencement in September 1937, and its collapse in 1939.

Chronicles more sensitive to the Jewish experience of the revolt emphasize, additionally, the role of Arab-on-Arab violence and intimidation in maintaining the strike and the rebellion, and may highlight Arab atrocities against Jews, such as the murderous assaults on Safed in August 1936 and Tiberias in October 1938. They also tend to reproduce the perspective of Zionist intelligence on the rebel movement and its personalities, and that of the Jewish Agency on British officials in Palestine.[4] Chronicles more concerned with representing the Arab experience of the revolt may call attention to episodes such as the collisions between British soldiers and Arab rebels at the pivotal Battles of Bal'a (near Tulkarm) and Beit Imrin (near Nablus) in September 1936, or at the Battle of al-Yamun (near Jenin) in November 1937. They are also apt to offer more sympathetic and subtle portraits of the rebel commanders and sub-commanders, and of the subversive institutions, such as the rebel courts, that proliferated across Palestine during the revolt's second phase.[5] Whatever the perspectives of these different studies, all of them absorb not only facts but also narratives from the sources upon which they draw. These narratives preordain certain events, persons, and developments as critical for understanding the rebellion, and in that way predetermine the basic character of the studies that assimilate them.

Then there are those histories of the Great Revolt that hew more conscientiously to a given theoretical perspective. These typically engage more critically and even skeptically with the archival materials relating to the rebellion. Over time, the general trajectory of these works has been away from top-down analyses of the rebellion and toward bottom-up analyses. Where the first emphasize elite political institutions and personalities as the driving forces of the rebellion, the second offer something closer to "peoples' histories" or "histories from below," which seek to reinstate the agency of peasants, proletarians, and other "subalterns" as decisive actors in the revolt's unfolding.[6]

The present book offers a crimino-national analysis of the rebellion, focusing on the under-explored area of overlap between the criminological and the nationalist dimensions of British imperial discourse in Palestine. British and Zionist discussions of the revolt both consistently represented it as a criminal affair only masquerading as a national uprising. This is the primary framing of the rebellion that one encounters in the British and Zionist archives. And it is therefore the framing that most chronicles of the rebellion reproduce, either wholly or in substantial part. But, as we will see, even the more theoretically sophisticated histories of 1936–39 have tended, often unwittingly, to reproduce the British and Zionist crimino-national framing of the revolt. Although the archives themselves contain ample evidence of the speciousness of this framing, the British and Zionist sources contain an abiding crimino-national narrative that mutes and marginalizes this evidence. Researchers who are less than vigilant in deconstructing this narrative therefore often reproduce, rather than remedy, these archival lacunae.

Consider the following example. The Great Revolt began as a largely peaceful general strike. With time, however, it grew violent. According to the standard narrative, the British initially followed a "policy of no repression," in Yehoshua Porath's phrase, and only belatedly resorted to violence in response to the increasingly violent tactics of the rebels. Yet, as part one of this book demonstrates, the "no repression" thesis is false. British repression in Palestine was rampant in 1936, and it got underway much earlier than most studies suggest.

Why have so many histories of the revolt gotten this point wrong? Because they have absorbed the depiction of 1936 that is latent in the British and Zionist archival materials. These materials include a vast number of situation reports and day-to-day telegraphic exchanges among and between officials in Jerusalem and London, and a handful of more detailed reports that are some of the earliest histories of the revolt. They contain multiple references to British violence, but the references are dispersed across a mass of material relating to other topics, and thus no narrative of British brutality emerges from them.

Many chronicles of 1936, for example, cite the summary report of R. E. C. Peirse, the British military commander in Palestine, but neglect to note the report's most damning disclosures.[7] These concerned the "village searches" that British security forces began conducting throughout the country in May 1936. The objects of these searches were supposed to have been weapons and wanted men, but Peirse acknowledged that the searches' real purpose was "punitive." He explained that on the pretext of "search," British police and soldiers were "actually" employing "Turkish methods" against the villagers. The point of these methods was to offer the villagers a taste of British terror, lest they became enamored of, or intimidated by, the armed bands then form-ing in the hills.[8] Peirse further divulged that the "Turkish methods" were sufficiently pervasive to cause "a grave crisis" within the Palestine police, whose Arab section nearly defected *en masse* in protest against the "searches."

All of this occurred in May and early June 1936. British repression only escalated with the spread of the rebellion thereafter. The April–October 1936 phase of the revolt was thus hardly a period of "no repression." The problem for researchers has been that Peirse did not do them the favor of underscoring the consequence of such disclosures. On the contrary, he made them only in passing, as though they were incidental to his larger narrative: the "no repres-sion" narrative. Similarly, significant revelations crop up elsewhere in the archival record, and in the same perfunctory fashion. For example, in discuss-ing the "considerable [Arab] resentment and criticism" of British repression in the villages, the deputy inspector general of police noted in a report of 23 June 1936 that "it would not appear that up to the present more than a small pro-portion of the villagers have taken arms against the forces of Government."[9]

To summarize, then, we have the military commander in Palestine acknowledging that in May 1936, British brutality against Palestinian villag-ers was pervasive to the point of causing a near-mutiny among Arab police-men. Additionally, we have the deputy inspector general of police conceding that, as of a month later, few of these villagers had attacked British security forces. When knit together, these and related facts suggest a narrative that runs counter to that found in the British and Zionist archives and parallel to that found in the Arabic sources. According to this narrative, British repres-sion in 1936 preceded and provoked widespread militant activity among the Palestinian population, not the other way around. British violence, that is, was a basic cause of the revolt, not a reluctant reaction to it.

By contrast, the logic of British imperial discourse in Palestine dictated that the rebellion be framed as an unprovoked outbreak of crime, to which London was merely responding. Palestinian militants, activists, and spokes-persons adapted, rather than rejected, this "crime wave" framing of the insurgency. In particular, they accepted its two core premises: first, that violence was justified when directed against criminals; and second, that peoples or nations were singularly competent to name the criminal. For the Palestinians, it followed not that the British nation was suppressing a crime wave in Palestine, but rather that the Palestinian nation was entitled to violently expel the British, whom they had rightly designated as criminals. Regardless of its application, in agreeing to this discursive framework, the Palestinians and the British reflected the prevalent understanding of nationalism as coded in international law and otherwise attested to in the international community of the interwar years. They thus committed themselves to demonstrating their own national and the other's criminal credentials.

This crimino-national discourse matters historically. Our appreciation of it enables us to approach the interwar archives with a deconstructive agenda that brings new facts to light. In the case of 1936–39, there are two groups of such facts. The first pertains to the archival, and by extension historiographical, absence of the British from key causal junctures of the rebellion, such as the watersheds noted above: the rebellion's outbreak, its temporary cessation, its recommencement, and its collapse. The village searches relate to the first of these. When we peer into the archive, we do not see the searches; we see the British seeing the searches. From their vantage point, the searches maintained law and order. Deconstructing that vantage point, we learn that the searches contributed to the breakdown of law and order. We learn, in other words, that the British were present at—that is, causally implicated in—the revolt's inception. The archival presentation of the village searches is but one instance of the "absence" phenomenon. Part one of the book examines other instances. The second group of facts that a crimino-national approach brings to light concerns the positive quality of the rebellion. Much of the scholarship on the rebellion presents it negatively, as an anti-British and anti-Zionist enterprise. No doubt it was these things, but it was also a constructive enterprise centered on state-building. By placing the criminological consideration of the Palestinian national movement at the center of our concerns, we become alert to the empirical indices of this fact, as part two of the book demonstrates.

Put briefly, the British and Zionist criminological framing of Palestinian nationalism succeeded in portraying a national rebellion as a crime wave only by cropping the British out of the picture. This is not to suggest that the archive contains no mention of British actions in 1936–39. It is rather to observe that the archive presents British behavior as reactive and causally secondary, while it presents Palestinian behavior as formative and causally primary. In this sense, at every critical moment of the archival presentation of the rebellion, the British go missing from their own story. This book returns them to their rightful place.

A word is in order with regard to the book's arrangement. The reader of chapter one can be forgiven if she puts the book down thinking that its argument goes as follows. The British were afflicted in Palestine by a kind of tunnel vision, which prevented them from apprehending their own causal implication in the disturbances they were attempting to manage. Their tendency to portray the rebellion as a criminal affair was a function of this tunnel vision. To have apprehended their own role in bringing about the revolt would have been to understand the revolt's nationalist character, something beyond the capacity of the imperial mind.

This understanding is a simplification, as the reader careful enough to carry it forward into subsequent chapters will learn. Chapters two and beyond present a range of Arab, British, and Jewish voices, and those voices suggest a diversity of views on the rebellion. For example, some British officials failed even to consider the possibility that His Majesty was suppressing not a crime wave but a national revolt in Palestine. By contrast, others were alert not only to the possibility but to the reality of this scenario. Many fell somewhere in between. This range of perspectives was evident not only in the voices of British civilian officials but also in those of British policemen, soldiers, journalists, politicians and dissidents. The same diversity characterized Zionist opinion. But if the British and the Zionists did sometimes apprehend their own causal implication in the rebellion, why should we preoccupy ourselves with a crimino-national discourse that seemingly excludes this possibility?

The answer is that the discourse elaborated in chapter one was a form of political logic, not a deterministic psychology. The people perpetuating this discourse did so with varying degrees of awareness. Some knew that they were framing the rebellion in a manner that served British imperialism and Zionism more than it did the facts. Others were true believers. Most were a mix of the two. But nearly all participated in the criminalization of Palestinian nationalism. This book is a history of that criminalization.

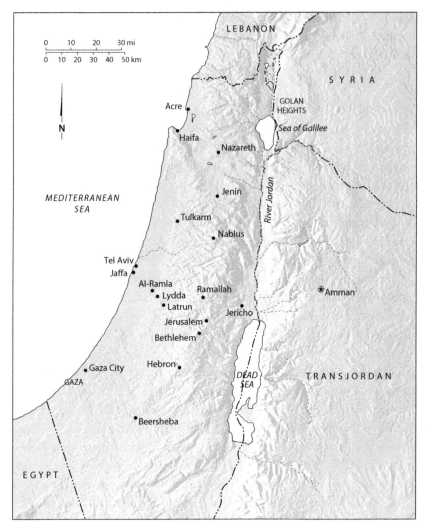

MAP I

PART ONE

April–October 1936

ONE

British Causal Primacy and the Origins of the Palestinian Great Revolt

19 APRIL 1936 WAS A SUNDAY, the first day of the Jewish week. Jewish and Arab merchants in Palestine began raising the metal shutters on their shops early that morning, as was their habit. Although tension between the two communities had been escalating over the preceding days, weeks, and months, it did little to slow the routine of their commercial interactions in the Old City of Jerusalem, where Jewish and Arab quarters were nestled together and the locals knew each other by name. Pinhas Zuckerman was therefore likely familiar with the Arab who remarked to another customer in his shop that morning, "It has begun. You [Jews] already killed two Arabs."[1] The man referred to a double-homicide of two days prior in Petah Tikvah. At the same moment, a curiously similar story was spreading out west, in Jaffa, according to which Jews in neighboring Tel Aviv had murdered two Arabs. Unlike the Petah Tikvah story, however, this one was false.

Because the ordinary person was in no position to verify such gossip, the emotional climate into which it drifted often determined whether it withered on the vine or "blossomed" into violence. Politically hot periods virtually yearned for the spark of an ominous rumor. Seven years earlier, for example, when a sensational report of rioting in Jerusalem reached Jaffa, Arab mobs there raped, tortured and hacked to death members of the Jewish community.[2] The atmosphere was similarly tense in the days before 19 April 1936. On 18 April, an Arab political activist noted in his diary that "various rumors" about Jewish violence were "spreading like wildfire," producing "outrage" among Palestine's Arabs.[3] At such times, gruesome episodes like those of 1929 lingered in local Jewish memory. Beneath the *shaloms* and *salams* Jews daily exchanged with their Arab neighbors, there stirred the unsettling awareness that such greetings of "peace" were prayers, not promises.

Arabs, meanwhile, harbored their own anxieties. A few days before the portentous tidings overheard in Zuckerman's store, some Arab highwaymen preying on passengers between Nablus and Tulkarm gunned down three Jews.[4] Jews retaliated the next day against Arabs in Tel Aviv and were presumed (correctly) by British authorities to be responsible for the Petah Tikvah homicides twenty-four hours later.[5] On the latter day, 17 April, some of the mourners departing the funeral of a victim of the Arab highwaymen proceeded from Tel Aviv towards Jaffa "with unlawful intent," according to the written testimony of the city's assistant superintendent of police.[6] When the mourners reached Jaffa, British police turned them away with baton charges. Back in Tel Aviv, a throng of Jews outside the Cinema Ophir battered an Arab gharry-driver named 'Abd al-Rashid Hasan, and several others trashed the shop of Ibrahim 'Ali Hatrieh.[7] A cascade of violence ensued. According to a British report, on that single day, "Cases of assault [against Arabs] took place in Herzl Street, ha-Yarkon Street, Allenby Road near the General Post Office, outside the Cinema Moghraby and at the seashore bus terminus."[8]

Despite these attacks, police station diaries recorded no Arab reprisals against Jews in Jaffa on either the 17th or the following day.[9] But by Sunday, 19 April, Arabs in Jaffa were prepared to believe the worst upon hearing the rumor begun early that morning regarding their two countrymen.[10] And having gathered for a 9 A.M. parade only to have the municipal authorities deny their permit request, they were already out in force (and frustrated) when the story of the murders started spreading. Shortly after 10 A.M., Arabs throughout the city began harassing Jews, who fled in panic to the bus station opposite the district police headquarters, whence they escaped on buses to Tel Aviv. A Jewish factory owner in the city shuttered his building as Arabs gathered outside. Several Jews emerged from the crowd, pleading with him for protection. One woman uttered fearfully, "I am a widow!"[11] In the teeming town square, a party of Arabs circulating among the mob set upon a Jew with knives, leaving his gored corpse within a hundred yards of the police station. Two and a half miles across town, a second group of Arabs bludgeoned a Jew to death in the vicinity of the Hasan Bey mosque.[12] Jewish counterattacks in Tel Aviv soon followed, and as vehicles carrying wounded Arabs pulled into the Manshiya quarter of Jaffa, Arab protestors hurled stones at the police, who in turn charged at them with batons.[13] By the following day, fourteen Jews and two Arabs lay lifeless in their families' arms.[14] Although no one knew it, the Palestinian Great Revolt had begun.

FIGURE 1. A Jewish family departing a "danger zone" in the Jaffa-Tel Aviv area, summer 1936. (Library of Congress)

BACKGROUND OF THE REBELLION

Certain questions press upon us in considering these and subsequent events. The most obvious concerns the larger context in which they transpired. In that regard, two developments in particular—both of which transformed Jewish and Arab politics in 1930s Palestine—require our attention. The first development pertained to the Zionist labor movement, which by the early 1930s constituted the institutional heart of the Jewish community in Palestine (henceforth: the Yishuv) in the form of the Jewish Agency and its filiations.[15] This movement's strategy of forging an Arab-Jewish workers' alliance so as to divide Arab proletarians against their effendi betters fizzled out in the 1930s. The sobering fact, Zionist leaders realized, was that class loyalty was no match for national loyalty among the Arabs.[16] As if relations between the two communities were not sufficiently strained, Arab and Jewish laborers would now compete rather than cooperate.

The second development concerned the efficacy of Arab nonviolent protest against the ongoing British implementation of the Balfour Declaration of 1917.

Many in the mandate believed that the "national home" His Majesty had famously pledged to prop up in Palestine was a nation-state in all but name. And while Jews anticipated it with joy, Arabs did so with dread. By the 1930s, more than a decade of peaceful Arab attempts to bring down Balfour had achieved nothing. The delegations to Britain, the protests in Palestine, the conferences across the region—all diplomatic routes reached a dead end in London.[17] When not ignoring Arab spokespersons, British officials would indulge them in dialogue, promise to consider their concerns carefully, and then carry on as before. On occasions when Arab protest veered into violence, the British would dispatch commissions of inquiry to Palestine. None of the commissions' recommendations included reneging on the Balfour Declaration, however, and any that implied Balfour's repudiation London effectively disregarded.[18] Noncooperation and nonviolent demonstrations proved equally unavailing, a circumstance so acidic to Arab political organizing that between 1923—when the British mandate for Palestine became official—and 1928, it ground to a virtual halt.[19] Nonviolence was futile, and by the 1930s, everyone knew it.

Of course, violence, too, had proven useless. Neither the Nebi Musa disturbances of April 1920 nor the Jaffa upheavals of May 1921 nor the Wailing Wall riots of August 1929 had produced any change in British policy in Palestine. But these local failings were belied by developments in the broader region, where Arab "lawlessness" in Egypt and Iraq (and in the French mandate for Syria) had extracted concessions from the governments of those territories.[20] The British, it seemed obvious, only understood force. The Arab consensus on this point, coupled with the mainstream Zionist abandonment of a Jewish-Arab labor alliance, rendered incidents such as those in Jaffa and Tel Aviv in April 1936 all but inevitable. It also ensured that these incidents would be construed quite differently by Jews, Arabs, and Britons.

And thus arises a second question regarding the debacle of April 1936 and after: whose fault was it? The answer to that question was everywhere the same: the criminals'. The Jews and the British bestowed that appellation upon the Arabs, who repaid both in the same coin. The accusation shaped out two entities: the lawless and, negatively, the lawful. To name the criminal was to name the chaotic, the unruly, the uncivilized, and thereby tacitly to designate not merely a political order, but order itself: the political transmogrified into the metaphysical. The revolt forced the question of who had the right to use force. To answer this question was to divide politics into order and chaos, and in more earthly terms, the licit and the illicit. This was the crimino-national game played by all.

Two circumstances occasioned it. First, by the 1930s, British intelligence regarding Arab political activities had become anemic. The 1929 Wailing Wall riots exposed the incompetence of the two British intelligence agencies responsible for Palestine: the "I" section of the Royal Air Force (RAF) Headquarters and the Criminal Investigation Department (CID) of the Palestine police. In the riots' aftermath, the inspector-general of police in Ceylon, Herbert Dowbiggin, arrived in Palestine to review police procedures and recommend changes in the police force.[21] His report of April 1930 spotlighted the inability of the CID to acquire reliable information on the activities of Arab "agitators."[22] Dowbiggin's reforms, however, proved no remedy.[23] Half a decade later, the former commissioner of police in Calcutta, Sir Charles Tegart, and the former head of the security service in India, Sir David Petrie, wrote in another report that the Palestine CID had once again "failed in its primary function, the collection of intelligence regarding, and the investigation of, terrorist crime."[24] As important, by the time of the revolt, the mandatory lacked a functional counterespionage apparatus. In consequence, Arab rebels thoroughly penetrated British intelligence (see chapter four).[25]

This breakdown of British intelligence in Palestine brought about a second circumstance. Without reliable information on Arab political life, the British could do little to manage Arab political expression but smother it beneath a blanket of draconian laws. Thus did a creeping criminalization of Palestinian nationalism set in. Crime would feature in the revolt as surely as it had in prior outbreaks of violence in Palestine. By the 1930s, however, the British application of the criminal label to Arab protest was becoming conspicuously expansive. This was most apparent when Arab protests threatened the stability of the political order in the mandate. The criminal law ordinance that the British put in place after the 1929 Wailing Wall riots, for example, not only criminalized disparagement of the British flag but also broadened state powers of collective punishment. The government proclaimed these measures in the name of "public order," where the public in question did not recognize the legitimacy of the mandate.[26] Likewise, the December 1933 Prevention of Crime ordinance—enacted after rioting late that year—permitted district commissioners in Palestine to take preemptive legal action against suspected troublemakers based solely on the "known characters" of the individuals in question. The accused were allowed no legal appeal to this charge.[27] While this increase in repression ostensibly served as a stopgap for the lack of actionable intelligence that might have enabled the

British to preempt violent episodes, it actually exacerbated the original problem by further alienating the Arab population from the mandatory.

The British had sought to mitigate such alienation early on by modernizing the Palestinian landscape, a project that was intended to benefit both Arabs and Jews. London gridded the country in railroads, highways and telephone lines, for example, and invested heavily in Arab schools and hospitals.[28] Arab access to the highest echelons of power in Jerusalem and London was, moreover, unprecedented in the history of British imperial governance.[29] But it did not compare to that of the Yishuv. As Gideon Biger observes, British and Jewish development of Palestine amounted to a "joint structure," whereby the British would "lay the infrastructure" and the Jews "depend on it for the success of their settlement endeavours."[30]

Palestinian Arabs were acutely aware of this "joint structure," and of the insidious imperialist ideology that it manifested. As Fredrik Meiton and Jacob Norris have recently detailed, the self-consciously "constructive imperialism" London brought to bear in its Palestine mandate centered, in Meiton's words, on "the material foundation of modern society: waterways, roads, bridges, ports and airports, railway lines and electric grids."[31] And, as Norris notes, the primary architects of the Balfour Declaration "all subscribed to [the] vision of European Jews acting as the drivers of colonial development in Palestine."[32] It was just this ideological project that enabled the British to sustain the conceit that a Jewish state in Palestine would uplift the country's Arab inhabitants even as it buried their national aspirations.[33]

The British believed that the key to Arab Palestinian quiescence was economic growth, and that the key to economic growth was the Yishuv. Mandate officials thus blithely excluded Palestine's Arabs from basic decisions regarding the country's future, even as they conferred with the Zionists about the same matters. As Naomi Shepherd observes of Arthur Wauchope, the British high commissioner in Palestine in 1936: "No High Commissioner became so intimately involved with the Zionist leadership, repeatedly taking them into his confidence in a way he never did the Arab leaders."[34] More broadly, the mandate authorities did not recognize Arab political organizations, and more often than not simply ignored them.[35] This created a distance between British and Arab political institutions much greater than that between British and Jewish political institutions, and made the preservation of "law and order" in the mandate—that is, the maintenance of the politically asymmetrical state of affairs—increasingly dependent on force.

Up through the period of the revolt, for example, the British neglected to forge connections between rural political structures and the mandatory state, leaving village elders and headmen bereft of any legal standing. There were no legal specifications for the status of mukhtar (village headman), for instance, a situation that placed many villages at the mercy of one powerful family, and without democratic representation. British "point-men" at the village level were therefore often out of sync with their supposed constituencies.[36] This limited the extent to which the mandatory could reach down to the level of the individual in these areas, both in terms of observing his political behaviors and of shaping his political sensibilities; that is, in Foucauldian language, the extent to which the government could individuate the rural population.[37] As a result, when the British authorities in Palestine faced rural rebellion and resistance, their menu of strategic options was limited to one: brute force, typically in the form of collective punishment. Such tactics only served to further alienate the peasantry, many of whom, by the time of the revolt, had not actually seen a Briton in decades.[38]

This dilemma was by no means restricted to the countryside. In 1925, for example, High Commissioner Herbert Plumer sought to extend a redraft of the prior year's Collective Responsibility Ordinance to urban areas. And as the colonial secretary confessed, applying this ordinance to towns "could not fail to lend colour to any criticism that the reason why we have to resort to such special legislation is that our policy is so much detested that the Arabs cannot otherwise be made to acquiesce in our rule."[39]

The British criminalization of Palestinian nationalism was an ontological claim regarding order and chaos. But the British failure to individuate the Arab population of Palestine—to incorporate them into a disciplinary apparatus that would naturalize the "criminality" of violent political protest against the government and its policies—left unveiled the discursive machinery underlying this claim.[40] The Arabs knew that they were being cast as criminals, and were therefore positioned to identify such casting as a form of power, which might be turned back upon the British and the Zionists.

JEWISH, BRITISH, AND ARAB PERSPECTIVES ON THE STRIKE AND REVOLT OF APRIL AND MAY 1936

Jewish, British, and Arab perspectives on the strike and emergent violence of the weeks and months after 19 April came quickly to revolve around the question of crime: that is, who the real lawbreakers were in Palestine, and what entitlements accrued to their victims, especially with regard to violence.

Evidence of the Jewish perspective on the violence of April and May 1936 comes from the files of the Jewish Agency.[41] Its legal committee transcribed the statements of Jewish witnesses to the events of those distressing days, which culminated in the commencement of an Arab general strike on 22 April. A Jerusalem shop owner named Naftali Barukh interpreted the strike as a hollow attempt to establish the Arabs' credentials as a nation or "people." He regarded this faux collective as something much closer to a rabble, as evidenced by local Arabs' harassment of a merchant from Hebron—an incident, he noted deploringly, that prompted no police response.[42] Yisrael Ligal, the mukhtar of the Old City, claimed that even in the days after the strike's declaration, Arabs and Jews in Jerusalem continued to have cordial relations. Both groups attributed much of the trouble to British mischief, as opposed to one another. But as the Arab press published and Arab leaders repeated allegations against the Jews, the calm began to crack, especially among the youth. Lamented Ligal: "Every day I see young punks interfering with vendors at Jaffa Gate."[43] These "punks," according to one H. Eden, were part of a "terrorist" vanguard, to whom the bulk of the Arab population of Jerusalem was quietly opposed. He specified that "in normal times," this youth element "sits at the cards and acts as intermediaries between the various criminals."[44]

Such street-level testimonies dovetailed with the claims of the Jewish Agency leadership. The Agency's highest body was its executive, which consisted of the heads of its various departments. The most important of these was the political department, whose director was the Agency's primary institutional link to the mandatory government.[45] In 1936, this was Moshe Shertok. Shertok's family had immigrated to Palestine in 1906, when he was a boy. He went on to study law in Istanbul and to serve as a translator in the Ottoman army during the First World War. His involvement with the Zionist movement dated to his student days at the London School of Economics in 1922–24, and led to his appointment at the Jewish Agency in 1933.

On that fateful Sunday, 19 April 1936, Shertok met with John Hathorn Hall, the British chief secretary—along with the treasurer and the attorney general, one of the three permanent officers on the high commissioner's own executive council—at approximately 1 P.M. Shertok had learned of the killings in Jaffa two hours earlier. He remarked in a memorandum concerning the meeting, "My main purpose ... was to make sure that the tenor and contents of the first Official Communique on the disturbances should not be given the usual wrong twist."[46] The secretary disappointed him, refusing to back away from his description of the events in Jaffa as "clashes" rather than what Shertok insisted they were: "an attack by Arabs on Jews."[47] This led to a discussion of the attempt by Jewish mourners on 17 April to enter Jaffa, a "story" that Shertok "refused to believe."[48] He likewise downplayed the attacks on "some Arab gharry drivers" in Tel Aviv by attributing them to "foolish youths." Hall was unmoved. Dissatisfied, Shertok departed in hopes of a more fruitful dialogue with the chief secretary's superior, the top civilian official in Palestine, High Commissioner Arthur Wauchope.

Wauchope had been appointed British High Commissioner for Palestine and Transjordan in 1931, at the age of 57. An enthusiastic civilian administrator, he had spent most of his adult life in the military, where he had proven himself a physically courageous man. His experience in the Middle East dated back to the First World War, when he commanded a British brigade in Iraq and was wounded in battle. While Shertok sought an audience with Wauchope, it was Chaim Weizmann, a British Jew and the president of the World Zionist Organization (WZO), who secured one two days later, on 21 April.

Weizmann was a tireless advocate for Zionism, and had been involved in a number of the movement's watershed victories, including the Balfour Declaration of 1917 and the awarding of the mandate for Palestine to the British at San Remo in 1920. At the same time, Weizmann's credentials as a British patriot were unimpeachable. He had resided in England since 1904, when his work in chemistry earned him an appointment at the University of Manchester. It was in his capacity as a scientist that Weizmann would place the British government in his debt, and thereby elevate his standing as a Zionist representative to London. In the course of the First World War, Weizmann developed a method for extracting acetone from maize. The breakthrough allowed British arms manufacturers to replenish their stocks of acetone at a moment when they had fallen critically short of the essential solvent.

In their meeting on 21 April, Weizmann learned from Wauchope that the Arab leaders, "one after another," had expressed both regret and surprise concerning the violence in Jaffa on 19 April.[49] The high commissioner likewise suggested in a letter to Shertok a few days later that the Arab leadership were not behind the disorders.[50] The Jewish Agency's own intelligence confirmed as much.[51] For his part, Shertok hardly regarded the Arab leaders as worthy of the name. He claimed that they had "seized the revolutionary chance for staging a big national show in the form of a general strike." He alleged further that their supposed followers were overwhelmingly opposed to the strike, and participated only under duress.[52] From these premises, it was a short step to the conclusion that the strike was a criminal affair. Shertok reported to members of the Jewish Agency in London, "We pressed [Wauchope] to declare the strike illegal in the sense that incitement to the strike and open organisation of it should become punishable."[53] Weizmann argued similarly to Wauchope's overseer and liaison to the cabinet, Colonial Secretary J. H. Thomas, during a confab at Claridge's Hotel in London on 18 May. He explained to Thomas that the high commissioner's belief that the work stoppage reflected Arab mass sentiment was mistaken, and that "if one was prepared to spend the necessary money, there would be no difficulty in calling off the strike." That is, there existed no deeply rooted national movement of protest among Palestine's Arabs, and lining the right pockets would reveal as much.[54]

In one respect, the British evaluation of the circumstances of April–May 1936 came quickly to converge with that of the Jewish Agency. While Wauchope's assessment of the state of affairs was more nuanced than the Agency's, he ultimately required little persuading with regard to Shertok's insistence that the strike be criminalized. The high commissioner wrote to Thomas on 18 April, suggesting that the present unrest was due in large part to Arab discernment of the fact that violent protest in Cairo and Damascus had led to negotiations with the British in Egypt and the French in Syria. He noted, moreover, that the British had promised the Arabs a legislative council in 1930, but were, as of 1936, still refusing them one.[55] But by 5 May, Wauchope's tone had changed. He was emphatic that the strike was indeed illegal and of a piece with other "criminal" behavior among the Arabs. He reported to Thomas that he had "initiated proceedings under the Criminal Law (Seditious Offences) Ordinance" against the issuing of a manifesto by the Arab Transport Strike Committee, which called upon Arab government employees to stay home from work.[56] In short order, he would begin arresting and incarcerating large numbers of Arab journalists, most of whom advocated for civil disobedience, not violence.[57] In the meantime, Wauchope urged members of the Arab Higher Committee (AHC) (about which more below) not to support the strike, and suggested, in all sincerity, that they send another delegation to London.[58]

In a second respect, however, the British evaluation of the events of April 1936 and after diverged from that of the Jewish Agency. While the Jewish Agency and many Jewish witnesses on the ground regarded the strike as a vacuous, pseudo-national gesture on the part of the Arab leadership, to which the Arab population at large was averse, Wauchope stressed in a 4 May memorandum, "The hands of the leaders are being forced by extremists and by the fact that the whole of the Arab population is behind the general strike."[59] The "extremists" he had in mind were the transport strikers, whose manifesto called explicitly for "a peaceful general strike."[60] Thomas communicated Wauchope's interpretation of events to the cabinet on 13 May, along with the high commissioner's reassertion (in response to earlier cabinet objections) of the need for the British government to appoint a commission to investigate the disturbances. Such a gesture, he insisted, "might enable the Arab leaders to call off the strike and the present unrest." The cabinet conceded Wauchope's point, but insisted that he make the appointment of a commission conditional on the restoration of "law and order," and that he announce this publicly.[61]

The high commissioner and his superiors were now agreed that the Arab leadership needed an excuse to call off the strike. They thus regarded it as a popular phenomenon—not, as the Jewish Agency maintained, as a ruse foisted upon the Arabs by their unscrupulous representatives. As Wauchope explained to Thomas on 16 May, "A demand was pressed upon [the Arab leaders] from all Arab quarters in Palestine that the strike should continue." The leadership was, he emphasized, "powerless to stop the strike unless [Jewish] immigration is suspended."[62] The RAF—which held supreme command over the armed forces in the mandate until September 1936—issued an intelligence summary for April 1936, which likewise concluded that the strike, having begun in Jaffa and spread to other towns, initially "lacked any central control."[63] The Arab "leaders" were following the strikers.

This was not news to the Arabs themselves, whose understanding of the circumstances of mid-1936—their nature and history—differed markedly from that of the Jews and the British. Three developments were especially salient for Palestinian Arabs in 1935–36. The first was a new, unprecedentedly large influx of European Jews—62,000 in 1935—who were fleeing the Nazi menace in Central Europe.[64] The Arab leadership in Palestine, operating with effectively universal popular sympathy, had for nearly two decades advanced three demands to the British: halt Jewish immigration, terminate Jewish land purchases, and establish a democratic government reflecting the country's Arab majority. As of 1935, the British had acceded to none of these demands, and the largest annual wave of Jewish immigration in Palestinian history was a painful reminder of that fact. This circumstance was aggravated by a simultaneous slump in Arab wages and surge in Arab unemployment.[65]

The second development pertained to the second of the perennial Arab demands, Jewish land purchases. As with Jewish immigration, the figures for

Jewish acquisition of land in Palestine peaked in the period preceding the strike and accompanying violence of 1936. By 1930, Jews held over one million dunums (four million acres) of land in the country. At 62,000 dunums, Jewish purchases in 1934 were greater than the previous three years combined, and they leapt to 73,000 in 1935.[66] Notes Ann Mosely Lesch, "In 1935, [the] high commissioner asserted that the fear that the Jewish community is 'eating up the land' is felt 'in every town and village in Palestine.'"[67]

The third significant development for Palestinian Arabs in 1935–36 was the nascent flowering of a public sphere, due primarily to the bootstrapping organizational efforts of the Istiqlal (Independence) Party, beginning in 1932.[68] As Weldon Matthews has shown, the Istiqlal played on and exacerbated the credibility problem of the traditional Arab leadership, whose fruitless protests and diplomatic missions the broader Arab population disdained. From late 1933 to the autumn of 1935, however, the Istiqlal and other youth-oriented Arab political parties were largely dormant. It was Jaffa port workers' interception of a Tel Aviv-bound shipment of weapons concealed in barrels of cement that reinvigorated grassroots Arab political networks in October 1935.[69] By then, Arab youths, intellectuals, and workers had become seasoned political activists, garnering press coverage for the national cause and staging popular demonstrations that brought pressure to bear upon the traditional Arab leadership.[70] The same elements compelled elite Palestinian families to set aside their differences and, in the days after 19 April, to form the Arab Higher Committee (AHC), with the mufti of Jerusalem (al-Hajj Amin al-Husayni) as president.[71]

The Husaynis had for generations occupied the upper echelon of Jerusalem politics, and the British (like the Ottomans before them) often depended on the family in their dealings with the local Arab community.[72] In 1912, the young Amin al-Husayni enrolled in the famous al-Azhar University in Cairo, where he first became involved in the anti-Zionist politics that would become his legacy.[73] His relationship with the British in subsequent decades teetered between harmony and hostility, but not to the point of disinheriting him of the mediating role London had long devolved upon his family. And thus on 21 April, the president of the newly constituted Arab Higher Committee assured the high commissioner that he would "do his best to prevent [the] continuance of disorder."[74] Wauchope would regard the mufti and the AHC as a "moderate influence on more extreme leaders" for some time yet. The AHC, in the high commissioner's view, was "not directly concerned with [the] organisation of strikes," which had been thrust upon it by the Arab masses.[75]

While the AHC awkwardly attempted to choreograph the actions of a popular movement it had neither initiated nor inspired, the Committee was in ideological accord with this movement on two points. The first was that the Arabs of Palestine were due the same legal recognition as the Arabs of Iraq, Egypt, and every other Arab territory: they were entitled to national independence. A number of AHC representatives stated this to the high commissioner and the chief secretary during a meeting at the government house in Jerusalem on the evening of 5 May. The mufti, for example, explained, "The Palestinians are not inferior in any way to the Iraqi or the Egyptian people, and while these two countries either have had or are about to have their rights recognized, the Jews are opposed to the slightest measure of reform that may be proposed in Palestine."[76]

The AHC's secretary and Istiqlal representative, 'Awni Bey 'Abd al-Hadi, then spoke. The 'Abd al-Hadis were prominent landowners in Jenin and Nablus, and 'Awni Bey—who had studied law in France, helped to found the Istiqlal party, and been appointed the AHC's liaison to the locally organized national committees—was a prominent figure in his own right.[77] Like the mufti, 'Awni Bey situated the local conflict in the larger Arab struggle for independence:

> While our neighbours in Syria and Egypt are fighting for their independence, the Arabs of Palestine are struggling for their bread. The dignity of the Arabs in this country and their freedom are exposed to danger, and we consider that it is the sacred duty of every one of us to defend his endangered bread and dignity.[78]

A few weeks later, on 30 May, the high commissioner and the chief secretary met with the mayors of major Palestinian towns and cities, who hammered away at the same theme. Allowing Jewish immigration to proceed apace, the mayors declared, posed a "danger to [Palestinian Arabs'] future existence" and constituted a "betrayal of . . . Arab rights."[79] Halting immigration would terminate the disorders. Absent that, "neither the [AHC] nor any other leader could . . . oppose the people without losing honour and credit."[80] A few days earlier, the high commissioner had opened a letter of protest from the First Arab Rural Congress. It also emphasized the "great danger to our national and racial existence" created by ongoing Jewish immigration, which it declared "completely illegal," as were the British "attempts to suppress the lawful voice of the nation ... by force."[81] Whereas everyone from Jewish merchants to the leaders of the Jewish Agency had stressed the pseudo-national and illegal nature of the strike, the many Arabs from whom Wauchope heard were adamant regarding their national standing and legal entitlement to resist British implementation of the Balfour Declaration.

When not parrying protests from Arabs and Jews, British officials mulled over the deteriorating security situation in the country. In the second half of May, His Majesty's troops encountered determined armed resistance in Gaza and Beersheba in the south and in Nablus and Tulkarm in the north.[82] Across the land, the silence of the Palestinian night was steadily succumbing to the hiss and crackle of gunfire and firecrackers.[83] While some authors have deduced from this circumstance that British security forces were under perpetual siege in May 1936, that appears to be an exaggeration.[84] As late as 23 June, the deputy inspector general of police would report that relatively few villagers had attacked British forces.[85] Nevertheless, the RAF intelligence summary for May 1936 did find that the AHC's attempt to maintain a peaceful strike was faltering, and that "more extremist elements were taking the law into their own hands." These "extremists," it is worth noting, aimed their attacks "chiefly against [the] police and military."[86]

At the same time, government crime statistics showed an astonishing increase in murders and attempted murders in April and May 1936, as compared with the same two-month period in the previous year. Murders numbered nineteen in April/May 1935, a figure which nearly tripled to fifty-three in April/May 1936. Attempted murders more than quadrupled, from twenty to eighty-seven. Crimes also shot up from earlier in the year. In March, there had been eleven murders and twenty attempted murders.[87] The data depicted a crime wave, a fact that colored the intelligence summary's portrayal of the "extremists," which it neglected to disaggregate from the common criminals committing murders. Thus, despite its observation that the bulk of the Arab violent attacks in May targeted military and police personnel—not exactly the magnets of the criminal class—the RAF report referred to the perpetrators of these actions as "gangs," a term that would become ubiquitous in British (and Zionist) discussions of the revolt.[88]

Arab leaders were meanwhile keen to distinguish themselves from those involved in violent actions. Both the AHC and the national committees advocated openly for a nonviolent campaign of civil disobedience.[89] They did so, moreover, with the backing of the Arab press. The pan-Arab *al-Difa*—

along with *Filastin*, one of the two highest circulation Arabic dailies in the country—editorialized in late April, "We want the Arab Higher Committee to act as Gandhi acted in India when he called for civil disobedience."[90] *Filastin* used the government's favored epithet ("disturbers of the peace") to designate those Arabs who were resorting to violence.[91] *Al-Liwa'* called in its 15 May edition for the Arabs to adopt only peaceful methods of protest.[92]

"TURKISH METHODS" AND THE VILLAGE SEARCHES OF MAY 1936 AND AFTER

Violence, however, was much more than an Arab problem, as Arab journalists and political leaders were quick to note. In fact, the problem of British violence was the second topic of agreement between the AHC and the Arab public. Thus, in the course of the mayors' 30 May conversation with the high commissioner and the chief secretary, Nablus mayor Sulayman Bey Tuqan complained of British police and soldiers' maltreatment of Arabs. He was particularly concerned about the so-called "village searches" that security forces were then conducting throughout the country.[93] British spokesmen announced that the purpose of these searches was to discover weapons and to apprehend wanted men. An abundance of Arab testimony, however, indicated that the searches were actually punitive expeditions, designed to frighten the population and thereby to re-establish "law and order"—just as the cabinet had directed Wauchope to do.

These "searches," moreover, were not limited to rural areas.[94] On 1 June, the high commissioner received a delegation of 'ulama', who drew his attention to an incident in the Bab Hutta quarter of Jerusalem, which the clerics had taken some trouble to investigate. They reported that soldiers and police, ostensibly searching for weapons in the area, had instead stormed through houses, destroying food and furniture and mortifying men in front of their wives. The 'ulama' had heard numerous tales of violent British exploits in Arab villages. Following their investigation at Bab Hutta, they now believed them. The men suggested to the high commissioner that these actions, coupled with the long-standing British policy of refusing to respond meaningfully to nonviolent Arab protest, were generating the present instability. "[I]f shooting and bombing is being done now," one of them explained, "it is not with the object of committing murder or because the Arabs like disorders, but simply with the object of letting their voice reach England."[95]

FIGURE 2. Residents of Bab Hutta, in Jerusalem, survey the wreckage of a British "village search," summer 1936. (Library of Congress)

These were not the first reports of police brutality that Wauchope had heard. Arab leaders had informed him as early as 21 April that officers had shot a sixteen-year-old youth in the back, and that "the attitude of the Police had given the impression to the Arabs that their real enemies were the British."[96] The Anglican archdeacon in Jerusalem related the same to the chief secretary. Anglican missionaries operated in villages throughout Palestine, and regularly reported back to the archdeacon and archbishop in Jerusalem regarding developments in the Arab community. On 2 June, the day after Wauchope's meeting with the 'ulama', the archdeacon wrote the chief secretary with concern: "It is believed amongst some at any rate of the British Police that they have been definitely ordered to 'Duff them [the Arabs] up'. (The phrase itself is significant to anyone who remembers, as I do, the days before the present Inspector-General)."[97]

The archdeacon referred to the notorious Douglas Duff, whose harsh tactics as a police inspector in 1920s Palestine had rendered his surname a byword for police brutality. Indeed, Duff's fondness for such torture techniques as waterboarding and "suspension" ultimately landed him in trouble with the high commissioner, who fired him in 1931 for the "ill treatment" of a prisoner.[98] The infamous former inspector had actually visited Jerusalem only a few weeks earlier, on 12–14 May, during his first trip to Palestine since departing the country in 1932.[99] Remarkably, Duff himself was taken aback by the violence to which the British openly subjected Arab civilians. After witnessing soldiers and police searching a caravan of Arabs wending its way out of the city's German Colony, he lamented: "If the sort of thing I saw . . . is usual in these days, then it is no wonder that we are laying up a great debt of active hatred against ourselves." As Duff described the episode: "The searching was none too gently executed, for I saw one Arab being savagely kicked by a brawny man in khaki, whilst an old man with a grey beard received a nasty cut from a leather hand-whip."[100] Evidence from Arabic sources suggests that the brutality Duff witnessed was, indeed, "usual" in those days. Bahjat Abu Gharbiyya, a schoolteacher and member of a militant underground organization in May 1936, wrote that British security forces in the Old City of Jerusalem were demeaning Palestinians by forcing them to stop and salute the same police patrols that regularly beat them up "for no reason."[101] *Al-Difa'* likewise reported that British police were "searching passersby for no reason" and "harassing them . . . when [they] show any form of resistance upon receiving rude, provocative insults."[102] Such smug behavior, writes Mustafa Kabha, "filled [Palestinians] with indignation and hatred for the English."[103]

The archdeacon received similar reports from around the country. He informed the chief secretary: "From every side complaints are reaching me daily of the unnecessary and quite indiscriminate roughness which is being displayed by the British Police in their handling of the native, and particularly the Arab, population."[104] In a subsequent letter, he disclosed that he possessed reliable reports that the repression was still worse in Palestine's northern districts.[105] The ubiquity of this unruly behavior led the archdeacon to surmise that the police had adopted a new "method" for dealing with Arabs. He dated its inception to one week before the death of Constable Robert Bird on 28 May at the hands of Arab rebels in the Old City of Jerusalem—an important detail, as Bird's killing served as "the usual defence" of police brutality.[106] Not incidentally, Bird's assailants appear to have targeted him in retaliation for the earlier British killing of an Arab man.[107] Similarly, a fortnight later, on 12 June, rebels attacked and wounded the British assistant police superintendent, Alan Sigrist, a man whose savagery towards Jerusalem's Arabs was legendary.[108]

The archdeacon's estimate of the introduction of tough new measures against the Arab community was on the mark. Duff had seen evidence of such tactics in mid-May. And by 24–25 May, police and troops were raiding villages near Nazareth and Gaza, on the assumption that they quartered men who had mounted attacks on government forces over the previous two days. These raids, a War Office report disclosed, "took the form of searches for arms and wanted men by troops and police and, being fairly severe in nature, had also a punitive effect which began to produce most satisfactory results in the more truculent villages."[109] The statement that the searches "had also a punitive effect" was disingenuous. In reality, punishing villagers was the searches' primary purpose, while weapons and wanted men were secondary concerns. As Air Vice-Marshal R. E. C. Peirse—the military commander in Palestine and the co-architect of the village search policy—divulged in a top-secret report: "Ostensibly these searches were undertaken to find arms and wanted persons; actually the measures adopted by the police on the lines of similar Turkish methods, were punitive."[110] In early June, the new colonial secretary, William Ormsby-Gore, spoke with Kenneth Williams, the editor of the publication *Great Britain and the East* and the author of a book about Ibn Saʿud.[111] Williams had received information from two sources of whose "bona fides" and "reliability and good judgment" he was certain, and who reported that "British troops in Palestine had been committing 'excesses' against the Arabs." He stated further that his informants "were under the impression that the conduct of the troops had the approval of the High Commissioner."[112]

While the colonial secretary assured Williams that Wauchope would not have authorized such tactics, the testimony of Duff and the archdeacon, the report of the War Office, and Peirse's disclosures all point to the widespread British adoption of "Turkish methods" in this early period. Wauchope's supposed ignorance of the fact warrants closer scrutiny. Echoing Ormsby-Gore, Charles Smith writes that Wauchope was "enraged" on learning of the "Turkish methods" being employed in the villages, and that he ordered Peirse and the inspector general of police, Roy Spicer, to "moderate the searches."[113] This occurred on 30 May, according to Peirse's own account.[114] It is curious, however, that Wauchope's private secretary, Thomas Hodgkin, wrote in a personal letter dated 28 May that he had taken the decision to resign his post the previous Sunday (24 May) to protest the "new repressive measures on the part of the Government."[115] The high commissioner's private secretary, then, knew of the punitive searches on the day they supposedly began, and attributed them, without qualification, to "the Government" led by his boss. This renders implausible, though not impossible, the idea that Wauchope only learned of the harsh treatment later and was then scandalized.

Regardless, the brutality of the village searches was sufficiently rampant as of early June that it had engendered, according to Peirse, "a grave crisis with the [Arab] section" of the Palestine police, who considered the severe measures "repugnant."[116] In one instance, soldiers "searching" Qaqun, near Tulkarm, handled the village so harshly that its residents called the police in desperation. The Arab officers who responded were appalled by the scene they came upon, to the point that they began fighting with the soldiers, one of whom shot and killed a policeman.[117] The dead man's fellow officers resigned in protest.[118] And within days, Arab policemen from several towns and villages convened a meeting in Jerusalem, which produced a series of demands to the general police authority. Among them: "Fair investigations into the crimes that British policemen have committed in light of recent events."[119]

It is worth noting that while Peirse and the archdeacon's chronologies indicated that the punitive searches began in the second half of May, a Jewish Agency summary of events from 7 May reported that "punitive posts"—"a most effective measure of teaching turbulent villages wisdom"—had already been installed in nine villages.[120] This was two weeks prior to the appearance of the first Arab "gangs."[121]

BRITISH VIOLENCE AND THE SCHOLARSHIP ON 1936

As the previous section demonstrates, the British began violently repressing the Arab population of Palestine within a month of the strike's declaration. Yet, when government officials later surveyed the revolt's first phase, they failed to factor this critical detail into their accounts. With a handful of exceptions—most notably, Matthew Hughes's pioneering work on British violence in 1936–39—much of the English- and Hebrew-language literature on the revolt has repeated their error.[122] Even Hughes writes that "the wide-spread use of punitive actions" in Palestine was "central to British military repression *after 1936*."[123] The scholarship more generally has taken for granted the truth of British officials' assertions that the few punitive measures police and soldiers did adopt in late May 1936 were discontinued in early June. But accepting this claim requires that one discard an abundance of testimony—both Arab and British—to the contrary. It also obscures a basic component of the causal machinery that determined the revolt's initial, and by extension ultimate, trajectory: namely, the mandatory itself.

Thus, Jacob Norris, who in a separate and very instructive capacity corrects the traditional understanding of the revolt, nevertheless writes that prior to October 1936, the British "[sought] to contain the rebel bands using orthodox civilian policing" (although the reality, as Georgina Sinclair notes, is that the British never successfully civilianized the Palestine police, which "remained essentially a paramilitary force").[124] In the same vein, Yehoyada Haim claims that Wauchope's policy of "protecting lives and property without the use of repressive measures" was "applied by the British during most of the Revolt's first phase."[125] Yoav Gelber writes that the British were "hesitant in the first phase" of the rebellion and that Wauchope "opposed a strong hand" approach to the disturbances.[126] Michael J. Cohen comes close to recognizing the inaccuracy of such statements. He cites the Peirse report in support of his assertion that the village searches in the revolt's first phase were "ineffective in the discovery of arms and were unpopular with the troops, against whom all kinds of charges were levelled." But Cohen then neglects to place these facts in the context of Peirse's admission that the real purpose of the searches was punitive—a truth which casts both the paucity of arms and the profusion of charges in a much different light. Cohen likewise takes it for granted that subsequent charges against British troops stemming from the village searches were mere "rumour and propaganda."[127] Yehoshua Porath, too, claims that "Government reaction to the strike and the revolt remained almost to the end rather reserved, in the hope that violence would die out and the strike would disintegrate before severe measures became necessary."[128] While acknowledging the existence of some "punitive measures" up to July, Porath goes so far as to state that a British "policy of no repression" existed in this period.[129] Likewise, Tom Bowden, citing a War Office file, suggests that the British abided by an internal security protocol in Palestine in 1936 that did not involve "strict repressive measure[s]."[130]

The government reports contained in the file Bowden references paint a similar picture. They consist, among other things, of a synopsis of Lieutenant General John Dill's "summary of events" for April-October 1936. Dill inherited command of the British forces in Palestine from Peirse in September 1936—thus marking the transfer of military authority in the mandate from the RAF to the army—and assumed the role of general officer commanding (GOC). His account of the time prior to his own arrival on the scene warrants some examination, given Bowden and others' effective reiteration of it.

According to the synopsis of Dill's report, several important points had been established as of October 1936: the strike had "developed into a form of open rebellion"; the loyalty of the Arab section of the Palestine police had become dubious; and the government had refrained from employing British troops in any offensive capacity.[131] The third point was a slightly inaccurate paraphrase of what Dill had written in the full report, but the error was inevitable. In the report itself, Dill emphasized that well into May 1936, British forces "had been dissipated on protective duties and little or no force was used for punitive work." Confusingly, he then stated that in June, when groups of armed Arabs began appearing, there occurred a "relaxation" in the use of "punitive measures" during the village searches, and that "combined with this relaxation . . . came definite signs of defection among the Palestine Police." A few sentences later, and more confusingly still, Dill claimed that on 3 June, "the Palestine Government decided 'to continue our present policy . . . of endeavouring to protect life and property without adopting severe repressive measures.'"[132] One might have thought that rebel sniping had led British forces to attack Arab villagers, which in turn had caused Arab police to mutiny. But on Dill's bewildering telling, armed Arab groups emerged, at which point the British for some reason "relaxed" the briefly operative (and hitherto denied) punitive measures and Arab policemen inexplicably began defecting. This causal picture was pure confusion, making the synopsis of it simplistic of necessity.

Each of Dill's three propositions, in any case, was specious. Concerning the first, while the strike *had* "developed into a form of open rebellion," this language obscured two crucial facts. First, in the strike's early days, armed revolt and refusal to work were largely unlinked. As noted, the AHC itself, as well as the national committees and the Arab press, advocated openly for a nonviolent campaign of civil disobedience.[133] The convergence of the strike and the revolt was therefore not a foregone conclusion as of May 1936. Second, Dill's language framed the armed rebellion as having evolved congenitally from the strike; it thus cropped out causal variables extrinsic to the Arab community, such as British violence.[134] This framing depended on Dill's second and third propositions: the questionable loyalty of Arab policemen and the supposedly purely defensive operations of British troops. Taking these in reverse order, British forces undertook offensive and intentionally "punitive" operations in Arab villages beginning in May. And these, as Peirse acknowledged, produced a "grave crisis" in loyalty among Arab police officers, who objected to the use of such measures against their countrymen.[135] As 'Abd al-Wahhab Kayyali observes, the same measures were "instrumental in bringing about a greater degree of cohesion and identification between the villagers and the rebels."[136]

British brutality alienated not only Arab policemen and villagers, but also the Arab population at large, which increased public sympathy for attacks on British police and soldiers. As Michael J. Cohen relates, in June 1936, when Emir 'Abdullah of Transjordan requested that his Palestinian interlocutors refrain from further violence, they "replied that the terrorism was itself in reply to the brutality of the Mandatory."[137] An organization of Arab priests argued similarly to the high commissioner, claiming that the government had "provoked the Arabs to resist it openly through the various ruthless and severe measures which it adopted."[138] Muhammad 'Izzat Darwaza, 'Awni 'Abd al-Hadi's successor as the AHC secretary, wrote that the search regime, coupled with the "violence and cruelty" with which the British repressed political demonstrations, only "added fuel to the [nationalist] fire."[139] The archdeacon said the same in a letter to MP Stanley Baldwin: "I am afraid . . . the rough-handling methods which prevailed for a time at the end of May among the British Police . . . were the direct cause of a good deal of the violence and shooting which has [now] to be suppressed."[140]

The gist of these testimonies is corroborated by Sir Hugh Foot, who served in Palestine as a junior assistant secretary in the Colonial Service during the revolt years, and later became the British governor of Cyprus. In 1959, Foot would recall:

> . . . [I]n Palestine and again in Cyprus there was often a tendency to attempt to make up for lack of intelligence by using the sledge hammer—mass arrests, mass detentions, big cordons and searches and collective punishments. Such operations can do more harm than good and usually play into the hands of the terrorists by alienating general opinion from the forces of authority.[141]

No reader of Dill's report would appreciate the role the British themselves played in stoking the rebellion. In scrutinizing Dill's three findings, one notices, in each case, the same element missing from the causal equation: the mandatory. The strike develops unaided into open rebellion; Arab policemen defect without apparent reason; and the British refrain from offensive operations in the mandate. The first two propositions gloss over, and the third simply denies, the causal role of the mandatory in the rebellion's unfolding.[142]

This blinkered imperial vision was pervasive among British officials. Among its more pristine manifestations was Wauchope's passing acknowledgement in a December 1936 memorandum that the government's casualty reports had hitherto failed to "differentiate between civilians killed and wounded by the Forces of the Crown and those who are the victims of riots or other forms of violence."[143] While the British had kept careful tabs on the number of Jews and Britons killed by Arabs, it apparently never occurred to them to count the number of Arab noncombatants killed or otherwise harmed by British forces. As for Arab militants, the notion that their deaths at the hands of the government could be anything less than justified was still further beyond the pale. One government official, having acknowledged the accuracy of an estimate of "1,000 ... Arabs killed during the [1936] disturbances," remarked in October 1937: "As the Jews point out these cannot fairly be described as 'murders' comparable with the figure of eighty Jews, since with few exceptions they represent casualties incurred while resisting Government forces."[144]

A November 1936 report of the supreme court of Palestine featured similar reasoning. The document concerned an appeal on behalf of two Arabs convicted of shooting a British soldier outside Bal'a, near Tulkarm. A lower court had sentenced both men to death. The high court did not deny that the defendants had been attempting to acquire water for their cattle when a British plane began firing on them, causing them to take shelter in a cave. Nor did it deny that a British soldier had then approached the cave and "fired two shots into the hole in order to investigate[!]." What the court did deny was the right of the men to defend themselves against unjustified and potentially lethal British force. On the contrary, the report asserted: "Yet another point was raised [by the appellants' lawyer], namely that it was the natural reaction for the appellants to shoot back when fired upon. This astounding theory, which allows men to retaliate when either police or military are doing their duty, is unknown to me."[145]

CONCLUSION

In viewing the "disorder" and "lawlessness" that plagued their Palestine mandate, the British gazed from the lofty perch of "law and order." This position required, as a matter of discursive coherence, that they be in no way constitutive of the "chaos" they sought to name as such and then sort out. The British could see the map of Palestinian politics, but they could not see themselves drawing it.[146] If an outbreak of Arab "criminality" was at the root of the instability that increasingly afflicted Palestine, the British could not be both implicated in it and at the same time positioned to identify and address it as such.

Yet, as the sources cited in this chapter suggest, a close reading of the government's own reports unearths evidence of the ubiquity of British violence in Palestine in 1936. Nevertheless, the British understanding of events in this period was generally consistent with the accounts of the military commander, the high commissioner, and the supreme court justices of the mandate, all of which presented the Arab rebellion as causally extrinsic to the behavior of the mandatory. As the next chapter will elaborate, the same was true of the majority of British soldiers, policemen, and opinion-makers, as well as the Zionists demanding greater British repression of the Arabs.

TWO

"A Wave of Crime"

THE CRIMINALIZATION OF PALESTINIAN NATIONALISM, APRIL–JUNE 1936

THE BRITISH RECASTING OF PALESTINIAN nationalists as criminals was not sudden. The pinch of the twin pincers of Arab and Jewish opinion, however, made it inevitable. Regarding Arab opinion, the League of Nations mandate instrument was holy writ for the Arab Palestinian political class. It stated that the inhabitants of the Middle East stood already on the threshold of national autonomy, and required only a last interval of British and French assistance in order to cross it. The British project in the region, in other words, was explicitly pro-nationalist. London was therefore poorly positioned to recognize its internal security woes in Palestine for what they were: an Arab movement for national independence from London. This dilemma rendered the Zionist tactic of portraying that movement as something else altogether—as a crime wave—increasingly attractive to the British.

Crime, as chapter one detailed, was a key point of convergence between British and Jewish portrayals of the revolt. This convergence was not total, however. There were, in fact, two crimino-national claims about Arab protest in 1936, which one might call strong and weak, respectively. The strong claim was that both the strike and the rebellion lacked popular Arab support, and endured only because thugs working for the Arab national leadership had cowed the docile masses into backing them. The weak claim denied that the strike was coerced, but affirmed that both it and the armed Arab attacks on British forces and Jewish civilians were, indeed, illegal. Zionist leaders promoted the strong claim from the first. Their British counterparts affirmed only the weak claim initially. With each passing month, however, London drifted toward the Zionist position. This chapter charts that drift.

On 24 April 1936, the Jewish Agency dispatched a telegram to "the Jewish people" at large, expressing resolve in the face of Arab attacks and observing, "This
is not [the] first time that our peaceful creative effort [is] being interfered with
by [the] assaults of instigated rioters."[1] This statement encapsulated the Zionist
case against the Arabs from 1936 forward, which was threefold: the rioters were
pawns of their devious leaders, not free agents acting on the basis of their per-
ceived interests and rights; the Jews were creators and the Arabs destroyers; and
the Zionist enterprise in Palestine was an entirely peaceful one. These three
themes converged in the criminalization of Palestinian nationalism.

Zionist leaders relentlessly promoted the "devious leaders" claim.[2]
Weizmann argued to Wauchope on 3 May that the "overwhelming majority
of ordinary Arab citizens" were secretly opposed to the strike.[3] Shertok and
David Ben Gurion wrote the high commissioner on 17 May complaining of
the government's refusal to dissolve the "rebellious body styling itself the
'Supreme Arab Committee' [the AHC]," a policy which they claimed gave
"further encouragement . . . to the acts of lawlessness carried out by its agents
throughout the country."[4] Ben Gurion was the chair of the executives of both
the Jewish Agency and the WZO, and a towering figure in the Zionist
milieu. He had founded the Histadrut (the General Federation of Labor) in
1920, and later led Mapai (the Israel Workers Party), which several Zionist
workers' organizations founded in 1930. The "acts of lawlessness" to which he
and Shertok referred included the previous night's murder of three Jews in
Jerusalem, although the two offered no evidence of the AHC's connection to
this crime. In a letter to Wauchope on 14 May, Shertok and Ben Gurion
likewise bundled together nonviolent protest and violent crime, and saddled
the AHC with liability for both:

> . . . open incitement to continue the strike, the call to civil disobedience,
> criminal acts including the murder of innocent people have not diminished
> . . . We cannot regard the guilt as attaching only to the miserable individuals
> committing crimes. The responsibility for this criminal activity rests upon
> the instigators and leaders who are kindling a fire of racial hatred and strife
> in the country.[5]

The pair stated unequivocally in their 17 May letter: ". . . [P]ersonal responsibility [must] be placed on [the AHC's] members as individuals for all terrorist acts which may be committed in the country."[6] Weizmann was meanwhile

FIGURE 3. The normally bustling jewelers' market in the Old City of Jerusalem, hauntingly empty as a result of the 1936 strike. (Library of Congress)

telling the high commissioner that "quiet" would never be restored in Palestine so long as the AHC continued to function. When Wauchope responded that he "needed rather more evidence ... before proceeding to take strong measures against them," Weizmann offered none, but proposed that "the disbanding of the Committee would make a strong impression on the country."[7] In a letter to Wauchope on 6 June, Shertok declared again that the AHC was "the mainspring of the whole campaign of strike, sedition, disobedience and terror."[8]

While insisting that the British recognize the AHC's unmitigated responsibility for the full spectrum of disorders then wracking the country, the Jewish Agency leadership was privately more ambivalent on this point. Shertok himself stated in a meeting of the executive in late May: "We have no evidence that the Committee of Ten (the AHC) are organizing the acts of violence and terror in the country, but it is clearly encouraging and provoking these actions."[9] Nevertheless, Agency members were united in their conviction that *if* the Arab leadership were personally responsible for all violence in Palestine, then organized Arab politics just was a criminal enterprise. Thus, regardless of the extent to which they believed that this conditional matched the state of affairs, Zionist spokesmen insisted the government adopt it as its framework for managing the disorders.

The Agency therefore demanded not only that Wauchope take sterner measures in combating violent crime but also that he "stamp out any attempt at civil disobedience."[10] The Agency's political secretary, Arthur Lourie, cabled Jerusalem from London on 7 June, suggesting that the Agency tap sympathetic members of Parliament to press the government publicly to outlaw the strike, the AHC, and the regional national committees—that is, Palestinian politics.[11]

Ben Gurion's 10 June reply to Lourie was revealing. He noted the efficacy of the government's deportations of leaders such as 'Awni 'Abd al-Hadi, whom he deemed the "moving spirit and principal organizer" of the Arab political community.[12] Ben Gurion had actually met with 'Abd al-Hadi earlier, in July 1934, on the understanding that he was a "patriotic, truthful, and incorruptible" Arab leader.[13] He claimed at the time that he and 'Abd al-Hadi had "parted in great friendship."[14] If he regarded him as a criminal by June 1936, he did not mention it to Lourie. Ben Gurion also disclosed that, in his view: "Even if the strike ends the acts of terrorism won't. That is not now (at any rate) in the hands of the leaders."[15] His insistence, then, that the Arab leaders were responsible for the criminal and other violence was tactical.

THE BRITISH DRIFT BEGINS

While the Jewish Agency relentlessly pushed the government to outlaw the strike and to unleash the full force of its counterinsurgent machinery against the rebels, British opinion was already moving in the same direction. The shift began at about the time of the government's escalation of repressive measures in the second half of May and early June. This is not to suggest that the framing of Arab rebels as criminals was simply a witting confection designed to justify in advance British ruthlessness. Something deeper and more discursively organic than this was at work, as evidenced by the unrehearsed quality, as well as the ubiquity, of the British conception of Arab political agitation from this point forward.

Consider, as a specimen of this conception, the words of the British director of education in Palestine, Humphrey Bowman. In a private letter dated 17 May, Bowman wrote vexedly of Arab violence, sabotage, and shop closures. Imagining the words of a more responsible Arab leadership, he ventriloquized: "They ought now to say to us: 'We have shown you we are honest and determined by keeping the strike going for four weeks. We have now done enough. Send your Royal Commission, and we will gladly abide by its results.'"[16] Bowman's faith in British commissions and distrust of the Arab "nation's demands" hinted at a broader British logic, as did his comments a few days later, on 24 May. These began with a list meant to illustrate that "crime has been serious throughout the country." It included "not so many murders, but shootings at buses and even at troops; bombs; telephone lines cut; railway sleepers moved; demonstrations daily."[17] His next entry, on 31 May, deemed the killing of Constable Bird "cold blooded murder."[18]

That Bowman brought military-style attacks on government security forces and infrastructure, not to mention political demonstrations, under the same "crime" umbrella as murder was not anomalous. Wauchope himself, in a 2 June memorandum to the colonial secretary, coupled the forces of British coercion with ordinary citizens, noting that "murders of innocent people and of police are almost of daily occurrence."[19] Nor was Bowman's seemingly cynical view of Palestinian nationalism an aberration. The major British papers took a similar line. *The Times of London* reported that the Arabs, far from having clear-sightedly identified the futility of nonviolent protest against the British, were mired in a fog of invidious rumor, which found them resorting to "rowdy . . . demonstration[s]" and general "unruliness."[20] They were also demanding a "national government," a term *The Times*, like Bowman, disparaged via quotation.[21] Nevertheless, the paper did acknowledge that another British commission of inquiry was probably pointless, as the fundamental problem in Palestine was the impossibility of establishing a Jewish "home" without infringing Arab rights.[22] These rights, however, clearly did not rise to a national status, as evidenced by *The Times'* recommendation the next day that the British might simply have to "crush" the Arab "unrest and disorder."[23]

When the punitive village searches began in late May, *The Times* promptly presented them as an unfortunate necessity.[24] On 30 May, a telling descriptor debuted in its coverage: "A military patrol on the railway to the north of Lydda had a lively affray last night with brigands, who opened fire on it from both sides."[25] *The Times*, then, had also begun referring without qualification to coordinated assaults on government forces as the actions of ordinary criminals. On 3 June it deemed the sabotage of British infrastructure in Gaza the work of "gangs."[26] On 8 June, it wrote that Arab "bandits" had engaged the Cameron Highlanders in a four-hour battle![27]

While the right-leaning *Spectator* also pointed out the vanity of another British commission and even acknowledged "the many injuries and illegalities done to the Arabs," it too implicitly downgraded the Arab standing in Palestine to something less than fully national, writing on 29 May:

> Whatever view be held on the broad question of the respective rights of Jews and Arabs in Palestine, there must be unanimity on one point, that the Mandatory Power will be abdicating its function if it fails to suppress with all the force at its command the Arab mobs who are resorting to destructive violence in Jerusalem and Jaffa and other centres.[28]

As with the government intelligence reports, the paper readily conflated this "mob" violence with the broader political instability, emphasizing, "The disturbance in Palestine is mainly of the nature of mob-violence."[29] The government's breaking of the strike by force was therefore "necessary and proper."[30]

A number of the *Spectator*'s readers took issue with these prescriptions. Among them was E. A. Ghoury of the Palestine Arab Party (whose president, Jamal Husayni, sat on the AHC). In a 12 June letter to the editor, Ghoury proposed that the behavior of British forces in Palestine—which included "beatings, destruction of property, insulting of women, invading homes," and so on—might usefully be juxtaposed with the attention the British press paid to "the cases of 'Arab snipers, marauders, rebels, bands,' and similar names given to the young Arabs who are trying to defend their rights and liberate their country."[31] He likewise told a British audience at Chatham House that the revolt was "not the act of terrorists or marauders or snipers," but was, rather, "a revolution" seeking "justice."[32]

But Ghoury's minority report could hardly be heard above the din of mutually reinforcing British coverage. The *Daily Herald* featured headlines such as "Arab Murder Campaign" (14 May) and "Gangsters in the Holy City" (19 May). Presaging Dill's later assessment, the *Daily Telegraph* editorialized in its 18 May edition, "What began as mere common crime . . . has [evolved] into a political exhibition of rueful hatred."[33]

MODERATE ELEMENTS

Although his was an audible voice in the chorus of criminalization, Wauchope was alert to the difficulties this chorus might create for law enforcement. Thus, while describing attacks on British forces as "murder," his

2 June memo to the colonial secretary also cautioned against adopting measures designed to "intimidate [the] Arab population sufficiently to bring lawless acts to an end." The high commissioner thus elided, as would GOC Dill, the fact that His Majesty's forces had already begun terrorizing Arab villagers. He nevertheless presciently advised that harsh tactics risked "alienat[ing] all moderate elements in this country, perhaps permanently."[34]

According to Air Vice Marshal Peirse, a few days before Wauchope's memo, on 30 May, the inspector general of police—along with Peirse himself, the other architect of the village search policy—relayed instructions to him from unspecified superiors to "modify the intensity" of the searches. Thus, he recorded despairingly, did "the only measure available for coercing the rebels [slip] away from us."[35] The record suggests, however, that this measure's indispensability in reality proved too precious to relinquish, official sanctioning aside.

The flow of reports of British brutality did not fall off in early June, after the supposed termination of severe measures. On 18 June, the AHC sent a telegram to the high commissioner, voicing more of the familiar complaints: ". . . Army men beat unarmed Arab villagers [and] destroy[ed] furniture [and] food supplies."[36] Two days later, Wauchope assured Yitzhak Ben Zvi, the chair of the Jewish National Council (Va'ad Leumi), that "where responsibility [for Arab attacks] can be fixed on any village severe measures are being taken."[37] Reports of such measures appeared contemporaneously in the Arab press, and included charges of theft, the destruction of food, and "ill treatment" of villagers.[38] On 23 June, the deputy inspector general of police wrote in a CID report that "summary action against certain villages" had "aroused considerable resentment and criticism." This took on added significance in light of his subsequent observation that "it would not appear that up to the present more than a small proportion of the villagers have taken arms against the forces of Government."[39] Peirse characterized the 24 June search of villages in the vicinity of the routinely sabotaged Jerusalem-Lydda railway line as having had "a good effect"—the familiar euphemism for terrorizing villagers into obedience.[40] By then, the government had conducted eighty-one village searches, nearly half of which had failed, not surprisingly, to recover any weapons.[41] In July, the high commissioner informed the colonial secretary that there were "accusations of undue military severity throughout the country."[42] He felt obliged to begin his 7 July address to the Palestinian public with a reference to the "misconception . . . that Government uses force wantonly and ruthlessly."[43] The next day, Reuven Zaslany, the Jewish Agency's liaison to the British army, reported to Haganah intelligence that "the government intended to reduce the weapons searches in Arab villages, in order to avoid further alienating the population."[44] If the authorities were still contemplating this course of action in early July, they had yet to undertake it, Peirse's assurances notwithstanding. It is therefore little surprise that on the same day as Zaslany's report, the AHC resolved to "complain to the League of Nations regarding terrorism and the killing of innocents by the British military" and "to prepare a report on the violent actions that occurred during searches."[45] Nor is it surprising that in August, the writer of a Colonial Office memorandum referred to "the numerous complaints we [have] received about outrages by the troops."[46] As the War Office itself ultimately acknowledged—almost in the same breath as it decried the Arabs' "successful protests against 'excesses' by troops"—in the absence of an official policy of repression in the revolt's first phase, "many repressive measures . . . crept in through force of circumstances . . . and mostly they were more severe in nature than would have been necessary . . . had a strong front been presented from the start."[47]

Such measures, coupled with the government's perpetual indifference to Arab demands, squandered whatever remained of its credibility among the Arab population, and placed "moderate elements" such as Arab government employees in an impossible position. On 30 June, Mustafa Bey al-Khalidi, a puisne judge at the supreme court in Jerusalem, along with 136 other Arab civil servants, signed a statement to the high commissioner and other top officials. Its essence was that the Arab officials could no longer usefully serve as a link between the British government and the Arab population, who with good reason disbelieved all of the officials' assurances as to London's good faith vis-à-vis commissions of inquiry and other such palliatives. British force would do nothing to change this situation, the statement insisted. In a poignant and representative passage, the officials asserted:

> It will be argued, we know . . . that Government cannot yield to violence
> without losing prestige. We would strongly have supported that argument
> had it not been for our belief that Government is itself in part to blame for
> the state of mind which has brought about the violence. We yield to no one
> in upholding order and authority as the foundation of all good government.
> But authority implies justice all round, and when justice is denied . . . then
> authority becomes undermined; and it shows a mistaken notion of prestige
> to suppose that it can be restored by the use of force.[48]

The statement prompted a delayed response from the president of the Committee of the Jewish Community of Jaffa and Tel Aviv, but one worth noting in the present context. It arrived on the high commissioner's desk with the endorsements of an array of Jewish groups, along with a request that it be forwarded to the colonial secretary and to the League of Nations Mandates Commission.[49] The letter claimed that the 137 Arab signatories of the statement had "wholly or partly ... identif[ied] themselves with the movement of civil disobedience and open revolt, with all its implications of cold-blooded murder, vandalism and the like." The government, it argued, should have fired them. To do otherwise was to yet again countenance "brigands, marauders and 'rebels.'" Incredibly, the Arab signatories had "even presume[d] ... to protest against the Government's policy of 'repressions.'" In a word, the Arab statement was "patently illegal" and the Colonial Office erred in deigning to acknowledge it.[50]

THE AMBIVALENT ZIONIST DEPICTION OF THE PALESTINIAN LEADERSHIP

The Jewish press beat the same belligerent drum. One newspaper, in a May special edition, proclaimed that the government had "surrendered the country to murderers."[51] On 19 June, the new colonial secretary, William Ormsby-Gore, relayed to Weizmann the high commissioner's opinion that Jewish newspapers' unrelenting calls for "ruthless repressive measures against the Arabs" had considerably "exacerbate[d] Arab feeling."[52] Indeed, two days prior, *Filastin* ran an article stating, "The Mandate authorities would clearly not have used these violent means were it not for the provocations of the Jews and the Jewish press."[53]

As Ian Black documents, a great deal of the Arab-related content of the Zionist press in Palestine originated from the political department of the Jewish Agency.[54] This was true in particular of the *Palestine Post*.[55] The *Post* claimed from the first that the strike was the work of thugs. Its 27 April edition, for example, contained headlines such as "Strike forced on Arabs" and "Business as usual in spite of hooligans." In a 29 April article titled "Deal with the instigator," the paper declared that "the inspiration for the strike is undisguised intimidation," and prayed that the British would not "lose themselves in admiration of what can easily be mistaken for a perfect organization, with its roots in some deep-seated grievance." On 20 May, the *Post* opined that arrest figures (800 Arabs, fifty Jews) during the recent "wave of crime" furnished "a simple index to the part of the population which supplies the aggressor and the criminal."[56] When the AHC publicly pled for nonviolent resistance to the British, the *Post* editorialized that the committee was either dissembling, or had "never exercised any real influence over [its] people" in the first place.[57]

This analysis contained a tension that was also present in the Jewish Agency arguments to Wauchope. These were resolute regarding the criminal nature of Arab political agitation in Palestine. When elaborating this claim, Zionists' rhetorical weapon of first choice was to lay responsibility for all violence in the country at the doorstep of the national leadership, whose national credentials they simultaneously belittled. The evidence for this inference was lacking, however, as disclosed in Jewish Agency members' private remarks (such as Ben Gurion's and Shertok's above) and in the *Post*'s desultory acknowledgement that the Arab leadership had, perhaps, sincerely advocated peaceful methods. But if they had, insisted the paper, that only exposed their "leadership" for the sham it was. Thus, to put it colloquially, the Arab leaders got it coming and going. They were either fomenting all violence or powerless to control it. Either way, what kind of leaders were these?

Of course, this choice was false. For the Arab leaders were neither responsible for all violence in the country nor empowered to prevent it. And the charge regarding their impuissance was, in any case, an afterthought in Zionist discussions. The primary indictment remained that the AHC had coerced Arab participation in the strike through thuggery and was likewise behind the attacks on British police and soldiers. As with the *Times*' coverage of encounters between Arab and British forces, the *Post* cast the Arab militants as mere outlaws, turning out headlines such as "Running fights with Arab bandits" and "Soldiers fight bandits."[58] Bandits and hooligans, not "some deep-seated grievance," were the real drivers of the strike. The *Post*'s 4 June edition heralded the government's "long-delayed recognition" of the strike's "essential illegality."[59]

BRITISH INTELLIGENCE ASSESSMENTS
OF THE REBELS

While the Jewish Agency and the Jewish press relentlessly reiterated the top-down (that is, AHC-directed) crime theme, British intelligence attempted to come to grips with some of the subtleties on the ground. Two were particularly significant. First, as noted above, Arabs mostly struck at British forces and infrastructure in May, although they also attacked Jews (sometimes fatally) and their property. The increase in "crime" therefore had a peculiarly military quality. Second, crime did not, in fact, increase dramatically from May to June. The number of murders was equal from one month to the next (twenty-one in each case), and attempted murders were comparable (moving from fifty-four to sixty). Cases of manslaughter, theft, and "other offences against the person" actually declined in June, while assaults and woundings increased from thirteen to seventeen and highway robberies from four to five.[60]

The RAF weekly intelligence summary of 17 June continued to refer to armed Arab groups engaged in sabotage and attacks on British forces as "gangs" and "marauders," but it also took notice of their organizational sophistication. Recounting an attack on a British railway patrol outside Dayr al-Shaykh, in the Jerusalem subdistrict, the report observed, ". . . the fire of the gang was organised and controlled—it was not mere indiscriminate sniping."[61] The following week's intelligence summary likewise remarked on "the improved organisation" of the "marauders" attacking British forces. It concluded, "The two main objectives of the Arabs now appear to be intensive sabotage of railway lines and formation of armed gangs to combat the military in the open."[62]

Peirse's report also commented on the more impressive rebel formations that appeared on the scene in June, particularly in what would come to be known as the "triangle of terror"—Jenin, Nablus, and Tulkarm. He wrote:

> Armed bands which a fortnight previously consisted of fifteen to twenty men were now encountered in large parties of fifty to seventy. The bands were not out for loot. They were fighting what they believed to be a patriotic war in defence of their country against injustice and the threat of Jewish domination.[63]

Such passing acknowledgements of the magnanimous (if misguided) motivation of what were otherwise referred to as "bandits" are rare in the record, and mark the boundary of mainstream British discourse on the revolt at the time.

CONCLUSION

By late June, then, the British and the Zionists were in firm agreement on the criminal nature of the burgeoning armed revolt—if not firm enough, from the Zionist perspective. With regard to the strike, London took a more nuanced view. On the one hand, as the high commissioner made clear verbally and via legal fiat, the strike was illegal and an open affront to the authority of the British government in Palestine. Those advocating it were therefore subject to prosecution and incarceration on grounds of sedition. On the other hand, while the British allowed that some of the strike's success turned on the work of criminally-minded young toughs operating at the behest of local strike committees, they were nevertheless certain that it had broad popular support. So much so that the Arab leadership would have discredited itself in opposing it. But as we shall see, this more moderate—and accurate—evaluation of the strike sat uneasily with London's pretense that it faced something other than a nationalist uprising in Palestine. And given that this pretense was indispensable to the legitimacy of the mandate, forfeiting it was impossible. Rather, the notion of a popular strike and insurgency would have to go.

THREE

"The Policy Is the Criminal"

WAR ON THE DISCURSIVE FRONTIER,
JULY–AUGUST 1936

THE TREND LINES OF THE REVOLT and the strike evident in June deepened in July. Increasingly robust and well-organized Arab military formations took the field, and the strike endured in defiance of its regularly forecast demise.[1] The government responded to these developments with air power, propaganda, and military reinforcements. In the course of the month, British planes assaulted the rebels assiduously, firing 8,000 rounds and dropping 205 bombs. Mandate authorities also circulated over 350,000 pro-government leaflets to nearly a thousand villages.[2] Mustafa Kabha relates that such leaflets tended to feature a mix of "veiled threats and promises." One read:

> In times of distress and drought . . . the government exempted you from paying taxes and lent you a helping hand in the form of subsidies. But now the government is spending its money arresting lawbreakers and maintaining order . . . Who loses as a result of violations of the law? The losers are you and your village.[3]

In addition to the bullets, bombs, and handbills, two more British battalions arrived in Palestine, raising the total to eight. They fortified road and rail, and set up permanent pickets at trouble spots such as the road between Jerusalem and Nablus and areas in the "triangle of terror" (Jenin, Nablus, Tulkarm).[4]

While the Jewish Agency and the Jewish press continued to regard the rebels as criminal gangs (*kenufyot*) and the strike as a contrived display of Arab "unity," it would be a mistake to suggest that the reverse was unqualifiedly true in either case. The rebels did sometimes harass, assault, and even assassinate those they considered an impediment to the movement for national independence, and thereby alienated many of their fellow Arabs.

And while the strike and the rebellion enjoyed broad popular support, there were Arabs who subverted both. The wealthy mukhtar of the village of Bidya, about twenty miles southwest of Nablus, refused to participate in the revolt on grounds that its proponents were lower-class delinquents.[5] The mukhtar of Silwan, near Jerusalem, defiantly offered his protection to the Yemenite Jews entering and leaving his village. The Arabs of Lifta, on Jersualem's northern outskirts, were likewise inclined to keep the intercommunal peace, and resented the push towards confrontation with the Jews.[6] Arab attitudes regarding what constituted national obligations thus varied. (Indeed, Arab ideas about what constituted Arab national identity in Palestine varied.)[7] Many Arabs were ambivalent about the strike, which placed their national and familial obligations at odds. The strike committees were alert to these difficulties and pooled resources to aid those most impinged upon by the work stoppage. Where beneficent tactics did not achieve their end, the committees resorted to intimidation.[8]

The Jewish Agency seized on such cases as evidence of the coercive and fundamentally criminal substructure of the strike. But the reality, as the British appreciated, was that while part of the strike's success turned on enforcement mechanisms designed to prevent those less willing or able to participate from undermining Arab solidarity, the political objectives of the Arab population at large were clear long before the disturbances began in April 1936—and they included halts to Jewish immigration and land purchases, both of which spoke to the fundamental Arab hostility to further Jewish economic encroachment in Palestine. Wauchope, for example, wrote Ormsby-Gore in mid-June: "Intimidation is responsible only in small measure for continuance of strike which has [the] full sympathy of all Arabs."[9]

While the British and the Zionists repeatedly admonished the Arabs that they would not meet their objectives through violent protest, such scoldings were disingenuous.[10] It was, after all, trivially true that the Arabs could not extract British concessions by violent means, for they could not extract them by any means at all, as the history of the mandate plainly disclosed. The general Arab response to this circumstance was well articulated three years earlier, during the October 1933 riots in Jaffa, when Musa Alami, then a mandate official, commented: "The prevailing feeling is that if all that can be expected from the present policy is a slow death, it is better to be killed in an attempt to free ourselves of our enemies than to suffer a long and protracted demise."[11] 'Awni 'Abd al-Hadi, writing to Wauchope from the detention camp at Sarafand (in Lebanon) in August 1936, gave voice to a kindred sentiment:

"The Arabs are aware that [the] Government is able to continue to pursue its present policy for another long period without showing any weakness. But they assert, on the other hand, that they have nothing to lose."[12]

All of this established the context of the escalating struggle between Zionists, Arab Palestinians, and Britons for discursive ascendancy vis-à-vis the rebellion, which the present chapter will chart. It will focus in particular on the boldest crimino-national claim of the Zionists: namely, that the revolt was literally the product of a criminal syndicate working in secret collusion with the Arab Higher Committee. In addition, it will detail how Britons and Arabs responded to this contention, and how Arab actions bolstered it.

CRIMINAL NETWORKS AND THE ORIGINS OF THE REVOLT

The most ambitious Zionist argument for the criminality of the strike and the revolt held that the apparently spontaneous disturbances of April 1936 were actually the premeditated outcome of known criminal elements working at the behest of the Arab leadership. In July, for example, a declaration "from the Jewish public in Israel to the civilized world" claimed that "the 'leaders' of the Arabs living in our country started making preparations for the recent agitations some time ago." The trouble began, the document continued a little further on, "with the operation of a gang of murderers."[13]

It is worthwhile briefly to address this charge, which was pervasive in 1936–39 and recurs in scholarship. The declaration's claim regarding "preparations for the recent agitations" was not without merit. According to the memoir of the Palestinian militant Subhi Yasin, the highwaymen whose 15 April murder of three Jewish motorists set off the sequence of events culminating in the slaughter of 19 April were motivated by more than loot. The men had, in fact, intended to trigger a popular rebellion against the British, and were members of a group that included two future rebel leaders, Shaykh Farhan al-Saʿdi and Abu Ibrahim al-Kabir.[14] Likewise, in his diary entry for 21 October 1935, the Istiqlal activist Akram Zuʿaytir noted his plans for a large meeting on 2 November (the eighteenth anniversary of the Balfour Declaration), the aim of which would be to "usher in a revolutionary campaign in Palestine."[15]

But despite the fact that some Palestinian groups were laying plans for a violent revolt well before 19 April 1936, the notion that the Arab leaders, much less a "gang of murderers," were behind the "agitations" was mistaken. Indeed, both Subhi Yasin and Akram Zu'aytir wrote disdainfully of the mufti and the AHC's reluctance to support even a peaceful strike.[16] And the most ambitious scholarly attempts to situate the armed bands in the milieu of the mufti and various criminal gangs have been unpersuasive.[17]

Even as they publicly characterized the militarization of the Palestinian national movement as the work of extremists, British officials privately acknowledged that this "extremism" in fact represented the mainstream of Arab opinion, which held that it was force alone that entrenched British policy in Palestine, and it would be force alone that dislodged it.[18] As the prolific pan-Islamist writer and activist Shakib Arslan put it in a February 1935 letter to the mufti, ". . . [T]he only language [the British] can understand is resistance."[19] The idea, then, that the rebellion was a mere "extension of traditional brigandage," the mischief of "irresponsible youths and criminals," or an assemblage of "terrorist nuclei" to which "youths from the villages" attached themselves, does not hold up.[20]

As Yehoshua Porath documents, a mere seven of the known rebels had prior criminal records, although these seven were prominent figures.[21] Based on interviews with former rebels conducted in the 1980s, Ted Swedenburg surmises that a greater proportion of lower-level fighters had criminal records predating the revolt than of rebel leaders, although he in no way implies that these comprised the majority of rebels. Swedenburg does note, however, that Palestinian histories conveniently ignore the criminal records of some insurgents.[22]

More broadly, Palestinian nationalist discourse has tended to retroject modern Palestinian conceptions of criminality onto the period of the revolt and prior. Until quite recently, this entailed the forgetting (or condemning) of erstwhile bandit-heroes such as Abu Jilda, whose violent and larcenous exploits in the 1930s were once the stuff of fearful and admiring Palestinian folklore.[23] Likewise, robbers whose victims lay outside their own communities were, in earlier times, locally revered among Arabs in Palestine. They occupied a liminal frontier between crime and adventure, which depended for its existence upon intercommunal fissures born of parochial loyalties, and which Palestinian nationalist discourse has therefore foreclosed.[24]

But while figures such as Abu Jilda largely vanished from Palestinian memory with the sealing of this frontier, their salience at the time of the revolt turned not only on a pre- or proto-national provincialism, but also on a dialectic in the Palestinian political imagination between the criminal and the national. This dialectic emerged naturally from the growing Palestinian conviction that the national government of the mandate was predicated on the illegal negation of Arab rights, and that it was only the maquillage of British sovereignty—flags, courts, uniforms—that concealed this ugly fact.

In his memoir of his time as a policeman in Palestine during the revolt, Roger Courtney recalls, "The names and fame of bandit leaders were treasured and revered everywhere in the Arab hills."[25] He goes on to tell of a twelve-year-old newspaper boy in Jenin, who adopted the moniker "Abu Jilda" and "led an 'army' of children, with the purpose of mocking and harassing the police and the government generally."[26] This "army," composed of youths aged seven to twelve, donned "tin hats" modeled on those the British police wore, and slung bandoliers around their shoulders, against which they rested sticks in lieu of rifles. They even carried drums. Courtney remembers the boys parading "through the dusty Jenin streets" and brazenly violating the curfew by running noisily from house to house after hours. In response, the police would cobble together slingshots and smack the children with stones ("*usually* in the rear"!), a tactic which succeeded in converting them into "law-abiding and law-respecting citizens."[27] Similar demonstrations occurred elsewhere in Palestine. In June 1936, a celebration erupted in the streets of Jerusalem. Its occasion was a rumor that the city's notorious assistant superintendent of police, Alan Sigrist, had been assassinated. Here, too, scores of children fashioned tin hats out of "trays and platters" and held aloft wooden swords as they chanted anti-colonial slogans.[28]

In willfully defying the outsider's law while reappropriating his symbols of national sovereignty, "Abu Jilda's" troupe reproduced, theatrically, tactics that Abu Jilda's troop had pioneered in its real-world skirmishes with British police. As another former Palestine policeman, Colin Imray, recollects in his memoir, Abu Jilda became a top law enforcement priority after his group of outlaws executed a four-man police patrol and made off with their horses, rifles, and bandoliers.[29] On a separate occasion, one of Abu Jilda's men apprehended a "senior legal officer" at gunpoint and demanded his pants.[30] When the police finally caught up with the infamous bandit and his longtime partner in crime, Salih al-ʿArmit, the two men emerged from their hideout "festooned with full police bandoliers and carrying police rifles."[31] An unwary observer might have mistaken them for policemen.

By the time of the revolt, bandits such as Abu Jilda seem not only to have straddled a line between criminal and adventurer but also to have sat astride the border of the criminal and the national—the very space the British inhabited in the Arab Palestinian political imagination. Indeed, both Abu Jilda and his attorney appear to have been keenly aware of this fact. The latter insisted at Abu Jilda's 1934 trial that his client's deadly assault on a policeman was "based on nationalist principles" as opposed to criminal proclivities.[32] This defense took for granted that the same actions, when coded as national rather than as criminal, took on an inverted moral significance. If the British could play this game, why not the Arabs? As for the bandit-hero himself, one of his fellow prisoners, Najati Sidqi, recalled in his memoir that Abu Jilda wore

> a military uniform decorated on the epaulettes with two swords and three stars in an attempt to distance himself and his group from the charge of being bandits. He also carried a long polished sword with a gilded handle and called himself chief of staff, while designating his colleague al-'Armit... as deputy with full authority.[33]

During the revolt, Arab insurgents employed the same strategy. Among the photographs that Palestine policeman (and great-nephew of Lord Allenby) P. J. De Burgh Wilmot kept in his scrapbook from the revolt years are a number featuring dead rebels in military attire. One such snapshot displays a mortally wounded Arab in button-down khaki trousers, khaki jacket, and high boots.[34] The private papers of the assistant superintendent of police in Jenin, G. J. Morton, include a revolt-era photograph of three rebels in the same outfits, with the caption: "Typical Arab gangleaders in the Jenin area."[35] As Morton's caption indicates, the wearing of such uniforms was common among insurgents. A CID report of 18 August 1936 noted, "... [A]ircraft report seeing men in some uniform decamping into the hills."[36] (The same report noted, not incidentally, that Palestinian "flag days have been held in Jaffa and other parts of the country.") One British soldier recalled of Fawzi al-Qawuqji, whom the British would come to regard as the commander-in-chief of the rebels, "I remember seeing him through the field-glasses, standing on a small hill at the Battle of Bala, in Turkish uniform, wearing his medals and carrying a sword."[37] Porath likewise notes rebel commanders' predilection for "uniforms and symbols of rank."[38]

It is worth pausing for a moment to consider Porath's explanation for the rebel uniform phenomenon, which is partially correct. He claims that rebel maltreatment of villagers in 1939 was "[t]o some extent... motivated by personal desire for status and wealth," and continues, "Otherwise, one can hardly understand the deep concern of the bands' commanders, who were leading an underground organisation, for uniforms and symbols of rank." Undoubtedly the uniforms served as a symbolic denial of rebel criminality, but not merely on account of some rebels' bad behavior. For the British equation of the rebels with "bandits," "marauders," and "criminals" persisted independent of the rebels' treatment of the villagers. And while the rebel armies were "underground" in the sense that they waged asymmetric war against a traditional police force and military, their uniforms signified—to the Arabs of Palestine, to the British, and to an international audience—that they were a national military, regardless of what the British might claim.

Arab rebels thus not only transgressed the law but also commandeered its legitimizing tokens in the form of military and police regalia, as well as flags, stamps, courts, and other such emblems of national sovereignty (as we will explore further in subsequent chapters). In so doing, they did not so much break the law as they did turn it back upon its ostensible guardians. The British responded with mockery and re-imposed upon the rebels labels such as "murderer" and "criminal." Thus, one of Wilmot's photographs of a uniformed Arab rebel is accompanied by a caption disparaging the idea that the man was a soldier of any kind. Wilmot refers elsewhere to a pair of slain Arabs in the same uniform as "murderers."[39]

The British eagerness to so name the insurgents had an anxious quality, the impetus of which is well articulated by the legal scholar Nasser Hussain: "As Walter Benjamin once noted, the law's fear of [generalized] violence is different from its fear of crime. Crime is a transgression against the law that may be checked by it. A more general unrest threatens not so much to upset the law as to set up an alternative logic and authority to it."[40]

While Arab bandits, rebels, and their young acolytes adopted police and military garb, British police and troops, as we have seen, frequently resorted to bandit tactics, and thereby embodied the conflation of the national and the criminal in the Palestinian political imagination. The bulk of the British officers imported from the disbanded Palestine gendarmerie into the Palestine police in 1926 were former Black and Tans from Ireland, whose reputation for "a certain ruthlessness," observed a 1939 War Office report, they "maintained" during the revolt.[41] The idea of employing Black and Tans in Palestine originated in the early 1920s, with then-Colonial Secretary Winston Churchill. Writes James Barker:

What Churchill envisaged for Palestine was a tough corps of fighters as a tactical reserve for the existing police force. As it happened, there were men available who matched this description: the thousands of ex-servicemen known as 'the Black and Tans' that Churchill himself had recruited as Secretary of State for War in February 1920 to reinforce the Royal Irish Constabulary. With both sides in Ireland seeking a negotiated settlement, these men, notorious for their brutality and indiscipline, would soon be out of a job. Churchill, unconcerned by their bad reputation, started planning their transfer en bloc to Palestine.[42]

Ex-Black and Tans became more, not less, prominent and influential in the Palestine police as time passed, holding five of eight district commander posts by 1943.[43] The group's notoriety was such that British officials began, in the course of the revolt, to use its appellation as a byword for illegal behavior among police.[44]

Criminal elements, then, existed on either side of the Arab-British divide, although neither party could be correctly described as simply criminal, and the bulk of those fighting—whether Arab or British—did not have criminal backgrounds. The Arab revolt could only be regarded as a criminal enterprise within a discursive framework that submitted the legitimacy of British force in Palestine as a given. British violence in Palestine was largely absent from the surface of texts operating within this framework, as did most British and Zionist analyses of the revolt. As detailed directly, however, Arabs challenged British and Zionist discourse in this connection, forcing the issue of British force (and its Zionist impetus) to the surface of the debate over the nature of the rebellion, and thereby pressing the criminal charge back upon the mandatory and those in whose interests it acted.

WAR ON THE DISCURSIVE FRONTIER: THE STRUGGLE TO CRIMINALIZE THE OTHER

In June 1936, Paula Ben Gurion opened a letter from London. In it, her husband David boasted that those making the Arab case in the city had singularly failed to expand "the ranks of our enemies" among the British political class. By contrast, Zionist influence was such that in the parliamentary debate of 20 June, "The speeches by Lloyd George, Leopold Amery, Tom Williams, Creech Jones, Herbert Morrison, James de Rothschild and Victor Cazalet were wholly or partly prepared by us." He regarded the debate as "almost entirely the fruit of our work."[45] But in early July, Lourie relayed to Shertok that members of the House of Commons, while "agreed that terrorism must be stopped," were nevertheless pondering the utility of reducing Jewish immigration into Palestine. And the Agency received a report the next day stating that Wauchope was all that stood between the British military and a death blow to the insurgents, no doubt exacerbating Shertok and others' sense of urgency regarding the British—and above all Wauchope's—perception of the rebels.[46]

Fear of British capitulation to Arab demands roused the Jewish Agency and its allies to apply greater diplomatic and popular pressure on the government to treat the revolt as a criminal affair: that is, to crush it. But doing so proved increasingly difficult for the British. By July, the rebels were launching twenty to thirty attacks on British troops and communications ("and occasionally . . . Jewish settlements") daily.[47] The CID periodical appreciation summary for 12 July logged "persistent reports" of "large armed bands in the hills between Nablus and Ramallah." Although the department regarded these as mere phantoms, it acknowledged the existence of such robust formations in the villages. The rebels' "courage," noted the summary, was not in question. It added poignantly, "[A] number are said to have gone to the hills taking their winding sheets [burial shrouds] with them."[48]

British forces countered insurgents via "pressure" on areas in and around Nablus and Ramallah, which generated still more insurgents.[49] The same undoubtedly resulted from the "bitterness . . . felt by the Rural and Urban population [over] the action taken by Government in sending large bodies of troops to villages, etc., and alleged shooting of unarmed peasantry," as the CID reported.[50]

On learning of some rebels' coercion of villages that failed to contribute "men or money" to the revolt, the CID averred that "the bandit ('Mujaheddin') spirit" was "still very much alive."[51] But the coercive tactics of the rebels were not, at this point, of primary concern to most Arabs, who were preoccupied instead with the behavior of British forces.[52] This included the comparable practice of levying collective fines on villages deemed insufficiently supportive of the government. A telegram from the village of Jabaʿ read aloud at a meeting of the AHC on 19 July described "soldiers bursting into the village and collecting fines."[53] Cities, too, were subject to fines. In June alone, the British fined Nablus, Acre, Safed, and Lydda.[54] Rebel manifestos referred to these actions as "infringements" (al-taʿaddi) and included them alongside robberies and murders in their list of indictments of the mandatory government.[55]

Apart from complaints regarding these often devastating financial impositions, Arab reports of British brutality continued unabated.[56] They frequently entailed a dual claim: the Arabs suffering such treatment were not criminals, and therefore did not deserve it; and the British meting it out were thereby advertising their own criminality. The Arab Women of Jaffa informed the high commissioner on 8 July that the British use of excessive force in the area was "common knowledge." Anticipating the charge of Arab criminality, their letter went on to assert:

> Your Excellency will realize that the Arab people are compelled in the present circumstances to defend themselves and their country by purely national motives without the least intention to commit crime, as Your Excellency may assume, and the only means for quickly ending this period of crime and disorder will be by the removal of the causes which have created them.[57]

'Awni 'Abd al-Hadi echoed this theme, addressing the high commissioner from the detention camp at Sarafand:

> I, personally, do not know any one person of those who fire from the mountain-tops or who blow [up] bridges or cut telephone wires but it appears to me that there is not one person amongst them who is actuated by any personal interest in all the acts which he does, exposing himself to many dangers.[58]

He also reminded the high commissioner, ". . . [T]he fact which cannot be doubted is that your troops have dealt with the Arabs ruthlessly and destroyed many Arab villages without any justification."[59]

The AHC wrote Wauchope on 15 July, "It is a matter of regret to the Committee that bitter complaints are still being addressed to it with regard to the ruthless and severe manner in which the troops are dealing with the situation under the pretext of 'search.'"[60] Wauchope received another such report three days later, this one from the Arab Orthodox Priests Congress for Palestine and Transjordan:

> The banishment of leaders, the confinement of people in prisons, the blowing up of houses with dynamite, the imposition of heavy fines on towns and villages, the looting of property, cereals and livestock, and other similar vigorous measures which are still being taken by troops and Police in all parts of the country are not only detestable measures which are prohibited by religion and inhuman and not befitting the civil forces of a great Christian and civilized power but are also unlikely to culminate in suppressing the rebellion and restoring order.[61]

While officials tended to dismiss such reports, it was not for lack of internal corroboration. A government welfare inspector reported to the chief secretary on 13 July that British troops had, a week earlier, killed an unarmed former policeman and father of five in the village of 'Abud, about ten miles northwest of Ramallah. 'Abud, wrote the inspector, had "always been peaceful and [had] not even been searched by troops." His sour commentary on the incident suggested that such episodes were not rare:

> Instead of pacifying the country by these tactics, bitterness and resentment is rapidly increasing in the villages and elsewhere. Whereas at the beginning of the trouble the fellahin were our best friends, we are steadily turning them into our worst enemies by these methods of ruthlessly killing innocent people and destroying their possessions and their stores of food.[62]

An internal Colonial Office memo dated 9 July noted "many instances of rash and dangerous shooting by Supernumerary Police," a particularly troubling development given the number of Jews among their ranks.[63] Testimony to continued British malfeasance turned up in private correspondence as well. Policeman Percy Cleaver wrote his aunt and uncle from Haifa on 6 July, "I've been on one or two of these [night] raids and it's quite good fun, especially turning the contents of the houses into the street."[64]

In addition to repudiating the charge of criminality emanating from British and Jewish quarters, articulate Arab opinion in the latter half of 1936 also reversed it, and not only with respect to Britons. Arab newspapers portrayed Tel Aviv as a "city of thievery, swarming with forgers and thieves," and made frequent reference to Jewish criminal conspiracies, often involving entanglements with world communism.[65] In reply to a Jewish newspaper's report that children throughout Palestine were suffering from nightmares of "an Arab criminal standing in front of their houses, trying to get in," a writer for *al-Difa'* observed: "This portrayal of the 'Arab criminal' is not surprising because every word in this newspaper, and in fact every word on the street and in official statements has painted this picture." The headline of the article read, in part: "The Arabs are not the criminals, you criminal!"[66] Arab newspapers also sought to transfer the criminal label to the British. *Al-Jami'a al-Islamiyya* argued, "... [T]he cases of the strike are not of the nature to which the criminal law is applicable, because criminal laws have been enacted . . . where the offence is committed on account of criminal habits."[67] The reality, declared *Filastin*, was that "the [British] policy alone is the criminal."[68]

While prior to April 1936 political cartoons featured sparingly in the Arab Palestinian press, they began appearing regularly in both Arab and Jewish newspapers during the revolt. Their caricatures often implied the criminality of the other by way of subtle visual cues that played on well-known physiognomical and phrenological codes.[69] One cartoon from the 19 June edition of *Filastin* depicted a British authority accepting a Jewish bribe while simultaneously exhorting the government to employ "all types of force" against the "Arab robbers and scoundrels." The official's deep-set eyes and compressed brow connoted his delinquency according to physiognomical conventions.[70] A second cartoon was more blunt. It depicted John Bull standing before a judge and flanked by two wives, one Arab and one Jewish. The judge advises him, "If you are sincerely looking for peace you must divorce your second wife [the Jewess], because your marriage to her is illegal."[71]

The Arabs were turning the charge of criminality back upon their accusers, and were thereby engaging the crimino-national critique: the nation reserved to itself the right to name the criminal, whether the criminal fell within or outside its ambit. To the extent that a "period of crime and disorder" was acknowledged by Arab nationalist groups (as it was by the Arab Women of Jaffa), it was a matter for the people to sort out—a process that began with diagnosing the external cause of the internal disorder, which was the long-standing, ongoing British and Zionist colonial penetration of Palestine.[72]

While the Arabs remonstrated against British policy and the means employed to enforce it, the mainstream British press continued to regard the revolt as a largely criminal affair, although this line of argument showed signs of faltering. The term "Arab revolt" appeared for the first time in *The Times'* coverage on 20 June, but it made no difference with regard to the paper's crime thesis; the same article marveled at Lord Winterton's minority opinion in a House of Commons debate that "the Arab revolt . . . was a national movement, not mere banditry," a view which led him to propose "the startling theory that nationalists were entitled to use all means, short of violence, to hold up the Government."[73]

The Spectator's coverage was more discriminating, partly because more of the column space it devoted to Palestine consisted of letters to the editor. Even its professionally authored "think pieces," however, gave evidence of a working hypothesis approach to understanding the revolt. A paragon of this genre was the 17 July article by William Blumberg, titled "The Arab and Zionist Policy." Blumberg contended that it was "no use trying to make capital out of Arab lawlessness as the Zionists do." "Revolutions," he continued, "have their own logic." He thus pointed out what *The Times* had ignored:

once the language of revolt and revolution was in play, talk of criminality became much more complicated. But the "proof of good will" that Blumberg suggested the Arabs rightly required was not that of the British but rather that of the Zionists. After all, setting aside the fact that the Arabs had done so for two decades, the British could not "concede demands raised at the point of the revolver."[74] Rather, Blumberg pressed the burden of surrendering to violence onto the Jews. The British position with regard to force was, once again, essentially invisible in its moral dimension. The very idea of the illegitimacy of British force was excluded in advance, even by someone capable of articulating the Arab case quite well in other regards, and who in fact sympathized with it. The dearth of analyses of the British presence in Palestine—and by extension of the legitimacy of the British use of force to maintain "law and order" there—was another instance of the discursive theme noted in the previous two chapters: namely, the absence of the British from their own calculations regarding the course of events in the mandate.

The same proclivity characterized the opposite pole of the mainstream political spectrum. The liberal *New Statesman and Nation*, for example, consistently maintained that the British could only do so much to help in Palestine; it was up to the Jews and the Arabs to put their intercommunal affairs in order. On 30 May, the weekly magazine editorialized that establishing peace in the mandate was

> a formidable task, in which the British Government and British officials in Palestine can play but a secondary part. They can be policemen and judges, they can advise and encourage. They can even in desperation appoint Royal Commissions to investigate complaints, to expose sham grievances and propose remedies for genuine ones. But they cannot work miracles. It is the Jews and the Arabs themselves who must find the way of settling their differences and making a Palestinian nation.[75]

The mandate may have been a British creation through and through, but the British role in its most basic functioning had somehow become "secondary," according to the writer. In a 13 June item, the magazine repeated that the government could do no better than to restore "law and order" in Palestine; the rest was up to the "disturbers of the peace."[76] "Law and order" was apparently a neutral state of affairs, which the British merely upheld, as a stage would actors.

The letters to the editors of both *The Times* and *The Spectator* became a forum of less narrow debate during July, evincing a divide between orthodox

THE POLICEMAN'S LOT

FIGURE 4. This political cartoon from the British publication *Punch* well illustrates the British crimino-national discourse vis-à-vis the Palestine mandate. The British policeman, who is composed and wields no instrument of coercion, separates two violent and enraged men, one an Arab and the other a Jew. The tussling "Moslem" and "Hindu" over whom the officer stands suggest that the British play this civilizing role throughout their empire. (Punch Ltd.)

professional opinion-makers and a heterodox section of their readership. John Poynder Dickson-Poynder (Baron Islington), the former undersecretary of state for the colonies and a man openly sympathetic to Palestine's Arabs, wrote *The Times* on 7 July, protesting, "[I]t is absurd and manifestly untrue to say ... that the recent outburst in Palestine is confined to a handful of Arab desperadoes and murderers."[77] This did not stop the paper from continuing to refer to the rebels as "bandits" and "marauders," but it did constitute visible dissent from this tendency within its pages.[78] Another letter, this one from House of Commons member Arnold Wilson, criticized those who "[referred] to the [Arabs] as terrorists" and who defamed "those ... who seek to do justice to the Arab inhabitants of Palestine."[79]

Meanwhile, the letters section of *The Spectator* was serving as the arena for a war of words between J. M. N. Jeffries, the former Near East correspondent for the *Daily Mail*, and Blanche "Baffy" Dugdale, niece and biographer of Lord Balfour himself and "gentile Zionist" par excellence.[80] Dugdale objected to Jeffries' apparent suggestion that the British "[yield] to the demands of the Arab extremists for the stoppage of immigration." Jeffries responded:

> I am sorry for the Jews driven from their homes by the tyranny of the Nazis, but we must not impose them on Palestine and try to cure tyranny with tyranny. Let us find room for them in our own Empire, not add to our reputation for hypocrisy by giving them a warm welcome to the shores of another people.[81]

This provoked a counter-volley the following week, including letters from Dugdale and one Benjamin Levy, who reiterated the charge that the so-called "strike" was nothing but a criminal campaign.[82] Another writer cited from a private letter he had received from a British official in Palestine, which claimed that government forces were "machine-gunning from aeroplanes those Arab patriots, called brigands by the Zionists."[83] This prompted a riposte in the 24 July edition from a man objecting to the testimony of any British functionary "openly sympathising with the lawbreakers" and perpetrators of "murder, arson and wanton destruction."

While *The Spectator* thus gave voice to a broader spectrum of opinion on Palestine than most major periodicals, its editor nevertheless felt compelled to state in its last July edition: "The policy of *The Spectator* has been, and is, to give a fair hearing to both parties ... We can neither defend nor condone the use of violence, whether by Arab or Jew."[84] Or Briton, he might have added, but did not.

THE PALESTINE MANDATE.

BRITANNIA. "THEY GAVE ME THE SCALES OF JUSTICE AND HER SWORD. I HAVE
USED THE SCALES; I HAD HOPED NOT TO HAVE TO USE THE SWORD."

FIGURE 5. Another *Punch* cartoon illustrating the British crimino-national self-conception.
Here Brittania does wield an instrument of coercion, but only reluctantly and alongside the
scales of justice. The artist has also positioned her at a physical (read: causal) distance from
the rioting Palestinian masses. (Punch Ltd.)

ARAB ATTACKS ON NONCOMBATANTS
AND THEIR RAMIFICATIONS

While peripheral voices challenging the conventional wisdom on the criminal nature of the revolt were becoming audible in the British press by July
1936, an undeniably criminal act at the end of the month rapidly replenished
the credibility of the mainstream. On 23 July, a bomb was pitched into the
playground of a Jewish day school on the Jaffa-Tel Aviv border, wounding
seven young children. British intelligence immediately concluded that it was
"unlikely that this isolated outrage was sponsored by any responsible Arab
leader," but added: "The Jews claim that the Arabs are responsible and it is
unlikely that we have heard the last of the incident."[85]

This was an accurate prediction. The Central PTA for Grammar Schools
in Tel Aviv made a public appeal on the day of the bombing, which stated,
"The government must put an end to this situation, in which gangs of murderers and savages have held this country for more than three months." It
ended with a plea for "all enlightened nations, people of science and learning,
teachers and writers, [and] defenders of civilization and humanity" to raise
their voices against such barbarism.[86] On 24 July, Shertok sent Lourie an
urgent cable, wherein he insisted that the episode be "made [a] lever" in the
effort to persuade influential officials that such actions "disqualif[ied] Arabs
for independence."[87] Simultaneously, the Council of Jewish Women's
Organizations dispatched a telegram to a number of prominent Britons,
including the colonial secretary and the president of the Women's Suffrage
Alliance in London.[88] It condemned the attempted murder, comparing its
horror to that of an earlier attack on a Jewish nursery. Both incidents pointed
to the same conclusion:

> To such moral deterioration [has the] Arab community descended under
> [the] leadership [of] men who tell well intentioned people in London it is [a]
> peaceful strike [the] Arabs are conducting while they and their press do not
> utter one word [of] condemnation [regarding] these outrages.[89]

The Palestine Post made the link between the strike and the schoolyard
bombing more explicit, proposing in a 24 July article that the indolence bred
by the work stoppage had corroded Arab moral sensibilities. The paper also
mentioned the "well-intentioned people in London"—echoing the language
of the Council of Jewish Women's Organizations, and thus suggesting that
the Jewish Agency framing of the incident was rapidly making the rounds.

The article went on to couple the attempted murder of children with attacks on British troops and police, asserting, ". . . [N]o Arab should be left under the impression that political concessions [can] be wrung by employing boys to throw bombs at defenceless school children or men to conduct guerilla war against troops."[90]

While eight Jews lost their lives to Arab assailants in July, thirty would be killed in August, a number of them in incidents that quickly became notorious.[91] On the evening of 13 August, for example, a group of Arabs snuck into the Jewish quarter of Safed from an adjacent cemetery. One Jewish family, fearing just such a scenario, had huddled together in a single room of their home, where they lay asleep on mats near an open window when some of the assailants approached. Spotting the opening, the men lobbed an explosive into the room, following it with a volley of rifle fire. The device detonated, blasting off the head of a 36-year-old rabbi named Walter Unger. Bullets meanwhile cut down two of Unger's three children—a boy and a girl, ages five and eight.[92] The number of Jewish children killed in the course of the revolt was thus raised to four.

Shertok met with Wauchope two days later—by which time the third Unger child had succumbed to her wounds in the hospital—and pled with him again to place responsibility for Arab terrorism on the mufti. Wauchope had, by then, begun considering more drastic measures, such as exiling Amin al-Husayni from the country.[93] Shertok telegraphed Lourie in London on 16 August, demanding that several members of the House of Commons, who on 30 July had publicly pledged to prevent "Zionist influence in Parliament and the Press" from derailing the recommendations of the newly appointed Royal Commission, be challenged to retract their statement in light of the murders of the Jewish children.[94]

The following evening in Jaffa, Martha Fink and Nehama Tsedek, nineteen-year-old Jewish nurses who worked at the government hospital in the Arab quarter of the city, were shot and killed.[95] The government immediately issued a communiqué condemning the killings, adding that the high commissioner was "confident that with the exception of some murderous individuals the whole people of Palestine share his detestation of these horrible crimes."[96] Both the mayor of Jaffa and the city's National Arab Committee did decry the murders, the mayor taking the opportunity to "[denounce] every act of this sort in which women fall victims" and the Committee claiming that "such an act proceeds only from men who are devoid of all human pity."[97] Lourie reported back to Shertok on 18 August, detailing his and others' attempts to "get into touch with a number of prominent people including some of the [Anglican] Bishops with a view to writing a joint letter of condemnation [regarding the attacks on children] to *The Times*."[98] In subsequent days, Lourie and the preeminent British historian Lewis Namier brought their concerns to representatives of *The Times*, *The Morning Post*, *The Daily Mail*, *News Chronicle*, and *The Yorkshire Post*, in addition to meeting with the prime minister and a number of high-level politicians.[99]

Ben Gurion and Weizmann, meanwhile, held a lengthy meeting with Ormsby-Gore and his private secretary, E. B. Boyd, as well as Deputy Undersecretary of State John Shuckburgh. The two adopted a hostile posture towards their British interlocutors, refusing to offer any input on Iraqi foreign minister Nuri al-Said's recent diplomatic interventions with the Arab Palestinian leadership, and stating in no uncertain terms that the Jewish Agency had lost all faith in Wauchope, who had yet to reckon with the fact that the "real government in Palestine [were] terrorists," among whom they included the mufti and ʿAwni ʿAbd al-Hadi.[100] On 20 August, Ben Gurion telegraphed former prime minister David Lloyd George suggesting that, in light of the "barbarous outrages being committed against Jewish women and children" in Palestine, he and Winston Churchill write their own letter to *The Times*, this one aimed at dissuading the government from "even a temporary suspension of Jewish immigration before the royal commission . . . reported" its findings.[101]

The cabinet did, indeed, shortly decide against a temporary suspension of Jewish immigration, despite the AHC's having agreed to call off the strike as a quid pro quo. The Jewish Agency received a report from London, the author of which regarded this as a fatal, if predictable, error on the part of the Arabs, who in insisting that the suspension precede the termination of the strike had succumbed to that "Oriental exuberance which the ordinary Englishman cannot stomach." But the Agency member reviewing the report took little note of this passage, instead underlining a section which read, "Government circles in England . . . are opposed only to Arab methods . . . but as far as the [Arab] claims themselves are concerned, the tide in England is running strongly in the direction of the Arabs."[102]

Regardless of the truth of this characterization of the state of opinion in England, it accurately conveyed the view of a large number of troops in Palestine. With four British regiments stationed in Jerusalem, Humphrey Bowman was afforded the opportunity to hear the thoughts of many soldiers. He recorded on 22 August, ". . . [E]very officer I have spoken to believes the Arabs have a case, and admit the bravery of the Armed Bands in the Hills."[103]

Such murmurings reinforced the Agency's anxiety regarding the need to shore up pro-Zionist voices in the British press and government.

THE ZIONIST STRATEGY OF COMPLAINT AND RESTRAINT

A key strategy in this connection was that of complaint and restraint. In August, a joint statement of the Histadrut and Poale-Tsiyon, directed to the Yishuv, declared: "We must repeat emphatically: Protest must be expressed responsibly, without intemperate outbursts that will do more harm than good."[104] The policy of non-retaliation or *havlagah* had been observed fairly consistently by all elements of the Jewish community since late April. These included the underground Jewish army, the Haganah, and its revisionist competitor, the Irgun (*ha-Irgun ha-Tsva'i ha-Le'umi*, or National Military Organization), although the latter preached against restraint.[105] Noting the tendency of "British and Zionist narratives" to efface entirely Jewish violence against Arabs in 1936, Charles Anderson writes that "in reality Jews attacked Arabs, if with less frequency," and offers a few examples.[106] The Arab press was aware of the policy of *havlagah*, and was quick to note its non-observance. In a 17 August article, for example, *al-Jami'a al-Islamiyya* reported on widespread anti-Arab violence in Tel Aviv, commenting:

> Those who are known to be "blessed with self-control" have completely lost it and started attacking all Arabs walking in the neighborhoods of Tel Aviv. They attacked 200 young men and a donkey cart on its way to Ras al-'Ain. The riders on the cart were all badly injured. There was also a young student riding a bicycle back home; they attacked him, took him inside a store, and beat the hell out of him. Then one person stabbed him, causing him to pass out.[107]

If such episodes did not, events in the 1940s would make clear that the Yishuv was by no means above using violence to advance its national objectives. In 1936, however, the Jewish Agency and others calculated that their ability to frame the revolt as a crime wave would be compromised by any Jewish action that reinforced the impression that Palestine was in the grips of a civil war between two national communities. Alternatively, observing *havlagah* enabled the Jewish community to juxtapose its own passivity with Arab aggression, especially on occasions when Arabs struck the softest of Jewish targets. The Council of Jewish Women's Organisations in Palestine illustrated the rhetorical benefits of *havlagah* in an August open letter, which declared:

> We Jews do not throw bombs at Arabs in the streets nor snipe at them along the roads, we do not burn Arab crops, nor uproot Arab orchards because we hold human life sacred and the fruits of human labour dear.

Apart from characterizing the revolt as an outbreak of unprovoked aggression against Jews, the statement also touched on the other two perennial Zionist premises, claiming that the Jews were creatively developing "a long neglected country" whose present Arab inhabitants had "destroyed ... hundred[s] of thousands of pounds[']" worth of capital directed to that end, and that the Zionists' real enemies were "those who purport to speak in the name of the Arabs of Palestine," as opposed to the Arab population as a whole.[108]

To be sure, the threefold Zionist criminalization of Palestinian nationalism—which contrasted Jewish nonaggression, economic creativity, and democratic idealism with Arab belligerence, economic blight, and demagogic authoritarianism—was much more than a rhetorical strategy. It ran to the roots of Zionist culture, featuring not merely in official statements, newspaper columns, and radio broadcasts, but even in the Passover *hagadot* of kibbutzim during the rebellion. As David C. Jacobson notes, "Settlements belonging to the kibbutz movement were at the forefront of the struggle with Arabs who rebelled," making these settlements' Passover *haggadot* a "particularly illuminating source for understanding the telling and retelling of the Zionist national narrative in response to the Arab Revolt."[109]

Kibbutz ha-Boneh produced one such *hagadah*. It read in part: "For in all other years we traveled securely on the roads of this land. This year—only crowded together in caravans, with policemen before us and behind us."[110] In earlier times, the stanza suggested, the Jews did not need armed escorts in Palestine. But this was only trivially true, for the enabling condition of Zionist settlement in Palestine was British force—albeit latent, and thus unseen, and thus unremarked. Again, the instruments of coercion rose to the surface of the text only when Arab violence (read: crime) was the concern. A few stanzas later, the *hagadah* continued:

> For in all other years we thought the English authorities ruled the land as they arrested every murderer or criminal and brought him to justice. This year the armed gangs took control of our land with murder and destruction; they murdered a hundred Jewish souls and hundreds of dunams of

planting... For the authorities have become too weak to arrest the murderers and no murderer receives his due.[111]

Kibbutz Givat Brenner composed another such Passover *hagadah*. Jacobson writes of its contents:

> In keeping with the suspicion harboured by many Jews at the time that the Arab Revolt was not a genuine grassroots expression of national will, the narrative speaks of "inciters (*mesitim*) [who] arose among [the Arabs]" to encourage them to attack the *yishuv*. The narrator characterises the Arab Revolt as a series of attacks by "criminals" (*posh'im*) and "gangs of robbers" (*havurot shodedim*).[112]

Regarding *havlagah*, the same *hagadah* stated: "And we were a wonder and an enigma, for the spirit of revenge did not move us and we controlled our spirit and learned self-restraint."[113]

Such sincere sentiments notwithstanding, exploiting the rhetorical force of *havlagah* became all the more imperative as reports of British officials' deliberations over the Palestine question—which seemed increasingly to ponder the legitimacy of Arab means and ends in isolation from one another—trickled into the Jewish Agency and its affiliates, who sought in response to drive home the intimate and necessary connection between Arab methods and objectives.

Henrietta Szold, speaking for the Council of Jewish Women's Organisations in Palestine, wrote the high commissioner on 18 August arguing that the "wanton cruelties" that the Arabs continued to inflict upon the Jews had "sprung from the seed of baseless hatred sown by irresponsible leaders." As the violence of the revolt had emerged organically from the same leaders who rallied the population to continue the strike, so too was Jewish *havlagah* "the outflow of [the] inherited Jewish way of life which demands respect for the soul and the life of others."[114] To separate Arab means from ends was to misapprehend the elemental difference between the Arab and Jewish communities in Palestine. It was, indeed, to mistake a crime wave for a national revolution.

As Rabbi Blau of Agudath Israel, the largest Orthodox organization in Palestine, expressed to the high commissioner in a meeting in late August, whereas Orthodox Jewry was "founded on the principles of the Torah," including "the commandment 'Thou shalt not kill'," the Yishuv's enemies in Palestine were "bands of brutal and bloodthirsty men," perpetrators of "murder and robbery" who did not "pity women and children" and "destroy[ed] the lives of peaceful and learned men."[115]

The Hebrew daily *Davar* lamented that the Jews of Palestine, in light of the murder of the young nurses, were self-evidently bereft of a negotiating partner in the Arab community:

> To whom should we speak? Should we turn to the murderers? To those who cannot be distinguished from predatory animals? To those at the core of whose souls have always dwelt sadism and slaughter, blood and the blade, but who appear now as teachers, priests, and leaders, donning the garb of heroes and nobles and holy men?[116]

The chairman of the Jerusalem Jewish Medical Society likewise indicated in a letter to Wauchope that the same "assassins" who had been rebelling for the previous four months were now "shooting down indiscriminately women, old men, children and even nurses." He beseeched the high commissioner to "[destroy] the nests of the murderers and the councils of agitation who are responsible for these acts of savagery."[117]

Such pleas did not fall on deaf ears. But their implication that the rebellion was little more than a crude campaign of murder, theft, and mayhem—that is, devoid of any political significance—was conspicuously implausible. For that reason, as we shall see in the next chapter, many British officials began privately to propose a more nuanced analysis of the rebellion, with important consequences for British policy in Palestine.

FOUR

The British Awakening to
the Military Nature of the Rebellion,
August–October 1936

AS OF AUGUST 1936, British intelligence had begun to emphasize the problem of Arab "terrorism" in Palestine, a term which, though common in the
British press, appeared in an RAF intelligence summary for the first time on 7
August. The word was employed ambiguously, but included threats to British
officials. The same report was the first to speak of rebel "murders," among
which it included the killing of two policemen, two Jewish watchmen, and one
supernumerary constable, thus counting (as had Wauchope) attacks on British
security personnel as ordinary crimes.[1] It did distinguish these "individual
murders" from deaths resulting from "long range sniping or ambushes."[2]

Although an intelligence report of 18 August observed that "villagers have
been forced to contribute towards the maintenance and shelter of gangs,
frequently unwillingly," the notion that the British were stamping out banditry in Palestine was losing credibility.[3] In the rebel bastion of Nablus, the
CID found that "although battening on the villagers for foodstuffs, etc., is
tolerated when it comes from genuine armed 'patriots', any robbers or others
who wish to take advantage of the people for private gain or revenge are given
short shrift by the rebels themselves."[4] RAF intelligence likewise concluded
on 28 August, "Throughout the present trouble the Arabs have obtained
singularly little pecuniary gain, either by robbery or by looting." It attributed
recent "minor raiding" in the Jordan Valley to "a few unscrupulous persons,
inspired less by patriotic than personal motives."[5] An 11 September intelligence report anticipated that, with the arrival of non-Palestinian fighters in
the country, looting was likely to increase. But it also acknowledged, "The
whole emergency has been characterised by the absence of looting."[6]

Such confidential admissions cleared the cobwebs from the British crimino-national perspective on the revolt, bringing Arab violence and "terror"

(as opposed to "banditry") into clearer focus as the government's central concern. On 8 September, the Colonial Office published a statement of policy on Palestine. Its thrust was contained in a single passage:

> ... [A]fter a careful review of the whole situation His Majesty's Government are satisfied that the campaign of violence, and threats of violence, by which the Arab leaders are attempting to influence the policy of His Majesty's Government cannot be allowed to continue, and that more rapid and effective action must now be taken in order to bring the present state of disorder to an end with the least possible delay.[7]

It went on to announce the imminent arrival of another division of soldiers (bringing the total number of troops in the country to 20,000) and the transfer of military command in the mandate to Lieutenant General J. G. Dill.

While the public statement placed the blame for the "campaign of violence" directly on the Arab leadership, the high commissioner's private remarks were less simplistic. He wrote the colonial secretary on 4 September: "The Arab leaders have done little to help and ... nothing to calm public opinion, quell resistance or assist Government to end disorder by any means except by force."[8] This depiction of a passive and uncooperative leadership was quite different than that put forward in the 8 September statement, which implied that the AHC was actively directing the revolt. It also hewed closer to the findings of British intelligence, which indicated that popular support for the rebels was spontaneous, and not the product of pressure from the Arab leadership. "[E]very Arab was either secretly or openly in varying degrees of sympathy with the rebels," noted a War Office assessment, which likewise found: "In semi-official and unofficial circles nearly every Arab gave the rebellion practical support in some form or other."[9] As the secretary of state for air reminded the cabinet in a 2 September meeting, the Arab leaders were "not ... those who control the actual terrorists" and were in no position to act as their proxies in negotiations with other parties.[10] Quite the contrary, the mufti began wearing a bulletproof jacket that month, so concerned was he that the rebels might assassinate him.[11] In mid-October, with the rebellion at an apparent end, Wauchope himself would caution Ormsby-Gore:

> ... [I]t would be the height of folly to imagine that by the removal of the Mufti or this Committee the danger of a fresh Arab rising will be ended or even greatly reduced. Compare the tenacity of villagers who have opposed us for six months with little pay and no loot, with the feebleness and a lack of any great qualities of leadership among the Committee.[12]

CRIMINAL + NATIONALIST = TERRORIST: THE CONVERGENCE OF BRITISH AND ZIONIST REPRESENTATIONS OF THE REVOLT

That the official policy statement of 8 September directly implied that the Arab leaders *were* in control of the rebellion was significant for two reasons. First, it marked a new point of convergence between the British and Zionist representations of the revolt. Private convictions aside, the British, like the Zionists, were now publicly insisting that the AHC was directing the revolt and should therefore be held responsible for its continuation. Secondly, this very fact disclosed an important feature of the "crime wave" framing of the rebellion: the credibility of the criminal charge depended on its specificity. It could not be applied to the entire Arab population, for this would inevitably prompt an unwelcome question: If the objectives of the rebels and those of the Arab population at large were the same, how did the British distinguish between nationalism and crime in Palestine?

Whatever their rhetorical pretensions, the British drew no such distinction in practice. The military mapping of "the enemy" in Palestine, as disclosed in Operation Instruction No. 23, regarded "armed bands" as just one of eight "hostile elements" among the Arab population. The others were: leaders and agitators, intelligence organizations, intimidators, saboteurs, terrorist gunmen or bombers, signaling organizations, and finally, "those engaged in a purely passive attitude." Including the last group amounted to declaring the entire Arab population "the enemy," as the War Office admitted in a classified report: "There was probably no Arab in Palestine who did not come under one of those headings."[13]

Two considerations led London to refrain from acknowledging this fact publicly, however. The first was the decline (not disappearance) in the post-WWI period of explicitly racist characterizations of nationalist movements. The second was the rise in the same period of moral regard for these movements. Both developments made criminalizing nationalists and the peoples they represented more difficult.

By the 1930s, British imperialist discourse had long nourished itself on the notion that the ethics of empire turned on the spread of law and order to the world's "lower races." The British considered themselves uniquely qualified for this task.[14] They had, after all, more or less solved the problem of crime at home. There was more to commend this view than one might think. Between the mid-nineteenth century and the First World War, for example, both serious and petty criminal offenses declined consistently in Britain—and this despite the fact that the government classified more behaviors as crimes and invested greater efforts into monitoring them.[15] The British were mindful of their success in setting the modern standard for social order. In 1883, Scotland Yard declared London the world's safest city.[16] In 1901, the well-known British criminologist Robert Anderson proclaimed that the permanent eradication of crime in Britain was simply a matter of incarcerating for life seventy known recidivists.[17]

All of this lent credence, in the British political imagination, to the enterprise of enlightening (or modernizing) the benighted (or backward) races on the fringe of the empire. Although historians typically speak of the British criminological tradition in Victorian and post-Victorian terms, this "colored" vision of modernity spanned the border separating the two periods. Popular Victorian literature, for example, cast the criminal threat in civilizational and racial terms.[18] From Charles Dickens to Arthur Conan Doyle, nineteenth-century British fiction unfolded against a backdrop of social stability, with the police and their newfangled forensic techniques supplanting the criminals of earlier narratives at center stage. The same literary works pushed scenes of social instability to the periphery of the empire, where modernity had yet to gain a foothold.[19] While late- and post-Victorian intellectuals would come to stress the biological and cultural determinants of crime—thus undermining the traditional Victorian emphasis on character and free will—they too presented the eradication of crime as a key index of modernity and order, and thus of civilizational development. Havelock Ellis, the influential author of the first English book on criminology (*The Criminal*, published in 1890), defined criminality in terms of modernity, characterizing it as a function of one's stage of historical development. Such stages were glimpsed in the "lower races," for whom much that moderns regarded as criminal (killing strangers, infanticide) was perfectly sensible. A criminal, according to Ellis, was simply a person in modern society who, for reasons of genetics and environment, behaved as though he were from an earlier stage of human history. He was, like the "lower races," a kind of fossil. J. Bruce Thomson, a surgeon at the General Prison for Scotland, put the point more forcefully in an 1870 article in the *Journal of Mental Science*: "The moral sense is absent in certain races of men, as the Bosjesman and the Australian, who simply follow their desires and objects of interest; and not only in certain races, but persons in the best races are moral idiots."[20]

This racial apologetic of imperialism was the intellectual context in which the British adopted the term "terrorist" to designate nationalists who threatened the empire. The first British use of the term dated to the 1860s, when London was attempting to suppress and marginalize Fenian dissidents in Ireland and England.[21] The first British legal measures targeting "terrorism" originated in the same period, as did the government's creation of the Criminal Investigation Department and a "special branch" of the Metropolitan police, both of whose initial purpose was to apprehend Fenian "terrorists."[22] G. K. Peatling correctly observes that "depicting terrorist or revolutionary movements as a minority of fanatics without organic relation to the surrounding community" was "a strategy etched deeply into the history of counterrevolutionary thought."[23] Nevertheless, the nineteenth-century credibility of racial stereotypes enabled the British to toggle between two depictions of "terrorists." One day they were a fanatical few hiding amidst an upstanding population; the next their fanaticism was representative of their racial group more broadly—that is, they were prone, like all Irishmen, Indians, and the like, to irrational violence. In theory, these two formulations did not accord. Within a discourse steeped in racism, however, their tension was not often apprehended. Thus, even as pillars of the mainstream British press downplayed the popularity of Fenianism in the 1860s, the notion that the Irish generally were a race of "unreformable savages" persisted.[24]

As a general rule, the same could not be said openly of Arabs in the 1930s, certainly not when the mandate instrument explicitly stated that they had "reached a stage of development where their existence as independent nations can be provisionally recognized."[25] More broadly, as Antony Anghie observes: "It is in the Mandate System ... that ... the 'uncivilized' are transformed into the economically backward; when international law begins to discard a vocabulary that appears racist and problematic and adopts a new series of concepts that appears neutral and universal."[26] Even privately, British officials were less inclined to invoke racist explanations of the instability in Palestine than one might expect. Charles Townshend claims that "large generalizations about 'the Arab', 'the Orient', and especially the 'Arab mind' ... reappeared constantly throughout the British attempts to cope with the events of 1936–39."[27] But while such judgments were by no means rare in British discussions of the revolt, Townshend exaggerates their frequency. More common than this racist rendering of the rebellion was a crimino-national one, which referred routinely to "gangs" and "bandits," and almost always placed military references to the rebels (commander-in-chief, army, and so on) in scare quotes. And this brings us to the key point. By divesting these criminological judgments of the racism that had historically animated them, British officials were able to maintain the pretense of a liberal agenda in the Middle East. But this divestment came at a cost; it left open the question of the basis for such criminological judgments. If Palestinian nationalists' racial inferiority did not make them criminals, what did?

This question was made more urgent by the second consideration underlying London's refusal to characterize as criminals the Arab Palestinian population at large: namely, the moral credibility that anti-imperialist forms of nationalism increasingly enjoyed in the post-WWI period. In nineteenth-century Ireland, the British encountered a less formidable foe in nationalism than they would in twentieth-century Palestine. It is true that even some British commentators in the nineteenth century took note of the incongruity of London's championing nationalist struggles in Europe while it sought to strangle the cause of Irish independence "at home."[28] Nevertheless, in the mid-1800s, British authorities had greater latitude in ranking different nationalisms according to their moral status. Some nationalisms were noble, others nefarious.[29] Such convenient compartmentalizing drew far more suspicion and scrutiny in the post-WWI period. Nationalist movements in the 1930s—especially those in the Middle East—were ticking time bombs of political autonomy. London was bound, by its own admission, to recognize Arab independence in Palestine. In nineteenth-century Ireland, by contrast, British authorities could acknowledge the existence of Irish nationalism without thereby committing themselves to an eventual recognition of Irish autonomy. By providing a conceptual link between crime and nationalism, "terrorism" enabled London to downgrade to the status of criminal enterprises those national movements that impinged on its imperial prerogatives. Although British commentators and officials similarly characterized the Palestinian rebels as "terrorists" in 1936, the link between nationalism and criminality was, by then, far less secure, and the "terrorists" designation therefore less potent.

The revolt years lay nearer to the age of nationalism than they did to the age of empire, to borrow Michael Mann's terms. As the former epoch approached, nationalism acquired a more muscular moral connotation. It was for this reason that the British disavowed the notion that their post-WWI occupation of Iraq and Palestine-Transjordan amounted to a covert colonialism, riding roughshod over the national aspirations of the region's inhabitants. Indeed, the very pretext of the British presence in the Middle East was the building up of independent nation-states there. This project preempted any British effort to characterize nationalists as criminals. By contrast, as Mann observes, "In the Age of Empire imperialists did not have to attempt 'nation-building' because the only nations were European ones . . . 'Third World' nationalism . . . only began to sustain broader-based rebellions in the twentieth century."[30] The revolt of 1936 was a case in point.

British imperialism was thus ill adapted to post-WWI ideological developments regarding race and nation. While it plodded along, continuing in practice to regard nationalist rebels as terrorist criminals, the "rebels" designation was accruing international legitimacy and the "criminals" designation suffering from a deficit of the overt racism that had historically given it force. And yet, only a crudely racist account of Palestinian nationalism could have enabled the British to equate it outright with criminality. Absent that, they could only insist that those claiming the nationalist mantle in the mandate were, in reality, not nationalists at all, but rather a criminal cabal operating among—and influencing for the worse—an otherwise law-abiding people. It was, in a word, a structural necessity of British imperial discourse in Palestine that a minority of individuals be singled out as the "criminals" with which the British were contending. As for the broader Arab population, the British cast them as two-dimensional, scenic figures, devoid of volition or political insight, and mere pawns of their nefarious leaders.

Zionist representations of the revolt conformed to the same logic. While fonder than the British of emphasizing the civilizational distinction between the Arab and Jewish communities in Palestine—and the "inferior" quality of the Palestinian nationalism resulting therefrom—Zionist leaders generally stopped short of suggesting that the Arabs at large were criminals. They tended rather to unpack the structure of the Arab political community in Palestine from the AHC down to the national committees and the "gangs," all of which they consistently characterized as criminal enterprises. Palestinian Arabs more broadly were passive, on this understanding. Those involved in criminal activity were the hapless patsies of their devious leaders, who stirred them to crimes of misguided passion against the British and the Jews.

"IT *IS* A WAR NOW": REBEL ORGANIZATIONAL SOPHISTICATION AND THE BRITISH RESPONSE

For the British, this framing of the revolt solidified in early September, when it became evident to military planners that more severe measures would be required to restore calm in Palestine. Given the already rampant charges of military and police brutality in the country, officials were concerned "to avoid anything in the nature of 'frightfulness'," as the secretary of state for air cautioned in the 2 September cabinet meeting. Having said that, he advised granting "wide discretion" to "military authorities on the spot," whose prerogatives should include "bomb[ing] the houses of criminals or their sympathisers."[31] These "sympathisers" were identifiable by the fact that the "criminals" firing on British planes used their homes for cover.

Such attacks had succeeded in downing and otherwise damaging British aircraft, which signaled the rebels' ascent to yet another level of military professionalism.[32] Other incidents pointed to the same conclusion. On the night of 6 August, for example, Arab gunmen staged an audacious raid on the El Hamme police post, overtaking the officers on duty and relieving them of their weapons.[33] Such sophisticated operations reflected the excellent quality of the insurgents' intelligence. Rebel agents had thoroughly penetrated the mandatory government. Military actions not executed within twenty-four hours of their initial planning were vulnerable to prior detection. Planners had to shepherd any intelligence furnished to translators or police guides carefully, and assumed grave risk in discussing operations over the telephone, even in code. Troop movements were invariably detected by the rebels, who employed an "extensive ... signal organization" consisting of "lights in houses, bonfires, and smoke signals," which British pilots could see flickering across the twilit landscape.[34] In a September report, the CID remarked that "the bandit movement" was displaying "more determination and better tactics," as well as "superior" marksmanship. It also offered a sketch of the larger, integrative structure emerging among the different rebel groups, naming six "principal leaders," only two of whom were Palestinians. The other four were Syrians, including the most important leader, Fawzi al-Qawuqji.[35]

Qawuqji was a former high-level officer in the Iraqi military. He entered Palestine from Transjordan in August with a contingent of 200 men, mostly from Syria and Iraq.[36] He travelled around the country, familiarizing himself with the terrain and visiting villages, which welcomed him and his men like heroes.[37] He recruited men and gathered provisions from the villages, which he then stored in mountain hideouts. The conscripted men underwent military drilling, which raised their morale and earned them the admiration of their fellow villagers.[38] By mid-September, Qawuqji's reputation was such that British civilian administrators in Palestine regarded him as the lone commander of the revolt.[39] The military reached the same conclusion.[40] It was apparently Qawuqji's men who had furnished the anti-aircraft guns that brought down the British plane in early September.[41] The War Office report on the first phase of the revolt would draw a distinction between the "bandit" tactics of the Palestinian fellahin and the more advanced tactics of these foreign fighters, whom it deemed "the better type of band."[42] An RAF assessment from 4 September put the total number of foreign militants in the country at between fifty and 300 men, and claimed that Qawuqji (whom it elevated to the curious rank of "soldier-bandit") and a Syrian named Muhammad al-Ashmar were "the leaders."[43] By the next week, though, RAF intelligence was focused entirely on Qawuqji, whom it credited with the "greater organisation and leadership" of the rebels, and who it claimed was "endeavouring to reorganise the gangs on a military footing."[44]

The Haganah acquired more specific intelligence: the heads of the six largest rebel groups had met with Qawuqji on 2 September in the vicinity of Bal'a, near Tulkarm, and there pledged loyalty to him as their commander-in-chief.[45] It appears that they had anticipated and previously agreed to his arrival.[46] Qawuqji's "command" of the revolt, however, was never complete. He had no contact with armed groups in Jerusalem and further south, and he was unable to control the Palestinians under his supervision.[47] He did set up a regional command of sorts north of Nablus, and drew on a network of hashish smugglers, among others, to acquire arms from Syria and elsewhere for his men.[48]

Regardless, the British perception of the situation was as consequential as the reality, and the idea that something like a war was underway between British soldiers and Arab rebels under a single command was in the air. Humphrey Bowman, the British director of education in Palestine, wrote in his journal on 13 September, "It is not an easy kind of war, but it *is* a war now—a real revolution of Arab Palestine versus the Jews and the British forces."[49] This view was common.[50] The British could not publicly acknowledge as much, however, and the reason was obvious. If what was transpiring in Palestine was a war, then British soldiers were not repressing a gang of Arab criminals, but fighting an Arab army. They were not managing disorder, but crushing an emerging order—one, moreover, that represented the interests of the majority of the country's inhabitants.

THE DEBATE OVER MARTIAL LAW

As the rebellion spread and the rebels came increasingly to resemble an integrated army (even if more in the British imagination than in reality), the default imperial solution—martial law—became a matter of urgent discussion among British high officials. Some expressed concern bordering on anxiety about the legal consequences of actions taken by the military authorities under such a regime. In the absence of a clear definition of martial law—a century-long desideratum in the British legal tradition—judicial prerogatives vis-à-vis martial law remained a point of some confusion.

In one view—that advocated by the legal advisor to the Colonial Office, H. Grattan-Bushe, who strongly opposed martial law—the key variable was war. If a state of war existed in Palestine, then the actions of the military authorities under martial law would not be subject to judicial review. If, however, a state of rebellion existed, retroactive immunity would not necessarily apply to the same actions. Who decided whether it was a state of war or a state of rebellion? The high court of Palestine, according to this line of thought.[51] This was of particular concern to military leaders in Palestine because the British high court there had publicly condemned some of the leaders' bolder initiatives. Most (in)famously, the chief justice of the supreme court in Palestine had issued a scathing and very public rebuke of the British decision to demolish a section of Jaffa on a "public works" pretext.

A second view, however, treated this supposed judicial supremacy with less reverence. This was the position of the judge advocate general and of GOC Dill, both of whom considered breadth of application to be the critical variable in determining the high court's authority with respect to martial law. On this understanding, if the government declared martial law over the whole of Palestine, as opposed to some section(s) of it, the court's say in the matter would thereby be negated.[52] This dispensed with the need to establish that a state of war existed.

On 15 September, the colonial secretary circulated a document entitled "Proposal to proclaim martial law in Palestine" to the cabinet. It addressed the 2 September cabinet conclusion that "at an appropriate moment Martial Law should be applied to the whole of Palestine or to selected parts thereof." The document endorsed the view of the chief of the imperial general staff and the high commissioner that any martial law declaration should be applied to the whole of the mandate (including Transjordan), although it did not mention the "breadth of application" rationale for this requirement. Indeed, it effectively split the difference between the "war" and "breadth of application" views, suggesting that because circumstances in Palestine had clearly not brought the civil government (including the courts) to a standstill, the high commissioner should be "given all the legal powers necessary ... to enable disorder to be suppressed"—"without a resort to martial law," however.[53] This would preserve Wauchope on his perch at the apex of the mandatory, and thus avoid the legal complications of handing power over entirely to the military.

But a week earlier Wauchope had himself endorsed the opposing position advocated by the War Office, according to which martial law had become indispensable to the restoration of order in Palestine, and should be applied regardless of the legal complications.[54] The Air Ministry concurred.[55] On the other hand, the attorney general for England and Wales, Donald Somervell, forcefully endorsed Grattan-Bushe's argument against martial law. Echoing the renowned nineteenth century British jurist Albert Venn Dicey, Somervell regarded it as "wholly foreign to our law and our methods to hand over the whole administration to the military." He reasserted the view that the military could not bypass the courts by way of a mere declaration of martial law. Its actions would still be subject to judicial review.[56]

Somervell chaired a conference at the Colonial Office on 19 September, at which he insisted that the wisest course was for the government to "confer greater powers on the military . . . in such a way as could not be challenged in the courts," something martial law would not accomplish.[57] Against this, Lieutenant-Colonel Henry Shapcott—speaking, along with Major-General Haining, for the War Office—argued that "the [military] commander [under martial law] could order the courts to close," to which Somervell replied that "the commander would be committing a crime if he did so"; indeed, "the idea that the civil courts could be closed by the military was quite unknown to English Law."[58] Thus did the attorney general place the threat of prosecution on either side of General Dill. For he claimed in a separate meeting of the cabinet's sub-committee on emergency measures that the same courts which Dill could not legally shut down would be positioned not only to review his actions, but also to find him "guilty of a criminal offence."[59] Shapcott's rejoinder to Somervell's "quite unknown" claim is worth pausing over; he "suggested that martial law was law as the military commander makes it."[60]

Law as one "makes it" articulated well one side of the ongoing quarrel over martial law; namely, that which furnished a conceptual space for "the power of real life" to "[break] through the crust" of anachronistic legal convention, as the German legal theorist Carl Schmitt put it.[61] Law, on this understanding, was abstracted to the breaking point when conceived in a manner that dichotomized the juridical and sociopolitical domains. Legal models that fell prey to this fallacy posited an objective legal order to which everyone, great and small, was accountable, including those constituting the state, with its apparatuses for creating, interpreting, and enforcing the law. The problem, according to Schmitt, was that the very idea of a freestanding, "objective" legal order left unsolved the problem of how, exactly, one went about discerning this order's objectivity. How, for example, was the individual to differentiate between a spurious order and this supposedly actually existing order? Political situations, hermeneutic interpretations, and other lived human realities were invariably bound up in and constitutive of any legal order. Extracting oneself from these processes so as to survey a legal order from a disinterested standpoint was impossible.[62]

That political situations and hermeneutic interpretations were constitutive of any legal order was demonstrated by the anxiety of the colonial secretary and others regarding the possibility that military actions under martial law in Palestine would be subject to the scrutiny of the chief justice. For this concern was rooted less in the office of the chief justice than in his person, as revealed when Ormsby-Gore "warned the [18 September] Meeting [of the cabinet] that there could be no doubt that the Chief Justice of Palestine would use all his legal powers as Chief Justice to give the Government and the Military Authorities the maximum amount of trouble and embarrassment." The colonial secretary was "very apprehensive of the serious legal and constitutional reactions that might be expected to result from the *attitude* of the Chief Justice."[63] Such considerations enabled a perennial truth—that law was, in the end, a human creation, and not an abstract "system of ascriptions to a last point of ascription" (Schmitt)—to cut through the misguided egalitarianism of contemporary legal discourse. Shapcott's view that under martial law, the law was whatever the commander said it was, took cognizance of this fact.

The nagging suspicion on the other side of the argument was that this was dangerously wishful thinking. Objective law lingered like an unwelcome apparition in the juridical imagination of the attorney general and many others. It could not be gotten rid of, even temporarily. Its many houses, the courts, could not simply be closed and then reopened, as though justice slumbered and awoke in a cycle of imperial convenience. Some course that navigated the imperishable legal order while simultaneously allowing for extraordinary repressive measures—"a kind of legal martial law," to quote the telling words of the solicitor general—would have to be charted.[64]

Somervell and others' concern over the criminality of the military's negation of judicial oversight paralleled their narrower preoccupation concerning the legality of the actions of soldiers under martial law. The difficulty in both cases was that the very term "martial law" was a misnomer—specifically the "law" part. As O. G. R. Williams at the Colonial Office divulged in the midst of the controversy:

> Martial law does not involve, as I understand it, supersession of one legal code by another, but the substitution of an arbitrary regime for the regime of law. There would appear, therefore, to be no particular point in taking steps with a view to giving an appearance of legality to the arrangements existing during the period of martial law.[65]

This did not worry everyone. Colonel H. J. Simson, GOC Dill's chief of staff, was a firm advocate of martial law in Palestine, which he readily admitted was "not real law" but "the rule of a conqueror."[66]

In so declaring, Simson drew on a long, if somewhat confusing, British legal tradition. As Charles Townshend documents, as early as the first decade of the nineteenth century, acts invoking martial law in British domains were "explicitly designed to prevent the ordinary law from inhibiting the operations of the army or protecting 'rebels'," though martial law itself remained a poorly defined legal concept throughout the century. One widely cited authority defined it as "the suspension of civil jurisdiction," which entailed "the sacrifice of the legal rights of a few." An influential opinion following the 1838 Canada emergency adumbrated Simson's language, holding, "Martial law is stated by Lord Hale to be in truth no law." Indeed, writes Townshend, "The whole drift of English legal thinking was towards banishing martial law from the confines of law properly understood—to say, in effect... that it was 'no law at all'."[67] This was the view articulated by Colonial Secretary Ormsby-Gore, who advised the high commissioner in June:

> Martial law, in effect, means no law, and is the suppression of the operation of the ordinary law so as to give the Government and the military forces unrestricted power to suppress rebellion. The acts of both under a state of martial law would, to a great extent, be illegal.[68]

But this could only be true if martial law was not "law as the military commander makes it." That Ormsby-Gore and Colonel Simson both acknowledged the lawlessness of martial law should not distract from the fact that Simson was in agreement with Shapcott, not the colonial secretary. The absence of the law under martial law was complete, for Simson, because "the rule of a conqueror" was the foundation of the rule of law. It always lay back of law and order, and only misguided democratic idealists (of which there were many) had lost touch with this fundamental reality. As Dill would

lament of the high commissioner's reluctance to declare martial law: "...
Wauchope loves greatly, administers with knowledge and imagination, but
he does not *rule*."[69] From Dill's perspective, Wauchope had forgotten that the
British, in the final analysis, just were law and order, and they need not have
been deterred from swift and decisive violent action by the nonsensical
notion that they were subject to a law which the forces of chaos were busy
destroying. Ormsby-Gore, by contrast, conceived of a freestanding legal
order, which martial law simply ignored. The order, therefore, could come
back to haunt the British, who thus required a guarantee of retroactive
immunity for their actions under martial law.[70] The immunity did not make
British actions legal; it made them unprosecutable. On the other hand, by
Simson's lights, the rebels had demonstrated their unwillingness to play by
the rules, and the British were therefore entitled to set them aside in order to
re-establish the conditions of their possibility. Arab violence defied the law,
British violence reified it.

The military leadership thus formed the vanguard of the criminalization
of Arab national protest. Simson was adamant that the revolt was a criminal
affair, a veritable "career of crime."[71] Dill, likewise, lamented the government's ultimate decision to refrain from imposing martial law upon what he
regarded as a "rebellion against law and order" itself and a "so called strike."
The Arabs, according to Dill, made poor soldiers but "good murder[ers]."[72]
Simson, too, downgraded Arab attacks on British troops from military
actions to criminal deeds—murders, specifically.[73] For Simson, Dill, and the
other advocates of martial law, criminal behavior on a sufficiently broad scale
in a given territory created a situation in which the rule of law itself had to be
introduced (or, in the case of Palestine, re-introduced) to that area. This
introduction required, paradoxically, the law's initial suspension vis-à-vis
British security forces. Disorder would give birth to order. The British would
violate the law in order to enforce it. London had long applied this lopsided
logic to its imperial domains.[74]

Jewish organizations across Palestine had been pushing the British to
declare martial law for many months, and their calls for harsher repressive
measures against "law breakers" continued in September. They put up fliers
to this effect in Tel Aviv and elsewhere, and some Jewish newspapers reported
that a declaration of martial law was imminent.[75] Such reports were widely
believed.[76] Blanche Dugdale, a key source of secret government information
for the Jewish Agency, met with Lord Cranbourne at the Foreign Office on
the 1st of September and tried to persuade him that martial law was the most

sensible course forward in Palestine.[77] When it became known that the government, rather than actually declaring martial law, had opted merely to announce that the high commissioner had the power to declare it, the *Palestine Post* urged, "If it is realized that the bandits will only yield to punitive measures these should not be delayed a moment."[78]

'Awni 'Abd al-Hadi contended in response to the 8 September government statement that the original lawbreakers were the British, whose mandate for Palestine was itself "an illegal instrument."[79] This sentiment was widely echoed. Douglas Duff, the former Palestine police inspector whose harsh treatment of the Arabs in the 1920s rendered his surname an epithet for police brutality, recorded many of his conversations with Arabs during the revolt in his 1936 memoir. On one occasion, Duff suggested to "one of the most senior of the Arab [mandatory] officials" that it was "the riff-raff who are making the trouble." He recorded the official's response:

> He looked at me, staring fixedly at my face. "Is that your opinion?" he said quietly . . . "Make no mistake," he said, "there is not an Arab in the land who is not a Nationalist. I do not wish to deny it; I am one myself."[80]

Speaking to another Arab acquaintance, Duff inquired presciently: "Aren't you afraid that the Government will copy the tactics of Dublin Castle . . . Concentration camps for you people, and Black-and-Tan methods for the population." The man replied, ". . . [B]y the time they arrest the last Committee of us they will have all the Arab population in jail."[81] If real nationalism, the kind a people would fight for, was a crime, then the Arabs of Palestine were all criminals.

Others of Duff's interlocutors made the positive case that the British were the criminals, as their "assassin" police were "paid to murder" Arabs.[82] Traveling through Lydda, Duff and a comrade received "cat-calls of 'British murderers'."[83] A woman in the village of al-Bira, near Ramallah, called Duff and his companions "English murderers."[84] Even talk of rebels offended some of those with whom Duff spoke. "Rebels?" asked one man indignantly, "I am a soldier of the fatherland, fighting foreign tyrants."[85]

The rebels themselves deliberately invoked legal arguments in their exchanges with the British authorities, which sometimes took the form of published refutations of British official statements. Not incidentally, the aesthetic presentation of these statements mimicked that of the government's statements. The documents displayed a stamp of Qawuqji's signature, along with the appellation "commander-in-chief."[86] On 11 September, Khidr al-'Ali

Mahfuz, writing "under the banner of Qawuqji" and in the name of the "General Command of the Arab Revolution in Southern Syria–Palestine," issued his own rebuttal of Wauchope's 8 September statement. Mahfuz offered a nuanced legal critique of British policy in Palestine, wherein he invoked the terms of the mandate instrument, citing a specific article and arguing that the British had neglected to meet their legal obligations to the Arabs as disclosed therein. He reasoned that the most sensible interpretation of the failure of Article 6 even to mention the political rights of the Arab inhabitants of Palestine was to assume that such rights went without saying. The instrument therefore legally bound the British to uphold the political rights of the Arabs, a duty which the government had entirely ignored.[87] As ʿAwni ʿAbd al-Hadi had claimed, the British broke the law first, although where ʿAbd al-Hadi suggested that the text of the mandate instrument itself violated a higher law, Mahfuz took the instrument on board and then offered a correction to the British and Zionist interpretations of it. Both men took up the legal gauntlet thrown down by their opponents and articulated a crimino-national narrative that countered and subverted that of the British and the Zionists.[88]

Moreover, this narrative intrinsically engaged the issue of martial law by challenging the basis for the British claim of emergency that would inevitably anchor any resort to martial law. For the claim of emergency, as Nasser Hussain notes, depended on "an interruption in the otherwise smooth functioning of lawful politics."[89] While the rebel military effort undermined this "smooth functioning," the rebel crimino-national critique called into question its lawfulness.

THE CLIMBDOWN

With the Arabs and the British vying to script themselves as the guardians of justice and one another as the lawbreakers, neither was particularly well positioned to pull back from the brink of a military showdown. For the Arab leadership, saving face meant not yielding to the British demand to call off the strike. A request to do so from the heads of the surrounding Arab states was another matter, however, and the precedent for this eventuality was already in place. Over the preceding months, first Ibn Saʿud of Saʿudi Arabia, then ʿAbdullah of Transjordan, and finally Nuri al-Saʿid of Iraq had all intervened in the affairs of the AHC. This allowed the Palestinian leadership to call on the Arab kings—ʿAbdullah, Ibn Saʿud, and Iraq's King Ghazi—for advice in September. By this time, the AHC's dwindling resources, coupled with the broader Arab public's fatigue and the onset of an agricultural season, motivated the Committee to find a dignified means of exiting the stage before a full-scale confrontation with the British commenced.[90]

Thus, when the Arab kings, with British encouragement, advised the Committee to call off the strike, the Committee quickly complied. Both the kings' appeal to the AHC and the AHC's appeal to the Arab public of Palestine were published on 11 October. The following morning, Arab and Jewish buses began running in Jerusalem, shops there and in Nablus opened, and life in Safed, Nazareth, and even Tiberias (where massive rioting had recently occurred) returned to normal seemingly overnight. Jews and Arabs appeared in the streets of both Tel Aviv and Jaffa, the twin cradles of the conflagration that had ravaged the country for six months.[91]

The British, too, sought a face-saving egress from all-out war against the Arabs. Dill, Simson, and their partisans did not win the day, but their opponents recognized that the rumors of imminent martial law made it politically impossible for the British authorities to simply back away from declaring it. It was for this reason that the government titled its 26 September order in council the "Palestine Martial Law (Defence) Order in Council." While including the term "martial law" in the order was "inaccurate," as the colonial secretary acknowledged, it was nevertheless desirable

> in view of the expectation of the declaration of Martial Law which has been aroused and of the possible impression (which would be quite false) that in not declaring Martial Law Government were weakening in determination to suppress the disorders.[92]

Although the British no doubt intended to stamp out further agitation, they were also anxious regarding the legality of this course of action, as the entire controversy surrounding martial law revealed. They could not afford to divulge as much, however, and thus intentionally obscured the issue of martial law before the public, rather than simply neglecting to declare it. Both sides, then, sought a dignified means of withdrawing from the precipice.

Many Zionists looked upon this development with despair. Colonel Fredrick Kisch—the Jewish Agency's valued liaison with the British military—captured their concern in his notes to the Zionist Executive on 2 October: "I feel that never again will there be such an opportunity for dealing radically with the Arab question, with England both willing and equipped to take strong measures."[93] On 12 October, someone at the Agency wrote Philip Graves—the famed Irish journalist and entomologist who had exposed the *Protocols of the Learned Elders of Zion* as a hoax in 1921—bemoaning at length the manner in which the revolt had been brought to a (no doubt temporary) conclusion. The writer was especially bitter that the "scoundrel-in-chief" (the mufti) had succeeded in "presenting himself . . . to the outside world as the representative leader of a suppressed people fighting for its national freedom." The "criminal acts" of the previous six months had, by virtue of the government's refusal to crush the strike and the revolt, been "glorified as noble deeds of national heroism." When the high commissioner issued the government statement in early September, it appeared that the British were finally coming to their senses and "placing the responsibility for the disturbances on those who were guilty of them." Alas, the Arabs had, in the end, been permitted to script their revolt as a national uprising, rather than the prolonged period of "anarchy and crime" that it was.[94]

For their part, the Arab leaders were concerned to erase whatever criminal taint the rebellion had acquired. Prior to the termination of the strike, the AHC expressed to Ibn Sa'ud their wish that the rebels in the hills receive amnesty.[95] The Committee's terms for peace likewise included a general amnesty for the Palestinian militants and the release of Palestinian prisoners.[96] Again, in their first post-strike meeting with the high commissioner on 24 October, the Committee began by requesting the release of political prisoners.[97] As Wauchope explained to Ormsby-Gore on 16 October, in spite of the hardship of the strike, the Arab population at large regarded "those Arabs who attacked our troops . . . as warriors in a holy cause, not as bandits or evildoers."[98] Interestingly, British intelligence belatedly (and tacitly) acknowledged a kindred distinction in the weeks after 11 October. In directly adjacent passages in its report of 16 October, the RAF concluded that there had been "no rebel activity since the calling off of the strike" and that "small gangs of desperadoes" and "gangsters" ("neither more nor less than common bandits") continued to wander the country.[99] In December, the high commissioner would state to the colonial secretary (by way of arguing against Dill's proposal to outlaw the Higher Committee) that the revolt ended not on account of the AHC's public plea of 11 October, but rather because "all Arabs except regular outlaws were bound to obey the call of the [neighboring] Arab rulers."[100]

Prior to his withdrawal from the country, Fawzi al-Qawuqji sent GOC Dill a note, in which he spoke admiringly, one old soldier to another, of the review of British troops the general had conducted before the King David

FIGURE 6. Lieutenant General John G. Dill, Air Vice Marshal R. E. C. Peirse, and a third military official chat during a military parade before the King David Hotel in Jerusalem, October 1936. Dill inherited command of the British military in Palestine from Peirse in September 1936, thus marking the transfer of military authority in the mandate from the Royal Air Force to the army. (Library of Congress)

Hotel in Jerusalem earlier in October. The rebel leader claimed to have been on hand, watching.[101] For a man of Dill's resolute convictions regarding the criminal nature of the rebellion, this was no doubt the height of insolence. But Qawuqji's departure from Palestine well illustrated the difficulty the British faced in taking too firm a line in this connection. A situation report of the 16th Infantry Brigade divulged that when British troops began closing in on Qawuqji's small army between 23 and 25 October,

> [H]is supporters came to his aid in cars from as far afield as Hebron and Khan Yunis. There is *no* doubt, however, that the Palestinians look upon Fawzi El Kawakji much more as a national hero than as a brigand chieftain who goes round terrorising villages.[102]

Capturing Qawuqji had become a political liability, and the British authorities therefore allowed him and his men to cross back into Transjordan in the early hours of 26 October.[103] The Jewish press was incensed. *Davar* observed bitterly that the British had arranged for "the head of the bandit gangs"—the "top commander," it noted parenthetically and in scare quotes—to depart the country without incident.[104] *Hadashot Aharonot* and *ha-Boker* demanded Qawuqji's extradition.[105]

If political literature directed to a young audience communicated the "big picture" or thrust of Zionist discourse regarding the nature of the revolt, *Davar le-Yeladim* (*Davar for Children*) was a bellwether of the times. Its 22 October edition explained that the Arab leaders had not "one representative among the working masses" and had carried out the rebellion by organizing "gangs of robbers—most of whom were criminals—murderers and bandits who had fled from their own countries to escape the arm of the law."[106]

Military leaders such as General Dill were similarly aggravated by the government's having drawn back from a decisive contest with the rebels at the last minute. In doing so, Dill observed acidly months later, the British authorities had merely postponed the inevitable.[107] In lieu of having his way with regard to martial law, the general attempted to have the last word on the revolt. He prepared a "special order of the day" for 12 October, which credited British forces with having brought the "campaign of murder and banditry" to an end via the infliction of "many severe blows" against the rebels.[108] Wauchope forbade its publication.[109]

Pillars of the mainstream British press, in the meantime, effected a quiet reversal in the waning days of the strike and after. With little fanfare, *The Times* acknowledged in late October that "the rapidity with which most of the armed bands have dispersed" indicated that they "were actuated by political motives and were not brigands."[110] As of September, the liberal *New Statesman and Nation* had, in the midst of averring that "order must be restored" in Palestine, conceded that the "Arab nationalists" could "[no] longer be dismissed as a handful of extreme malcontents."[111]

While the Zionists were embittered by Qawuqji's escape from Palestine and that of many rebels from punishment, they had achieved important economic gains over the previous six months and had largely succeeded in hewing to the principle of *havlagah*.[112] Their attention, in any case, soon shifted to the importance of persuading the Royal Commission—whose investigation into the causes of the rebellion was shortly to commence—of the Zionist case.

One exception to *havlagah*, however, illustrated that another struggle—that for discursive ascendancy in Palestine, the victor of which would succeed in criminalizing the other's national aspirations—was proceeding as before. Early one morning in mid-October, two men on bicycles sidled up to a taxi on Eliezer Ben Yehuda Street in Tel Aviv. They fired three shots through the windows, wounding two of the four Arabs sitting inside. Before racing away, the assailants scattered some leaflets, which declared in Hebrew: "There is no right of way for murderers in Tel Aviv. No Arabs shall be seen in the streets of Tel Aviv." The incident occurred in the light of day, and on a crowded street, but the would-be assassins fled without interference, and the 257 Jews that police interviewed afterward stonewalled them.[113] The still volatile question of who the real criminals in Palestine were simmered beneath the delicate calm of the post-revolt months. General Dill was not alone in believing that some future disturbance would reignite the country.

PART TWO

1937-39

FIVE

The Peel Commission Reconsidered

1937 WAS THE YEAR of the Palestine Royal Commission, whose unpopular July proposal to partition Palestine into two states, one Arab and one Jewish, created the immediate preconditions for a renewed Arab rebellion. This chapter argues for a revised understanding of these preconditions, one taking into account the policy of "vicarious punishment" that the British initiated in the aftermath of the report's publication. It also argues for a revised understanding of the most prominent British critic of partition, the Foreign Office's George Rendel. Rendel's posthumous reputation has suffered dearly at the hands of Elie Kedourie, who has characterized his anti-partitionist stance, as well as his critique of the British criminalization of the revolt, as the peculiar preoccupations of a delusional mind. I suggest, on the contrary, that Rendel was among the least deluded of British high officials in 1937–38. While his estimation of regional Arab loyalty to Palestine proved erroneous, his judgment regarding the folly of British repression in Palestine proved sound. The primary consequence of increased British repression in 1937–38 was the strengthening of popular Arab support for the revolt.

PRELUDE TO PEEL: THE POLITICAL DYNAMICS
SHAPING THE POPULAR RESPONSE TO THE REPORT
OF THE ROYAL COMMISSION

By the conclusion of the Royal Commission's hearings in January 1937, British officials were pessimistic about Palestine. On the first day of the new year, Colonial Secretary Ormsby-Gore presented to the cabinet a summary of the sobering state of affairs. Among his observations were the following points.

First, "non-political" crime—highway robbery in particular—was trending upward. The high commissioner claimed that he expected as much given that many rebels were newly unemployed, but he also acknowledged that such activity mostly victimized Arabs and was "contrary to the wishes of the Arab political leaders." The Jewish press nevertheless adopted a "policy of exaggerat[ing]" these incidents, apparently with the intention of "impress[ing] the Royal Commission with the lawlessness of Arabs." Ormsby-Gore's second point concerned a letter he had received from the commission chair, Lord Peel, which he regarded as unobjectionable, with one exception: Peel contended that "nobody makes any attempt to bring about a reconciliation between Arabs and Jews." Surely, the colonial secretary averred, the commission chair would agree that "no one could have done more than Sir Arthur Wauchope . . . to bring about an improvement in the relations between the two races." Yet, despite the labors of the British, intercommunal tensions were intensifying, making "the prospects for the year . . . very gloomy."[1]

While thus persisting in the illusion of Britain's playing the disinterested arbiter in Palestine, both Ormsby-Gore and Wauchope remained, for the moment, clear-eyed regarding the spurious conflation of the Arab leadership with criminals. The Colonial Office continued to believe that the AHC's roles in stoking criminal activity and in fomenting the revolt were minimal. On 6 January, a government official met with Selig Brodetsky, the well-known mathematician and head of the WZO's political department in London. Brodetsky complained about Wauchope's kid-gloves approach to the Arabs, suggesting that the high commissioner should have dissolved the AHC. "I knew, however," the official recorded,

> that the High Commissioner held the view (and this was accepted here also) that the disturbances were not an artificial movement organised by one or two leaders, but something much deeper and widespread throughout the Arab people in Palestine; hence, the apparently simple procedure of removing the Mufti and a few others at the top would not have put an end to the outbreak.[2]

Declaring martial law might have put an end to the outbreak, but as detailed in the last chapter, Zionist and British officials' arguments for that course of action failed to persuade the government. And by late January 1937, even civilian officials' compromise solution—the deceptively titled Palestine Martial Law (Defence) Order in Council of September 1936—had come back to haunt the British. One of their own courts of criminal appeal found that the order in council had rendered a tranche of prior emergency regulations inoperative, thus suggesting, in the words of one official, that "there must . . . be a number of people in prison who . . . ought not to be there."[3]

On this point, most Arabs agreed. In his 13 January testimony before the commission, ʿAwni ʿAbd al-Hadi maintained that British policy in Palestine "was based on force."[4] The large numbers of Arabs imprisoned in the course of the revolt, including ʿAbd al-Hadi himself, were evidence of this fact. He was nevertheless willing to hear Wauchope's concerns about Arab violence in the country. Along with the mufti and Raghib Bey al-Nashashibi—the leader of the National Defense party (NDP) and the mufti's perennial rival on the AHC—ʿAbd al-Hadi agreed in early February to sign a public repudiation of "recent assassinations and crimes of violence."[5] Despite sensationalist reports and a general focus on Arab violence in the British press, however, such incidents were in fact declining.[6]

Nevertheless, by March 1937, Wauchope was anxious about the possibility of a "sudden recurrence of crime and murder."[7] At the request of Chief Secretary John Hathron Hall, the AHC thus issued another statement "expressing their abhorrence of all acts of terrorism and assassination" and calling the perpetrators of these misdeeds "enemies of the nation."[8] Two looming realities overshadowed this otherwise welcome proclamation, however.

First, Arab-Jewish tension showed no sign of subsiding, despite earlier indications that it might. In his testimony before the Peel Commission, for example, Ben Gurion had made a surprising statement: "If Palestine were uninhabited we might have asked for a Jewish state, for then it would not harm anyone else. But there are other residents in Palestine, and just as we do not wish to be at the mercy of others, they too have the right not to be at the mercy of the Jews."[9] By February, Ben Gurion had reached such heights of magnanimity as to concede, for the first time, that the "Arab inhabitants of Palestine should enjoy all the rights of citizens and all political rights, not only as individuals, but as a national community, just like the Jews."[10]

Alas, these sentiments were fleeting and, more importantly, shared by few Zionists. As the chief secretary lamented on 11 March, the Zionist papers had adopted a "highly undesirable [tone] for some weeks past," to the point that on 8 March he suspended the widely read, and typically tame, *Haaretz*. The paper had implied "that Government [was] assisting murderers and agitators" and "supporting rebellious people."[11] Only the previous day, Hall had suspended the Arabic daily *al-Liwaʾ* because of "an editorial which in unvarnished terms congratulated the Arab Community in Tiberias for . . . the disorders which occurred in that town on the 19th [of] February."[12]

Wauchope wrote the colonial secretary in April, observing that "our political troubles at the moment . . . are concentrated in mixed [Arab-Jewish] areas not, as during the [1936] troubles, mostly in purely Arab areas."[13] He bemoaned "the continuous growth of bitterness" between Arabs and Jews.[14] *The Times* reported in May that an Arab café in the Old City of Jerusalem was prominently displaying a picture of Hitler, alongside images of King Ghazi and Mussolini. The article related, "The Arabs explain that they naturally acclaim . . . Herr Hitler because he dislikes the Jews."[15]

The second reality that diminished the value of the AHC's condemnation of violence was the Committee's evident lack of control over the armed groups, to say nothing of ordinary criminals. Regarding the latter, Wauchope observed in late March the rising sense of insecurity in the country, mainly due to the actions of "small parties of bandits" and (a first) "anarchists." But the high commissioner's own analysis left doubts as to the true identities of these actors. He claimed, for example, that the difficulty in capturing such persons resulted in part from the fact that "the [rural] Arab population is in general sympathy with the criminal." But this supposed sympathy was hard to square with Wauchope's unqualified assertion in the same report that the "bandits" were "attacking law-abiding citizens in the country districts." The high commissioner also considered the "strong National feeling existing throughout the Arab population" inimical to British policing of the country.[16] Crime and Palestinian nationalism were again converging.

As for the Higher Committee's ability to control the armed bands, the entire subject should have been considered from the other end. That is to say, the issue in 1937 was less the AHC's influence over the bands than it was the bands' influence over the AHC. In April, a Qassamite group sent menacing letters to Amin al-Husayni, one of which included a death threat.[17] The mufti received two more death threats the next month, which he turned over to the police.[18] Similar warnings were issued to other Committee members, as well as to local Arab officials.[19] Prior to the coronation of George VI in May, for example, Nablus city councilmen received threats that they would be executed if they took part in the celebrations.[20]

Neither the persisting intercommunal antagonism nor the AHC's inability to rein in the rebels boded well for British "law and order" in the mandate. And a third factor exacerbated these two: the British themselves. In May, a British constable stationed in Jerusalem stated in a letter home that "most of the trouble out here is caused by the police and the army."[21] He referred to the security forces' brutality. As he would disclose in a subsequent letter, "Most of the information we get is extracted by third degree methods, it is the only way with these people."[22] Meanwhile, in the cramped central prison at Acre, the British were holding nearly fifty prisoners in each of the cells— an "appalling number," one official remarked.[23] In June, airborne attacks on Arab villages recommenced.[24] These and other repressive actions fueled Arab enmity towards the British. *The Times* reported on 13 May: "The Arabs are making no public observation of the Coronation: no prayers for the King and Queen have been said in the mosques and even the Arab Anglicans are not holding services."[25]

While many Zionists also viewed the government—and particularly its failure to deal more harshly with the Arabs—with hostility, their resentment must be understood in the context of certain institutional realities that were intrinsically advantageous to the Jews. Most importantly, as Yehuda Bauer relates, the Haganah had, by 1937, "become a de facto partner of the army in Palestine."[26] Among other things, it had begun exchanging intelligence on the AHC and the rebels with the R.A.F.[27] This was a year, moreover, in which the Haganah held command over the majority of Jewish youth in Palestine.[28] The Yishuv therefore stood in radically different relation to the mandatory than did the Arab community.[29] This disparity shaped both communities' responses to the July release of the Peel report. For the Arabs, its injustice provoked outrage at the report's partition proposal. For the Jews, its reality inspired the confidence to negotiate with the government for better terms.

THE PEEL REPORT

Appointed in July 1936, the Royal Commission conducted its investigation in Palestine from November of that year to January 1937, and published its findings that July. It was the last of three commissions headed by Lord Peel, the twice former secretary of state for India and one-time lord privy seal, by whose name it became known. A cursory glance at the Peel report might raise doubts about a key assertion of part one of this book; namely, the claim that British officials and opinion-makers tended not to see the mandatory as a causally primary factor in the unfolding of events in Palestine. The commission's very terms of reference, after all, placed the actions of the mandatory front and center. These were to ascertain the underlying causes of the disturbances which broke out in Palestine in the middle of April; to enquire into the manner in which the Mandate for Palestine is being implemented in relation to the obligations of the Mandatory towards the Arabs and the Jews respectively; and to ascertain whether, upon a proper construction of the terms of the Mandate, either the Arabs or the Jews have any legitimate grievances on account of the way in which the Mandate has been or is being implemented; and if the Commission is satisfied that any such grievances are well-founded, to make recommendation for their removal and for the prevention of their recurrence.[30]

Among the "underlying causes" mentioned at the report's outset, the commission would include "Arab distrust in the sincerity of the British Government" and a "general uncertainty as to the ultimate intentions of the Mandatory Power."[31]

As indices of the British perspective on the causal implication of His Majesty's Government in the revolt, however, such general observations were less telling than the report's more specific assertions. The latter were reminiscent of the assessment of the *New Statesman and Nation* quoted in chapter three, which located final responsibility for the state of the mandate in the inability of the Jews and the Arabs to come to terms, despite the best British efforts to facilitate that outcome. The commission likewise concluded:

The sincere attempts of the Government to treat the two races impartially have not improved the relations between them. Nor has the policy of conciliating Arab opposition been successful. The events of last year proved that conciliation is useless.[32]

The report thus reproduced in its findings the standard British discourse on the revolt. Absent from its calculations vis-à-vis "impartiality" and "conciliation" was the perennial British refusal to grant any of the Arab majority's demands, regardless of whether they were advanced peacefully or forcefully.

Among the commission's key criticisms of the "execution of the Mandate" were the Palestine government's over-employment (given their dubious loyalty) of Arabs and under-employment of Britons, as well as its failure to declare martial law. Significantly, given what previous chapters have documented, the commission also suggested that more "punitive" police posts should have been stationed in Arab villages, in order to enforce the collection of fines.[33] In sum, had the British presence in Palestine—and the violence that underwrote it—been augmented, the revolt might have been averted. It had not, however, and the only feasible solution was therefore to partition the mandate into two independent states, one Arab and one Jewish.

Despite the above-noted disparity between the Arab and Jewish communities' respective institutional relationships with the mandatory, signs of discontent with the Peel report were conspicuous among both groups even prior to the report's release. While Ben Gurion and Weizmann favored a partition scheme on the condition that it met certain criteria, they faced substantial opposition in the broader Zionist community.[34] Weizmann in particular came in for caustic criticism. In a 27 June letter to Va'ad Leumi member Avraham Katznelson, he remarked acerbically: "I can see . . . that the floodgates of demagogic eloquence are wide open and the zealots are gnashing their teeth and clenching their fists. I suppose I'm the 'traitor', etc."[35] In reality, the WZO president was apprehensive regarding the particulars of the partition proposal, which he did not know. Ben Gurion, too, was in the dark. He wrote his wife on 12 June: "I am extremely concerned. We've been told that the Commission's conclusions were adopted unanimously—and I can't believe that all the members of the Commission would agree on something that is good for us."[36] On 1 July, Weizmann was informed that Ormsby-Gore had opted not to furnish him a copy of the report until three days before its publication. He reacted by launching a red-faced tirade, refusing to speak to Wauchope, proclaiming, "They shall not strangle us in the dark," and threatening the colonial secretary with noncooperation from the Jewish Agency.[37]

The Arab community expressed equally grave misgivings regarding the Peel report. On 7 July, the day the report was published, the postmaster general of Palestine sent a memo to his regional subordinates, advising them to be vigilant for "a large number of most seditious pamphlets [which] have been prepared for despatch through the post in case the report of the Royal Commission is unfavourable to Arab interests."[38] As Wauchope would relate to Undersecretary of State Cosmo Parkinson two weeks later, "large numbers" of Arabs opposed the partition scheme "quite apart from the Mufti."[39] The mufti, in the meantime, had come to hopeless loggerheads with his longtime adversary, Raghib Bey al-Nashashibi, who departed the AHC in early July.[40] But even Raghib Bey opposed partition, having buckled, it would appear, under popular pressure.[41]

The discord between Amin al-Husayni and Raghib al-Nashashibi was part of a broader rivalry between their two families. Like the Husaynis, the Nashashibis had long moved in the inner circles of Jerusalem's elite. Raghib Bey, for example, had been the Jerusalem representative to the Ottoman parliament in 1914 and had then served as the mayor of Jerusalem for over a decade—an office he acquired after the British dismissed his predecessor,

Musa Kazim al-Husayni, in 1920, and which he then lost to a Husayni partisan in 1934. The general—and generally accurate—perception among the British, the Palestinians, and the Zionists was that the Nashashibis were more inclined than the Husaynis to compromise with the British in the interest of avoiding violent conflict and also of maintaining their privileged position as mediators between His Majesty and the Palestinian public.[42]

General Dill proposed that Raghib Bey be bribed into reversing his position on partition. Wauchope cautiously concurred, noting "there is little doubt that [Nashashibi] could be bought."[43] A British intelligence agent likewise regarded both Raghib Bey and his political ally, King 'Abdullah, as "men of straw," and divulged to Wauchope: "I am led to believe that there are few Arabs who cannot be bought and that the price is not usually very large. If that be so it seems that now is the time to spend money in a righteous cause."[44] The British consul in Damascus had the same idea. In correspondence with the Foreign Office's George Rendel, he subtly boasted that his judicious spending was responsible for the fact that "the two [Syrian] papers which carry the most weight in Arab politics, 'Al Kabbas' and 'Alef Ba', have not joined in the general condemnation" of the Peel proposals.[45] The significance of the discussion's having turned to buying Arab support for partition was not lost on British high officials. The colonial secretary wrote Wauchope in late July, "It now appears from what you report that all Arab Parties in Palestine oppose partition and that no 'moderate' body of opinion has yet emerged."[46]

While the Colonial Office pondered the utility of "buying" Raghib Bey, as well as planting pro-partition articles in *Filastin*, it also began considering more seriously the possibility of ridding itself once and for all of the partition plan's most prominent critics, the mufti and the AHC.[47] This would require a plausible pretext, however, and as Wauchope acknowledged, while the mufti was "the fomenter of discord, agitation and 'reprisals' . . . no one has ever produced any proof of his instigating assassinations, or indeed any evidence."[48] In a revealing telegram, the colonial secretary, after mentioning the government's attempt to arrest and deport the mufti on 17 July, laid out the dismal state of affairs:

> The [coup] attempt failed and now we have a new situation to deal with. If [the] Mufti were arrested now or later, [the] question of justification would assume much greater importance, but . . . I understand that [the] behaviour of [the] Mufti and his party since [the] publication of [the] Report has not been such as to justify drastic action.[49]

Wauchope's reply was equally telling, particularly his conclusion that it was "[un]necessary to declare the Arab Higher Committee an illegal organisation at present."[50] Not legally unjustified, but simply unnecessary from the perspective of British objectives. The law, that is, was not the issue.

Nor, for that matter, was the legitimacy of the Arab case against partition. In its published response to the report of the commission, the AHC protested:

> The Royal Commission recommended the establishment of an autonomous Jewish State. They propose that its limits should include the most important and fertile plain lands ... the coastal region and the large agricultural area bounded by the northern frontier. In the section so delimited there are some 300,000 Jews and 325,000 Arabs. In the Northern sector of this area there are districts which are entirely Arab. An instance is the Acre district where there are 50,000 Arabs and 63 Arab villages, but only one Jewish village with 300 inhabitants ... It appears to us in the highest degree anomalous that the Royal Commission, while finding it impossible that a Jewish minority should be placed under the rule of an Arab majority, should yet find no difficulty in the reverse process or even in placing an Arab majority under a Jewish minority.[51]

Even the director of the Jewish Agency's settlement department, Arthur Ruppin, could see the problem. "The difficulties of putting [the partition proposal] into effect seem—in light of the large number of Arabs in the Jewish state—almost insuperable," he noted in his diary.[52]

Wauchope and Dill themselves were both of the opinion that "the sacrifices entailed by [the] terms of the Report, particularly [in] Galilee and Acre, are soaking in among all Arabs to the detriment of the principle of Partition."[53] Not only was this portentous development occurring "independent of ... the Mufti," but it was also rousing a hitherto quiescent section of the Arab population. The colonial secretary summarized the contents of a private letter he had received from a commission member in June:

> The Jews, he says, have a very old traditional contact with Galilee and until recently the Arabs of that region have never been stirred up against them, but he thinks, nevertheless, that there is bound to be violent feeling at the first intimation that the Arabs in Galilee are to come under Jewish rule.[54]

The Times went further, reporting that the Galilee provision was the partition plan's fatal flaw:

> Before the publication of the Royal Commission's proposals to include Galilee in the Jewish State, the plan to give the Jews an autonomous canton

or independence for predominantly Jewish areas would probably have found wide acceptance outside the Higher Arab Committee and its immediate supporters; but since then Arab opinion has become much stronger, and any form of partition is now entirely rejected by all parties.[55]

All of this was to say nothing of the commission's proposed solution to the demographic fiasco its partition scheme entailed; namely, an "exchange" of populations between the Jewish and Arab areas. While registering important points of difference between the two cases, the commission explicitly invoked the forced transfer of populations between Greece and Turkey after the First World War as the model to emulate in Palestine:

> The numbers involved were high—no less than some 1,300,000 Greeks and some 400,000 Turks. But so vigorously and effectively was the task accomplished that within eighteen months from the spring of 1923 the whole exchange was completed. Dr. Nansen was sharply criticized at the time for the inhumanity of his proposal, and the operation manifestly imposed the gravest hardships on multitudes of people. But the courage of the Greek and Turkish statesmen concerned has been justified by the result.[56]

The AHC's response is again worth quoting at length:

> How this came to be considered a feasible suggestion is past comprehension. The Royal Commission admits that as against 1,250 Jews owning a negligible quantity of property in the proposed Arab area, there are resident in the suggested Jewish State (according to the Royal Commission's own report) some 225,000 Arabs, in addition to the 100,000 Arabs who are resident in the towns of Haifa, Acre, Tiberias and Safed. Since no "exchange" is possible from the Jewish side we cannot but take it that this means the more or less forcible expulsion of the Arab inhabitants of the Jewish State and the expropriation of their property.[57]

This suspicion was well-founded. In a 14 August letter, Weizmann assured Pierre Orts, the president of the League of Nations' Permanent Mandates Commission, that while the Peel Commission's "transfer" proposal was of "the greatest importance" to the Zionist leadership, it should be implemented "without recourse to constraint, or . . . any coercion whatsoever: only those who wish will be transferred." The latter eventuality, he then acknowledged, was likely to apply to many of the Arabs residing in the proposed Jewish area.[58] But Weizmann's allusions to transfer were often less qualified. In another letter, he referred simply to the desirability of "a partial removal of

FIGURE 7. Members of the Arab Higher Committee. Front row, starting from the left: Raghib Bey al-Nashashibi, the chairman of the National Defence Party; al-Hajj Amin al-Husayni, the mufti of Jerusalem and president of the AHC; Ahmad Hilmi Pasha, the general manager of the Jerusalem Arab Bank; 'Abd al-Latif Bey al-Salah, the chairman of the Arab National Party; and Alfred Roke, an influential landowner. (Library of Congress)

Arabs, say from Galilee and Judea (even though the process is a slow one)," and in yet another to the "crucial importance of transfer for the success of a partition scheme."[59]

Such statements must also be interpreted in the context of Weizmann's vision of a future, Jewish Palestine. As he wrote the head of the American Jewish Congress, Stephen Wise, in June 1937: "It is our destiny to get Palestine, and this destiny will be fulfilled someday, somehow. Our present task is to get a fulcrum on which to place a lever . . . leaving the problems of expansion and extension to future generations."[60] Ben Gurion said much the same thing at the twentieth World Zionist Congress in Zurich on 15 August, arguing that partition was the most sensible short-term step towards the long-term goal of a Jewish Palestine.[61] While in New York in September, he told some Jewish labor leaders that the Jewish state's borders would "not be fixed," and wrote his son Amos the next month of partition's "boost to our historic efforts to redeem the country in its entirety."[62] He used the same language in an October letter to his wife.[63] By January 1938, *The Times* would be reporting the Zionist "anxiety" over "the refusal of [the] British Government to contemplate the compulsory transfer of the Arabs from the Jewish Zone."[64] And within a year, the Zionist leadership as a whole would come, in Benny Morris's words, to a "virtual consensus" that the Arabs should be "transferred" out of Palestine.[65]

Well before then, important elements of the British government had become aware of the mirage-like quality of the partition scheme, given its role in the strategic calculations of leading Zionists. George Rendel, the head of the eastern department at the Foreign Office, wrote in a 13 October memo:

> Since the issue of the [Peel] Report ... evidence has been accumulating to show the overwhelming difficulties in the way of a solution by partition. Not only has the whole Arab world reacted violently against the suggestion, but it has become clear that partition will not mean what we at first imagined—i.e. a separation of the Jewish and Arab spheres—but will mean the creation of a new jumping off place for the Jews ... The Jews make no secret of this, and it has become clear that it is one of the main objections of the Arabs to the partition proposals.[66]

Thus, as August 1937 got underway, things were not as they appeared. The World Zionist Congress had "accepted" partition, but only on the assumption that the designated Jewish territory would, in future, expand into the designated Arab territory.[67] This assumption, along with the partition scheme's "exchange" provision and its delegation of the country's most fertile lands to the Jewish state, underlay the AHC's rejection of the Peel plan.

Unfortunately, British policy failed to engage with such niceties. Instead, in the face of a relatively modest uptick in intercommunal violence in the wake of the Peel Report, the government resorted to the ham-fisted tactic of "vicarious punishment." That is, it willfully incarcerated innocent persons, both Arabs and Jews, in lieu of apprehending or even identifying the actual perpetrators of various violent actions, which it lacked the intelligence to do. As in 1936, the British attempted to compensate for feeble intelligence with brute repression, finally outlawing the entire Arab Palestinian political establishment—including the AHC and the local national committees—in October 1937. And, as in 1936, such repression only nourished popular support for the revolt.

VICARIOUS PUNISHMENT: THE FAILURE OF BRITISH INTELLIGENCE AND THE CRIMINALIZATION OF PALESTINIAN NATIONALISM (AGAIN)

While partition's most diehard Arab detractors harassed and even assassinated Arabs suspected of sympathizing with the Peel plan, as well as those accused of selling land to Jews, the AHC's public position in August 1937 was that Arabs should refrain from acts of violence. Late in the month, after a spate of intercommunal killings, both the AHC and Va'ad Leumi published manifestos calling for peace.[68] Shertok made a similar appeal to the Yishuv, as did mosques to the Arab community. OAG Battershill informed the colonial secretary that he "doubt[ed] whether the Arab Higher Committee or the Jewish Agency can effectively control the extremists on their [respective] sides." As evidence, he listed several attacks that "were perpetrated *after* the manifestos . . . had been issued."[69]

British authorities had virtually no success in apprehending the responsible parties in either camp, but made arrests nonetheless. As one official stated bluntly:

> The police action in connection with the recent series of murders and attempted murders has led to the arrest of nobody against whom there is any satisfactory evidence. On the other hand, certain Arabs and Jews from near the places where the murders were carried out have been consigned to twelve months' preventive detention in Acre Gaol. The methods of "martial law" could hardly be more arbitrary.[70]

He nevertheless approved of these methods, and assumed they had the support of the colonial secretary. Another official pointed out that while handling Jews in this manner would not go unnoticed, "no one is likely to object to the vicarious punishment of Arabs."[71] Arabs objected, of course, but the British ignored them. When Hasan Dajani, an Arab lawyer and member of the municipal corporation of Jerusalem, wrote Battershill complaining of the government's routine resort to the collective punishment of Arabs and its simultaneous failure to employ the same tactic against Jews (offering many examples), Battershill suggested the colonial secretary politely acknowledge that he had received the complaint, as it was "unnecessary to attempt a detailed commentary." One official speculated: "It is possible, I suppose, that the Police cannot escape having a different psychological approach to Jewish disorders and therefore a different manner with the persons concerned."[72]

The AHC also objected to the vicarious punishment of Arabs, appealing directly to the prime minister via telegram on 19 August:

> While [the] country enjoys tranquillity and political Arab bodies urge for quietness a number of honest Arabs have been arrested or are menaced by arrest by [the] arbitrary decrees of [the] local administration without any judgment or [the] slightest proof of culpability in any illegal act[.] [The] Arab Higher Committee considers [it] its duty to draw respectfully His Majesty[']s Government[']s attention to [the] regrettable consequences of such measures and to a policy of provocation and contempt to the feelings of an afflicted nation and honestly believes that such a policy . . . may produce grave repercussions.[73]

Many of those arrested were reportedly abused in detention. *Al-Jami'a al-Islamiyya* reported numerous instances of "police officers beating up and brutally insulting" inmates at the prison in Acre. The paper urged the authorities to "do something."[74] As in 1936, Arab spokespersons placed repressive British actions—and the policy that actuated them—at the center of the instability plaguing the mandate, whereas all such actions were, from the British perspective, the inevitable response to said instability.

As ever, the latter conviction made crime a basic British preoccupation. Despite the flurry of intercommunal violence in August, the government's own statistics did not show a dramatic increase in crime during the month. Murders were up, from fifteen in July to nineteen in August. But they remained within the range established in the first half of the year. There had been nineteen murders in March as well, for example, and seventeen in May. Likewise with attempted murders. There were twenty-four in August, as compared to twenty-two in July. But there had also been twenty-four attempted murders in May, and thirty-four in June. Manslaughter was down. Robberies and break-ins were up, but they had been higher in the first few months of the year. Serious assaults were down from the previous month, from 262 to 234. Possession of firearms cases were at a six-month low.[75] Narrowing the criminological scope to "terrorist" attacks on Jewish and British persons and property, the British report to the League of Nations for 1937 would list twenty-six such incidents for the July–September quarter—which was higher than the figure for the April–June quarter (nineteen), but well below that for the January–March quarter (forty-six).[76] As Wauchope himself stated privately on 2 September, ". . . [T]he country remains wonderfully calm."[77] In testimony before Parliament, the colonial secretary spoke of "a quiet August" in Palestine.[78]

The British press nevertheless featured headlines in August such as "Renewed crime in Palestine," "More disorders in Palestine," and "Lawlessness in Palestine: need for sterner punishments."[79] In the last article, *The Times* disclosed: "The authorities are trying to stem the decline in public security which has been evident in the past few weeks by interning under the emergency regulations persons suspected of encouraging lawlessness." The article went on:

> Recent crimes have been quite varied. In comparatively few cases have the objects of attack been Jews. There have been several deliberate attacks on the police, as, for instance, the murder of a police tracker in his house yesterday at Beisan and a volley fired from the dark at a party of police in a village near Nablus last night.[80]

No mention was made of the fact, probably unknown to *The Times* reporter, that many of those interned had no known connection to any criminal activity. Also noteworthy was the fact that the paper referred without qualification to organized attacks on police as crimes and, when fatal, murders. The categories of rebel and criminal were again converging. Indeed, the full 13 August headline read: "Renewed crime in Palestine / Arab bands reorganizing."

As in May, the same convergence continued to feature in Wauchope's thinking. He wrote Parkinson on 25 August: "... I feel sure Police are taking all measures possible to prevent crime and to catch criminals, but catching criminals amid a sympathetic population is a hard job."[81] At a minimum, this suggested that Palestinian Arabs preferred criminals to the British authorities pursuing them. It also left open the possibility that many of the "criminals" in question were, in fact, rebels enjoying the sympathy of the Arabs among whom they lived and moved.

In the early evening of 26 September, as he approached the courtyard of the Anglican church in Nazareth, Lewis Andrews, the forty-one-year-old assistant district commissioner in Galilee, was suddenly set upon by four Arab gunmen. They fired nine bullets at Andrews, killing him instantly and mortally wounding his bodyguard, Constable Peter McEwan.[82] The incident marked the highest-ranking British official to be killed by rebels in Palestine, and it shook the mandatory. As those involved in the Arab-Jewish violence had eluded the authorities, so did Andrews' killers. Four days after the assassination, Deputy Undersecretary of State John Shuckburgh chaired a meeting at the Colonial Office, during which he acknowledged, "The difficulty in the present situation [is] that there [are] murders but no evidence [is] forthcoming and it [is] impossible to catch the criminals."[83]

The Jewish Agency was convinced that regardless of the specific criminals in question, the persons ultimately responsible for their crimes were the same as those causing the trouble in 1936. In both cases, the mufti and the AHC were to blame. Prior to the Andrews assassination, Bernard Joseph, Shertok's deputy at the political department, wrote Weizmann that the mufti had, through force of terror, become the "master" of the Arab community in Palestine. Joseph claimed that the opponents of Amin al-Husayni were all agreed that, were the British to expel him from the Supreme Muslim Council and strip him of the "mufti" title, "the whole atmosphere [would] be changed." Somewhat contradictorily, several of the same men also cautioned that driving the mufti out of the country might "make a greater national hero out of him."[84]

The Andrews assassination swung British official opinion back in the direction of the Jewish Agency. Mandate authorities expanded the policy of vicarious punishment to include the AHC itself. Having approved an official declaration (to be issued on 1 October) outlawing the AHC and the national committees, the colonial secretary advised OAG Battershill to arrest the members of the Higher Committee, adding, "I do not think it practicable to make distinctions between individuals or to confine action to leading members only."[85] The incarceration of prominent Arabs had already gotten underway. Naji 'Allush estimates that the authorities arrested 200 clergymen and national committee members at this time.[86] Moreover, according to reports that reached Muhammad 'Izzat Darwaza in Damascus, "the authorities [were] seeking to terrorize the people in the process of the mass arrests."[87] This prompted the mufti to write Battershill on behalf of the AHC, protesting the imprisonment of "notables, professional men and Sharia Qadis" and reminding him:

> The Arabs have condemned the attack [on Andrews] instantaneously following its occurrence and expressed their deep sorrow for it, and the Palestine Broadcasting Service has announced the Supreme Arab Committee's [the AHC's] statement to that effect ... The Supreme Arab Committee wishes to intimate to Your Excellency that the entire Arab population of Palestine ... have been greatly astonished at the measures to which Government has resorted in arresting a large number of notables and Qadis, without any charge or guilt, because law and justice demand that the aggressors be sought and not that innocent people and religious men be punished ... [S]uch arrests will make the situation more complicated.[88]

The aggressors in question were, in fact, Qassamites operating independently of the AHC.[89] (Recall that it was Qassamites who had earlier sent the mufti a letter informing him of his imminent demise.)

The mufti's modestly worded warning that the wave of arrests would "make the situation more complicated" had little impact upon Battershill and other British officials. They interpreted the quiet of early October as a sure sign that no new revolt would materialize.[90] As the high commissioner had remarked on the "wonderfully calm" atmosphere of early September, so the colonial secretary wrote OAG Battershill on 5 October, "I am glad to learn that ... [the] country generally is quiet."[91] Battershill reassured him three days later, "The country remains quiet and as far as I can see there is no prospect of a change."[92]

The mufti's forecast rang hollow. The British therefore ignored it, instead relieving Amin al-Husayni of his official duties and arresting and deporting his associates on the AHC. Two days later, Akram Zu'aytir would note in his diary: "The killing of Andrews can be considered a breakthrough for the renewal of the revolution." Not because the assassination was the opening salvo of a new Arab offensive, but because the mandatory's response—in its "abuse of power and oppression"—was "fueling the spirit of national liberation."[93]

Zu'aytir's observation is worth pausing over. Bayan al-Hut argues that the first and second phases of the revolt shared a basic feature: both began with assassinations carried out by Qassamites.[94] Yet, while Qassamites may have intended for the highway murders of 15 April 1936 to spark a rebellion, there is no reason to believe that they succeeded. What the murders did do was exacerbate intercommunal tensions, which led to the slaughter of 19 April, which led to a countrywide strike, which—when faced with rampant British repression—produced a rebellion. The chain of events was contingent, and well outside the control of the handful of Qassamites apparently responsible for the 15 April operation. In keeping with al-Hut's characterization, virtually every chronicle of the Great Revolt regards the Andrews assassination as the beginning of the rebellion's second phase. But this, too, is misleading. Zu'aytir's reflection on the state of affairs as of 10 October 1937—a full two weeks after the Andrews assassination—indicates that it was not the assassination itself that triggered the rebellion, but rather the policy of vicarious punishment that the British adopted in response to the assassination.[95]

Aware of his precarious circumstance as of mid-July, when the authorities first attempted to arrest him, the mufti had since then taken refuge in al-Haram al-Sharif. He correctly assumed that the British would not dare attempt to apprehend him there. When he absconded to Lebanon in mid-October 1937, it was a moment of truth for the Jewish Agency and the government, both of which had anticipated that the mufti's absence from Palestine would deplete his political capital and pacify the Arab population. According to Yehoshua Porath, the mufti's departure did indeed diminish his "influence inside and outside Palestine since it was regarded as an act of cowardice."[96] Mustafa Kabha's careful survey of the Palestinian press from this period undermines Porath's claim, however. As Kabha writes, after the mufti's escape, his "traditional opponents . . . in the press, headed by the newspaper *Filastin*, which was long considered the journal of the mufti's opponents, displayed their support of him, stating that he was their sole leader and that his acts embodied the wishes of the Palestinian people."[97] British criminalization of Amin al-Husayni rallied Arab popular opinion in his favor, rather than undercutting him.

The same held with respect to the armed bands, whose violent actions shortly surged in the mufti's absence, contrary to expectations. The British office of the censor had to compel Palestinian newspapers to stop printing admiring stories of the rebels' exploits, and force them instead to publish government accounts of incidents involving the armed bands, which referred to them as "'hooligans' (*ashqiya'*), 'terrorists' (*mukharribun*) and law breakers."[98] As Kabha documents, the authorities were quick to suspend the publication of Palestinian newspapers, making coverage of local politics in their pages conspicuously sparse and typically cautious. The papers' praise for the rebels was therefore remarkable in itself.

While the Arab press made the case for the legitimacy (non-criminality) of the national leadership, others went further, charging that the British were the criminals. A group of prominent Arabs from Gaza wrote Kings Ghazi, Ibn Sa'ud, and Farouk in early October: "The British government has applied the oppressive policy of terrorism in Palestine. Leading members of the nation have been arrested and deported."[99] The "terrorism" accusation began appearing more frequently in October, as illustrated in the following parliamentary exchange between Ormsby-Gore and the ardent left-wing MP Aneurin Bevan:

> MR. BEVAN: Has the right hon. Gentleman seen reports in the Press of reprisals carried out by the police authorities in Palestine? Is there any truth in these reports, and if so, does he condone that conduct?
>
> MR. ORMSBY-GORE: Certainly the military authorities and the police will have my and the Government's full support in dealing with a campaign of murder and outrage.

MR. BEVAN: Does the right hon. Gentleman seriously suggest to the House that it is the policy of His Majesty's Government to carry out reprisals on innocent persons for misdeeds committed by others?

MR. ORMSBY-GORE: Certainly not. But the particular incident was that the local people burnt and destroyed the buildings and entire equipment of the civil airport at Lydda, and in my view the police and the military were quite right in destroying the houses of the people who committed that act.[100]

Vyvyan Adams then spoke up, changing the subject. One might infer, however, that the colonial secretary's last word on the matter did not satisfy Mr. Bevan, who had inquired regarding "reprisals" (plural) only to hear exculpatory details of a "particular incident."

Both the Zionist and the British press were, to be sure, in the corner of the colonial secretary, whatever reports of "reprisals" may occasionally have appeared in the latter's pages. In the second of two September articles titled "The Murder of Mr. Andrews," *The Palestine Post* acknowledged that the AHC had "not hesitated to denounce the murder of Mr. Andrews," but added: "Yet it stopped short . . . of raising its voice against gangsterism and of calling upon the people within reach of its voice to cease offering shelter and comfort to the assassin." As a result of the British determination to "avoid . . . repression," neither the terrorists nor those supporting them had "been given reason to fear just retribution."[101] British repression, then, not only failed to feature in the *Post*'s analysis of the Arab resort to violence, but its alleged absence was made the explanation for Arab violence.

The mainstream British take on the state of affairs in Palestine in the aftermath of the Andrews assassination was well summarized by the right-wing *Spectator* when it wrote:

The recent assassination of Mr. Andrews and Constable McEwan at Nazareth, following other murders and attempted murders, brought things to a head. A government cannot rest upon conciliation alone when those whom it would conciliate take kindness for weakness or fear and simply redouble their criminal activities . . . Crime must be punished.[102]

The rebels were murderers, insisted the *Spectator*. *The Times* wholeheartedly agreed. Its first headline regarding the Andrews assassination read, "Terrorism in Palestine: three murders at Nazareth." In a 28 September article titled "The Palestine Murders," the paper delineated "four classes" of murder: personal, racial, murder (by Arabs) of Arab policemen and notables, and murder of British officials. The administrators of the British empire—

including Andrews, an "energetic official" whose "active . . . measures to suppress the disturbances in 1936" endeared him to the Zionists and won him the ire of many Arabs—were on a par with the victims of street crime. Thus, in a 30 September article ("The Murders in Palestine"), *The Times* made mention of a "police inspector who was murdered recently," "officials murdered on duty," and "murdered officials." The liberal *New Statesman and Nation* titled its 2 October article on the Andrews assassination "The Nazareth Murders," and affirmed that "resolute measures must be taken for the maintenance of law and order and the protection of human life—whether it be the life of a British official or of the humblest Jewish or Arab citizen."

Unlike the other periodicals, however, *The New Statesman* made room for a minority view in the letters section of its 9 October edition. It issued from the pen of Thomas Hodgkin, Arthur Wauchope's private secretary of a year earlier, although he did not identify himself as such. His letter is worth quoting at length:

> However much one may disparage killing for political ends, it is surely misleading to describe an action like the assassination of Mr. Andrews as a "dastardly murder." (The *Times*, in a leading article of October 2nd, describes it so). Would any liberal-minded person speak in such terms of the killing of some prominent Gestapo official by an opponent of the Nazi regime? Yet that is exactly the light in which the assassination of Mr. Andrews would appear to most Palestine Arabs. Mr. Andrews was a very competent official, who, because of his good knowledge of Arabic and wide contacts with influential members of the Arab and Jewish communities, was in the position of an unofficial secret service agent to the British Administration. From the point of view of the Administration he was a valuable and loyal officer: from the point of view of the great majority of Arabs he was a spy, who represented the hated British autocracy in its most objectionable form.
>
> It must not be forgotten that the Arab villagers of the Galilee district have suffered severely at the hands of the British during the last eighteen months. Their young men have been shot; their houses destroyed; their crops and animals confiscated to pay heavy collective fines. And they are still no nearer than they were to the national independence which it is their aim to achieve. Partition would mean for them the alternative of leaving their homes and lands and being settled in Beersheba, the Jordan Valley, or Trans-Jordan, or inclusion within the frontiers of a Jewish State. These are the political conditions which give rise to terrorism. It cannot be cured by the deposition of the President of the Supreme Muslim Council and the transportation to Seychelles of some of the most respected Arab leaders on the charge that they are "morally responsible" for these terrorist acts.

While utterly radical, this defiant missive actually found support at high levels of the British government, where one group of officials—those working in the Foreign Office under eastern department head George Rendel—agreed with Hodgkin's contention that the equation of the rebellion with crime was simplistic. Any policy premised on this equation, they believed, would require repression, and would therefore stir, rather than quell, the forces of rebellion.

RESCUING RENDEL: THE FOREIGN OFFICE AND ITS CRITICS

The British government had first integrated its Middle Eastern policy with the formation of the Middle East Department, under the Colonial Office, in 1921. Prior to that time, London's policymaking in the region had been split among the War Office, the Foreign Office, and the India Office. But while the Colonial Office was technically ascendant in Palestine at the time of the revolt, from the beginning of the strike in April 1936, the Foreign Office became increasingly engaged in the Palestine issue.[103] And by 1937, the Foreign Office had elevated its regional status such that its eastern department was in charge of foreign relations with Iran, Iraq, Syria, Sa'udi Arabia, and Turkey, in addition to managing the foreign policies of Palestine and Transjordan.[104] The department's head, since 1930, was George Rendel.

Rendel had been urging the government to consider more seriously the Arab perspective on British policy for much of 1937. Reading Hodgkin's *cris de cœur*, he commented, "I think this letter has a great deal of good sense in it, though it is, of course, written from a very 'Left' and 'anti-Imperialist' point of view." Another department official conceded, "There is unfortunately a lot of truth in this letter."[105] Rendel appreciated, for example, the dilemma giving rise to the "reprisals" about which the colonial secretary was briefly queried in Parliament. It resulted, he reasoned, from the universal Arab opposition to British policy in Palestine, which, as in Ireland, made it "impossible to obtain any evidence upon which to base any conviction." The only response available to the authorities was "to carry out reprisals, which . . . fall to a large extent on the innocent." Such actions were, nevertheless, "necessary if we are to cow the population into some kind of acquiescence."[106]

Cowing of the population was indeed on the rise in October, as noted obliquely in various *Times* stories coming out of Palestine. An article from

21 October ("Palestine Quieter") reported the "severe measures taken by Government against villages in the neighbourhood of which there has been sabotage or shooting." Another from 27 October ("More Violence in Palestine") mentioned "drastic measures . . . against fellahin who are suspected of sabotage or sheltering armed bands," which included "punitive police posts." It mentioned specifically "the village of Dahariya [just north of the Negev Desert], which was severely punished." Porath notes that the government introduced "tougher measures" against the rebels in late September and early October, and that "District Commissioners were energetically using their powers to inflict punitive measures."[107] Somewhat hyperbolically, but nevertheless tellingly, al-Liwa' accused the government of "[performing] acts that even Hulagu [Khan, grandson of Genghis] did not contemplate."[108] In acknowledging that such repressive measures fell "to a large extent on the innocent," Rendel had tacitly confirmed the Gaza leaders' accusation that the British were pursuing a "policy of terrorism in Palestine."

Rendel and others at the Foreign Office believed that the pro-partition elements of the government—including the War Office, the Colonial Office, and the Air Ministry—were "living in comfortable illusions."[109] At an interdepartmental meeting on 29 October, Lieutenant-General Robert Haining, the director of military operations and intelligence at the War Office, claimed—as had Dill and Simson before him—that the "conditions under which [British] rule existed" in Palestine were "hardly relevant," given the fact that said rule had been "challenged by a band of criminals."[110] The Air Ministry representative argued that "no nationalist movement against [the British] or even against the Jews" existed in Palestine![111] In reply to Rendel's suggestion that "the distinction between criminal and nationalist elements was a very difficult one to establish," the Air Ministry spokesperson asserted that the British were contending in Palestine only with "criminals" and "thugs."[112]

As in 1936, the rebels themselves rejected such characterizations. Fawzi al-Qawuqji channeled the voices of many Palestinian Arabs when he wrote in the 13 October edition of al-Istiqlal: "The Arabs are seekers of right and justice; they are not murderers."[113] A rebel manifesto from 29 November declared that the British claim to be upholding "law and order" in the mandate was merely a pretext for illegally attacking nationalists. It protested the incarceration and exile of those opposed to British rule, whose activities were "legal," despite the British attempt to frame them as "ordinary criminals."[114] Some Arabs suspected that the British were secretly aware of this fact. Decades later, one erstwhile rebel sympathizer would declare adamantly to the researcher Zeina Ghandour: ". . . [T]he English knew it was a rebellion. They knew very well that we were not criminals."[115]

This was certainly true of Rendel, who made a point of keeping his views on the revolt out of the public, and recommending that others of his persuasion might do the same. In correspondence with Gilbert MacKereth, the British consul in Damascus, Rendel suggested that MacKereth's "recent references to the Arabs as 'bandits', 'bad hats', and 'thugs'" glossed over the fact that "the Palestine problem is . . . very far from being merely . . . a rebellion by criminal elements against constituted authority as such."[116] His concern, however, was not so much the government's public portrayal of the rebels as criminals as the fact that the British were drinking their own bathwater:

> It may, of course, be wise to continue to take the line in dealing with the Syrians that any Arabs who cross into Palestine to take part in the campaign are merely ordinary criminals. But I am not sure that it will help us to get over our difficulties if we are too ready ourselves to assume that this is the case.[117]

MacKereth himself was meanwhile organizing the killing of Arab rebels crossing into Palestine from Syria.[118] And despite his recognition of the misguided criminalization of Palestinian nationalism, Rendel was quick to affirm that MacKereth "should not for one moment relax" his "efforts to . . . prevent the nationalist Arabs of Palestine—who, after all, are fighting the British Government as well as the Jews—from receiving assistance from Syria."[119] Thus, even Rendel, in the final analysis, affirmed the government's a priori equation with law and order.

By November 1937, the eastern department had come decisively to oppose partition.[120] It is possible, as Elie Kedourie demonstrates, to paint Rendel as a man whose fevered imagination got the better of him and the department he led.[121] While acknowledging the intrinsic dangers of prognostication, Rendel did pontificate at some length (and with some implausibility) about the disasters likely to beset the British in the broader Middle East and ultimately Europe should the government press forward with partition.[122] It is nevertheless unfair and inaccurate to depict Rendel as simply deluded, while leaving untouched such figures as the above-mentioned Air Ministry representative, whose denial of an anti-British nationalist movement among the Arabs of Palestine would certainly give him an equal claim on utter confusion. Moreover, despite Rendel's "lurid catastrophism" (quoting Kedourie), his voice, when placed in the broader context of interdepartmental exchanges on the topic of partition, was often among the more sober. As seen above, this was especially so when the conversation turned to the "criminal" nature of Arab resistance to British policy.

Although Rendel failed to persuade those outside the Foreign Office of the error of equating Arab political agitation with crime, his arguments regarding partition's likely fallout in the broader Middle East made substantial headway in London in December 1937. In a cabinet meeting on 8 December, Prime Minister Neville Chamberlain proposed that a new commission be dispatched to Palestine, and that its terms of reference allow it to discard the partition scheme if necessary.[123] When the British government officially appointed the new commission (the Woodhead Commission) in January 1938, the Colonial Office looked upon it skeptically, regarding it as the Foreign Office's anti-partition Trojan horse.[124] Zionist leaders had similar misgivings.[125]

They were right to worry. Rendel's legacy vis-à-vis British policy in Palestine would lie, in fact, in his strategic arguments against partition, which lived on even after Charles Baxter replaced him at the Foreign Office in mid-1938. The Woodhead Commission arrived in Palestine in March 1938. Hitler had just annexed Austria, and London was surveying developments in Europe with unease.[126] With a European war appearing more probable, the anxieties about alienating British allies in the Middle East to which Rendel had long given voice began resonating more broadly in official circles. They would contribute substantially to the British decision, later that year, to renege on partition.

By contrast, Rendel's concerns regarding British repression in the mandate left almost nothing in the way of a bureaucratic legacy. Even as it discarded the Peel proposal, the government continued to regard the rebel movement as a criminal, rather than a political, problem. In fact, a number of top officials ceased to limit the criminal charge to the rebels and the Arab leadership, and began privately to predicate it of the Arab population at large.

REPRESSION REDUX

As detailed in chapter four, the British framing of the revolt in 1936 restricted charges of criminality to the Arab leadership. This was a function of British imperial discourse, which held that the Arabs of Iraq and Palestine-Transjordan were on the verge of national consummation, and that the "mandate" of the British was to shepherd them into the community of nations, an eventuality that had transpired already in Iraq. While technically the mandate instrument for Palestine did not mention the national autonomy of the Arabs—indeed, it did not mention the Arabs by name—by the time of the revolt, the issue was no longer whether the Arabs would achieve self-determination, but rather when and in what form. As the AHC told Wauchope in May 1936, the government "knows ... that Palestine is ... among those countries that fall within the guarantee of independence provided to the Arab territories by the British government in section twenty-two of the covenant of the League of Nations, and that it is to enjoy the same rights as do the other Arab countries."[127] By endorsing the 1937 partition proposal, the government openly committed itself to the establishment of an Arab state. Although this state would consist of an expanded Transjordan, the British were nevertheless promising some form of national autonomy to Arab Palestinians, and thereby attempting (or at least pretending) to meet the mandatory obligation to grant them statehood. Any perception that London was militarily targeting a popular national movement in Palestine was therefore unacceptable. The natural recourse, under the circumstances, was to disparage the "supposed" Arab national leadership as demagogues who did not truly represent the Arab masses, and to pin the criminal charge—that is, the reason for the repression—upon them.[128]

Chapter four also identified racism as both the driver of British crimino-national discourse in the age of empire and the dead weight of that discourse in the age of nationalism. In the latter period, race was typically sublimated into an economic idiom. This had the merit of undermining the charge that the British were behaving with their usual colonial chauvinism in territories such as Palestine. In the event of a national rebellion, however, the sublimation had the liability of leaving open the question of how the British distinguished nationalism from crime. Whereas in the nineteenth century the British could refer, in such circumstances, to their own elevated position in the hierarchy of races—and thereby downgrade to the status of "terrorism" the nationalisms of select "lower races"—in the twentieth century, the British were both less able and less inclined to do this. Nevertheless, under sufficient pressure, race resurfaced as the critical criminological variable, if only when the curtains were drawn.

Palestine was a case in point. Officials' awareness of the popular base of the revolt, and of the far-reaching measures that would be required to repress it, had, by late 1937, taken its toll on the pretext that the "criminals" with which the British were concerned were the Arab leaders, not the Arabs at large. As OAG Battershill—who was then standing in for the absent Wauchope—confessed in a private letter in November 1937, "I doubt whether any Arab really has any ethical feeling against murder."[129] Such sentiments were not anomalous among top officials. In October 1937, the chief secretary opined that most Arabs were "prevented . . . from expressing such feelings as [the Andrews assassination] may have . . . touched" by their general "callousness for life and the absence of any word for murder in their colloquial language."[130] Charles Tegart, whom the government brought to Palestine in December 1937 to advise on counterinsurgency, suggested in his January 1938 report that the Arab "public conscience" in Palestine was "undeveloped."[131] Battershill "frankly admit[ted]" that the government was resorting to "most repressive" and even "distasteful" measures against the Arabs, but deemed them "essential."[132]

Thus, while the mandatory's public statements continued to adhere to the "crime wave" framing of the revolt, the private British assessment of law and order in Palestine began, from the Andrews assassination forward, to fracture. On the one hand, the obsession with Amin al-Husayni as the driving force of the rebellion persisted. On the other, claims of a pervasive criminality among Arab Palestinians became more frequent. A third view, of course, was Rendel's, which remained at the margins of official thinking.

In November 1937, the Colonial Office recommended that the government in Palestine disregard Arab opposition to partition and employ whatever force proved necessary to see the policy through.[133] Not surprisingly, there was a deluge of Arab testimony regarding repressive measures that very month. Raghib al-Nashashibi himself denounced the government's adoption of "most severe and stringent measures towards the Arabs," which he characterized as "even more drastic" than those the British had employed in 1936.[134] The Arab Women's Committee protested "recent measures . . . directed towards the Arabs with a view to intimidating them, and compelling them to agree to a policy which aims at their eviction from their country and their replacement by another people."[135]

As before, the authorities were in no way deterred from these tactics by the fact that, as Battershill informed Shuckburgh, "The Government cannot trace the wrongdoers and bring them to justice."[136] Thus, in the village of Silwan (near Jerusalem), the suspected home of insurgents who had killed two British soldiers, members of the Black Watch regiment were permitted by their superior officers to conduct an eight-hour "search," during which they beat to death twelve Arabs.[137] Constable Sydney Burr wrote his parents from Haifa regarding a similar incident in December, in which the district superintendent of police allowed Burr and his fellow officers to "beat up a village" where "a band of the bad boys" had reportedly "stayed the night."[138]

He also related, ". . . [A]ny Johnny Arab . . . caught by us now in suspicious circumstances is shot out of hand."[139] Not long after composing this letter, Burr wrote his brother, ". . . [R]unning over an Arab is the same as running over a dog in England except we do not report it."[140] While in England in late November, the Anglican bishop in Jerusalem, George Francis Graham Brown, received a note from a personal acquaintance, which included two letters from Britons in Palestine reporting episodes of police and military brutality.[141] Official reports made almost no mention of such incidents, and the government forbid Arab newspapers to publish the details of British repressive actions.[142]

Following the Andrews assassination in September, the government had announced the establishment of a military court system, as well as provisions making the mere carrying of arms a capital offense and stripping condemned persons of the right to appeal.[143] Whereas the trend was towards commutation of death sentences in the first half of 1937, by the end of the year it had shifted back in the direction of implementation. On 3 January 1938, the BBC launched its first Arabic broadcast in Palestine. In a grim omen of things to come, the station's debut story concerned the hanging that day of an Arab convicted of weapons possession, and sent tremors through the region.[144]

The left-wing MP Thomas Edmund Harvey wrote Ormsby-Gore a week later, suggesting that executing individuals merely for possessing arms was likely to strike the Arabs—a people with a "generation-old general habit of keeping arms in the house and on the person"—as "tyrannous and unjust."[145] Indeed, no less an authority that the general officer commanding conceded privately that the "large majority of folk [in Palestine] have always carried fire arms."[146] The colonial secretary reassured Harvey that sentences for arms possession were carefully vetted, but also essential given the "campaign of terrorism and murder" that the British faced in Palestine.[147]

The British were at least partly successful in managing this campaign in January 1938, during which murders were cut in half (from twenty-three in December down to twelve).[148] Harvey, however, was not the only one wondering at what expense London secured such short-term gains in security. After sitting in a military court in Nablus where two Arabs, a father and son, were convicted of weapons possession, a British expatriate wrote deploringly of the government's tendency to "call the whole movement by such names as terrorists, bandits, robbers, and so on." This approach, he was certain, would "only add fuel to the fire of hatred, and really encourage people to resist."[149]

REBEL SOLDIERS AND GOVERNMENT GANGS:
TEGART, WINGATE, AND "THE TOUGH TYPE"

His was a voice in the wilderness, however. When Charles Tegart—the former head of the security service in India and newly appointed advisor to the Colonial Office on the rebellion in Palestine—handed his report on the security situation in the mandate to the colonial secretary in late January 1938, the recommendations contained therein made ample reference to Arab "gangs," "terrorists," and "criminals."[150] Tegart's proposals included the creation of an "irregular force" of men, more suited to the "rough work" of handling "gangs of banditry" than were ordinary policemen. "What is required," he wrote, "is the tough type of man, not necessarily literate, who knows as much of the game as the other side."[151]

Several people working in the Colonial Office were quick to note the implication. One warned that such a force would be "rather like the 'Black and Tans', with some of the original personnel of that body, and might easily supply material for the same kind of reputation as they, rightly or wrongly, obtained in the Irish troubles." Another official wrote, "This 'irregular' force into which Sir C. Tegart wishes to import 'the tough type of man, not necessarily literate' is none too welcome from my point of view."[152]

Such worries were misplaced. Tegart's proposed "rural mounted police" would in no way introduce Black and Tan tactics to British forces in the mandate, who were conversant with them already. Likewise, Palestine policemen and other elements of the existing British counterinsurgency apparatus proved more than capable of handling the "rough work" of which Tegart wrote.

The other elements in question would come shortly to include the clandestine groups of Haganah men operating under Captain Orde Wingate, a British intelligence officer recently arrived to Palestine. Orde was an oddity. He ate onions obsessively, cooled off in polite company by stripping nude, and scrubbed himself with an oversized toothbrush to avoid the trouble of bathing.[153] But the captain was also a committed Christian Zionist, champion of empire, and unabashed advocate of war against the armed bands and their supporters.[154] As such, he won the friendship and confidence of Chaim Weizman, Moshe Shertok, and other leading Zionists. And in May 1938, Wingate secured the approval of the general officer commanding for the formation of "Special Night Squads" (SNS).[155]

The SNS were composed mostly of Haganah men, with a sprinkling of British soldiers. In his proposal for their establishment, Wingate indicated that the squads would have two targets, the armed bands and the villagers who sustained them. The aggressive tactics of the SNS would, he reckoned, "persuade the gangs that, in their [nighttime] predatory raids, there is every chance of their running into a Government gang which is determined to destroy them, not by an exchange of shots at a distance, but by bodily assault with bayonet and bomb." With regard to the villagers, Wingate wrote:

> It can be pointed out to them that terror by night will in future be exercised, where necessary, by Government, whose forces are close to hand and able to visit any area at a moment's notice; that, consequently, failure to notify the presence of a gang will be regarded as evidence of complicity, since the excuse of terrorism will no longer be valid.[156]

While the Colonial Office pondered the possibility of creating units comprised of "the tough type," Wingate led the SNS on nocturnal raids into Arab villages, and put on coercive demonstrations for his men that would have made many a Black and Tan blush. On one occasion, Wingate forced sand into an Arab captive's mouth until he vomited, and then instructed one of his soldiers to shoot the man (which he did).[157]

Soldiers and police, too, did not hesitate to don the mail of British repression in the first half of 1938, by which point the government's village search policy of 1936 had been resurrected.[158] One difference, of course, was the absence (via exile) of the Arab political organizations that had, in 1936, protested and publicized the abuses that occurred during the searches. But the authorities continued to receive evidence of such abuses from reputable British sources. Charges of torture and the destruction of property reached the Colonial Office from a network of Anglican missionaries who worked among the Arabs. They furnished officials with photographic evidence and testified in detail to the reliability of their sources. And unlike many of the Arabs reporting atrocities in 1936, these British expatriates regarded Arab resistance to British rule in Palestine as terrorism and criminality, which made them all the more credible from the government's perspective.[159]

Palestinian rebels meanwhile continued to take the field in uniform, thus implicitly identifying themselves as soldiers and not bandits. In response, government statements were bowdlerized of any language suggesting that a state of war existed between the troops and the rebels, which might have lent credibility to the enemy's attempt to portray itself as an army.[160] GOC Wavell (who replaced Dill in September 1937) advocated the death penalty for any Arab "wearing [a] uniform or equipment likely to be mistaken" for a Briton's.[161]

While the government did not adopt this proposal, soldiers and police took it upon themselves to administer capital punishment to rebels in the field. Constable Sydney Burr wrote home in March 1938: "... [T]he Ulsters and West Kents caught about 60 of [the rebels] in a valley and as they walked out with their arms up [as would surrendering soldiers] mowed them down with machine guns." He added, "No news of course is given to the newspapers."[162] Indeed, the majority of British journalists in Palestine rarely left Jerusalem, and received most of their information regarding security operations in the rest of the country from the government.[163] While the British press thus dwelt at length on rebel atrocities, British residents of Palestine indicated in private letters home that "many more people have been killed by troops and police . . . than have been killed by brigand bands in the hills."[164]

THE BRITISH RESPONSE TO ATROCITY CHARGES

Despite the minimal attention accorded such charges in the press, the British authorities proved increasingly sensitive to them. The more that allegations of police and military misconduct emerged, the more hotly the government denied them. Officials in Jerusalem and London knew many of these accusations to be, at a minimum, plausible. The bishop in Jerusalem personally informed the chief secretary that he "had been receiving an increasing number of very serious complaints regarding third degree methods practised by the Police Authorities on those arrested under Emergency Regulations." These included reports of "physical torture."[165]

The chief secretary was likely unsurprised by the torture allegation; the government itself had purchased Dobermans from South Africa for use in interrogations.[166] Indeed, according to the memoir of the then-governor of Jerusalem, Edward Keith-Roach, the torture of Arabs was not only sanctioned but actually set in motion at the highest levels of the mandatory. Sometime between the death of Andrews in September 1937 and Wauchope's retirement in February 1938, disclosed Keith-Roach, "[Tegart] started what he called 'Arab investigation centres', at which 'selected' police officers were to be trained in the gentle art of 'third degree', for use on Arabs until they 'spilled the beans', as it is termed in criminal circles."[167]

On 25 February 1938, the bishop in Jerusalem wrote a letter to the chief secretary, in which he insisted that such actions could "[not] be hushed up indefinitely."[168] He met with the chief secretary and the inspector general the next day, this time in the company of the Anglican chaplain in Haifa, David W. Irving. Irving, having personally surveyed the damage British forces inflicted upon the village of Ijzim (south of Haifa) in the course of a search, told the men, "It is not that . . . some things are damaged: everything in most houses searched in [Ijzim] was broken or destroyed."[169] According to several eyewitnesses to the same search, British soldiers shot a villager named Muhammad Shambur in cold blood, then split his head in two with a bayonet in front of his wife.[170] There were, as well, reports of Arabs being forced to stand for extremely long periods, a Russian technique that inflicted profound physical and psychological trauma upon its victim while leaving his body externally unscathed.[171]

Despite all of these facts, when confronted with a letter of protest from the Arab Ladies of Jerusalem, which charged that British policemen were torturing Arab detainees and British soldiers were "destroying house articles and food" during searches, the Colonial Office insisted that there was "no ground for the allegations."[172] When the London-based Arab Centre produced a tract detailing the same charges, the claims were fiercely disavowed at all levels of the British government, including the Foreign Office.[173] Under questioning in Parliament regarding "Arab propaganda alleging ruthless and lawless behaviour of troops and police in Palestine," Ormsby-Gore stated:

> I consider that such propaganda is sufficiently discredited by its own obvious falsity and extravagance, and I do not propose to add to the many burdens of the Palestine Administration that of investigating each reckless and unsupported charge against British forces who are endeavouring to combat a campaign of murder and outrage.[174]

It appeared, in the wake of the Peel report, that the British had finally committed to the full-blooded crackdown that the Jewish Agency and press had long advocated, and were making no apologies for it. But, as in 1936, the very repressive measures by which the British hoped to quell the rebellion instead fortified it. So much so that rebel institutions began, in the revolt's second phase, to take on the aspect of a state. As chapter six will detail, this presented a formidable challenge not only to British policy, but to the very British presence, in Palestine.

SIX

Towards a Rebel Parastate

THE ARAB REJECTION OF PARTITION
AND THE EFFORT TO INSTITUTIONALIZE
THE REVOLT, 1937–38

INTRODUCTION

As detailed in chapter five, in the months following the July 1937 publication of the Peel report, the British adopted increasingly repressive measures against the Arabs of Palestine. This was a welcome development from the Zionist perspective, as were a series of subsequent turnovers in the British government. Malcolm MacDonald succeeded Ormsby-Gore as colonial secretary in May 1938, an appointment Blanche Dugdale deemed "the best . . . that could be made from the Jewish point of view."[1] Likewise, Harold MacMichael replaced Wauchope as high commissioner in February of the same year. MacMichael communicated to Weizmann his support for the Zionist plan to secure a rump state and then expand into Arab territory. After all, he explained with reference to the Arabs, "[Y]ou can turn a goat into the desert and it will carry on."[2] Wavell's successor as general officer commanding, Colonel Robert Haining, offered Weizmann more encouragement, reassuring him that there was "no need to worry about Galilee."[3] Haining also officially sanctioned the formation of the SNS, which would operate under the leadership of the above-mentioned Orde Wingate, and consist mostly of Haganah men.[4] The machinery of British repression thus appeared to be advancing in a direction the Yishuv had long hoped it would.

Yet, the repression generated still more sympathy for the rebellion among the Arab population. Government reports indicated that, notwithstanding the rebels' coercion of Arab civilians in many parts of the country, Arab sentiment at large was in sync with rebel objectives. One official therefore cautioned against optimism on the subject of "moderates": the same hopes have been entertained, fruit-lessly, since 1 October 1937, and (as the [Royal Commission] point out) there are no "moderates" on the major political issues, so that any who would be produced by the restriction of terrorism would be simply (a) personal enemies of the Husseinis or (b) neutral people tired of disorder. There is no great <u>political</u> function for the Army in Palestine to fulfill: only a police function.[5]

Others made the same point. Daniel Oliver, a British Quaker in charge of schools in the village of Hammana in Mount Lebanon, was well-known in and moved freely among Arab communities in Syria and Palestine. He wrote the secretary of the British Commonwealth Peace Federation in August 1938: "There is no such thing now as a moderate or loyalist party. The whole country of Palestine is entirely with the rebellion . . . The situation in Palestine is an exact duplicate of what took place in Ireland."[6] Regarding another of Oliver's reports, Lacy Baggallay at the Foreign Office minuted, "Mr. Oliver's views confirm the reports which are pouring in upon us from all sides."[7] The secretary of the Peace Federation passed Oliver's comments on to the Colonial Office, along with a report concluding:

A new authority has been established among the Arabs in charge of opera-tions and while a criminal element has attached itself to the National cause, the Arabs—as a people—whether Moslem or Christian, are united. The Arab villages are heart and soul with the rebellion.[8]

This included many Arab policemen. Hiring of Arabs into the Palestine police therefore ceased, and the government initiated a process of shifting the existing Arab police officers to unarmed work, as well as reducing their over-all numbers.[9] This made Tegart's proposed "rural mounted police"—consist-ing of "the tough type of man"—increasingly attractive to both the high commissioner and the general officer commanding. MacMichael explained to the colonial secretary that this select force, should it come into being, could partially displace "the existing regular police."[10] GOC Haining also endorsed the creation of a mounted police force, whose commanders he thought "should be soldiers who have learnt a little police work rather than police who have learnt a little soldiering." Haining suggested employing Circassian and other mercenaries for the force rank and file.[11]

As they had in January, Colonial Office personnel noted this proposal's ominous implications, particularly vis-à-vis the British claim to be upholding law and order—as opposed to waging war—in the mandate. Haining's mer-cenaries struck J. S. Bennett as especially problematic:

[S]o long as these forces are <u>British</u>, it is at least open to us to maintain, with very great persuasive force, that they are the friends and servants of the law abiding section of the community, concerned simply in restoring order and protecting all and sundry against (Arab) terrorism. But draft in a force of mercenaries, and I gravely doubt whether any Arab could hesitate for a moment in concluding that the British had definitely "declared war" on the Arabs.[12]

Bennett also expressed the familiar fear that the proposed force, especially if composed of mercenaries, "might well be less scrupulous than British personnel about 'Black and Tan' methods in the villages."[13]

This concern again glossed over the fact that British police and troops were already less than scrupulous regarding the use of Black and Tan methods in the villages and elsewhere. A British doctor working at St. Luke's Hospital in Hebron wrote up an account of the night of 20–21 August, for example, in which he disclosed that "a great number" of Arabs had come in with cracked craniums, the result of blows delivered by British forces during a village search. There were also six gunshot casualties. The doctor commented:

It would be difficult to argue that these casualties were inflicted on dangerous enemies or their allies . . . [O]f those whom I saw in life, two were old men, three were children, and the only "shab" [youth], if his story be true, was shot from a distance, inside his own house.[14]

While mentioned in private reports, such incriminating eyewitness testimonies received negligible attention in broader forums. This was no accident. In August, the authorities notified all Palestinian newspapers that they were forbidden to mention military or police operations (or rebels) unless the details were furnished to them by the government.[15] The occasion for the decree appears to have been the assassination of the assistant district commissioner in Jenin, W. S. S. Moffat. While *The Times* referred to Moffat's killing as a "terrorist's crime," Arab testimony indicated that the assistant district commissioner was himself a bad actor.[16] As Matthew Hughes details, Moffat reportedly "lined up Palestinian villagers . . . and shot every fifth man when hidden rifles were not produced."[17] Constable Burr heard from a colleague returning from the Syrian border that British forces in the north had wiped a number of villages clean off the map.[18] Al-Bassa, where soldiers forced a busload of Arabs over a land mine before reducing the village to ash, was a case in point.[19]

MacMichael wrote MacDonald on 5 September: "I have been much concerned lately by [the] occasional emergence of Black and Tan tendencies."[20] Three days later, the British vice-consul in Damascus, Frank Ogden, relayed more specific information regarding "police atrocities in Palestine" to Lacy Baggallay at the Foreign Office:

> Third degree persuasion is used by a picked body of men, all British, who are sworn to secrecy. The victims are taken to a house outside Jerusalem which used to be the house of [Roy] Spicer, the former Inspector-General of the Palestine police. Here the G-men, as I am told they are called, are permitted to inflict every form of torture they can think of.[21]

The extent to which such brutality resulted from British score-settling (as occurred in al-Bassa), on the one hand, or British terrorism meant to generate greater Arab fear of the government than of the rebels, on the other, is difficult to determine. What is clear is that the repressive measures failed to subdue the rebels, whose audacity had, by late 1938, reached new heights—the heights of state-building.

WIGS, WARDERS, AND WITNESSES: REBEL INSTITUTION-BUILDING AND THE BRITISH AND ZIONIST RESPONSE

In May 1938, the high commissioner sent word to the colonial secretary that in the area of the country north of Tel Aviv's latitude, "outrages against life and property" had become the norm. The Galilee district, MacMichael elaborated, was under the control of "gangs," who had succeeded in convincing the villagers that they, and not the government, were to be feared and obeyed. The rebels' executions of uncooperative mukhtars were particularly persuasive in this connection.[22]

Such coercive tactics evinced a lack of political unity within the Arab community, a problem the exiled Arab leadership did little to ameliorate. Village leaders complained to Amin al-Husayni, then in Lebanon, about rebel atrocities. In consequence, the exiled AHC issued pamphlets denouncing the bands' maltreatment of their fellow Arabs.[23] Likewise, the Headquarters of the Arab Revolt in Palestine, the closest thing to a unified rebel command as of August 1938, sent out orders to band leaders forbidding them to execute traitors without prior authorization.[24] The most prominent commander associated with the Headquarters was a Tulkarm-based grain merchant named 'Abd al-Rahim al-Hajj Muhammad, or Abu Kamal. Abu Kamal had fought in the Turkish army in the First World War, and then alongside Fawzi al-Qawuqji in 1936.[25] He now issued a series of instructions to local rebel leaders, including: "[You] do not have the authority to sentence a man to death, whatever the incriminating evidence."[26] Neither the Headquarters of the Arab Revolt in Palestine nor any other coordinating body, however, succeeded in exerting control over the various rebel formations.[27] Not that such control would have eliminated the violence. The AHC itself ordered the rebels to kill any Arab in contact with the Woodhead Commission.[28] Neither was local sanction for such deeds difficult to obtain. A blacklist of informers was posted in Haifa mosques, for instance, which included a religious authorization for the informers' assassination.[29]

British officials were largely of the opinion that the mufti was orchestrating all of this villainy from his new residence in Junieh, outside Beirut. But they had yet to obtain solid evidence for this supposition. Many of their Arab informants were of questionable reliability.[30] And in private, officials ruefully acknowledged the paucity of "positive evidence of the mufti's complicity in the plots of the Arab conspirators" and confessed they were "quite unable to produce any proof of his criminal activities."[31] They were nevertheless convinced on the basis of circumstantial evidence that Amin al-Husayni sat at the center of the "criminal" network responsible for Palestine's "inundation by propaganda, accompanied by money and arms, from over the [Syrian] border."[32]

The British consul in Damascus characterized the claim that the bulk of captured arms in Palestine came from Syria as "mere supposition, not to say invention."[33] He was more concerned about anti-British propaganda, particularly in the local Syrian press, whose "sympathetic tone towards banditry in Palestine" he was at pains to modulate.[34] MacMichael produced several examples of this troubling tendency from Syrian newspapers, which included: mention of "rebel courts" (his scare quotes); an interview with Fawzi al-Qawuqji, which lionized this "dangerous brigand"; claims that the Palestine police were torturing and executing people; and one report in which "a man about to be hanged urged that the enmity shown by the British against the Arabs should never be forgotten." The high commissioner concluded:

In spite of their obvious absurdity, these reports obtain wide credence and cause a disproportionate swelling of anti-British feeling as well as magnifying to the importance of a Holy War the relatively insignificant achievements of a few groups of brigands.[35]

MacMichael was seemingly unaware of the contradiction produced by his and other officials' positing of an elaborate rebel network—orchestrated by Amin al-Husayni and, evidently, expert at thwarting detection—and their simultaneous insistence that the courts, commanders, and patriotic zeal of said network amounted to little more than the paltry handiwork of a few criminals. From May 1938 forward, the sheer scale of rebel activities rendered the latter claim increasingly untenable.

As noted, Arab political unity in mid-1938 was partly a function of rebel coercion of the Arab population, and the rebels themselves did not operate according to an integrated command structure. Nevertheless, the rebels' institutions had acquired substantial popular support—their courts, above all. A War Office report disclosed:

. . . [T]here can be no doubt that an anti-government feeling on the part of most of the populace developed throughout the rural districts during June and July, largely on account of what the Arabs considered to be the imminence and inevitability of "Partition". Symptomatic of this was the effort made in Samaria to set up independent Courts of Law, systems of tax collection, etc. These organizations were run by the gang leaders in the hills and have met with success in proportion as the anti-government attitude produced a more united front.[36]

Mustafa Kabha observes that at the high-water mark of the second phase of the revolt, the rebel courts implemented few death sentences. Their popular legitimacy was such that they rarely felt compelled to.[37] In the same period, notes Yehoshua Porath, the courts operated as an integrated system, the nucleus of which was a central court whose "decisions were heeded by the various [rebel] factions" and which "even the [rebel] commanders considered themselves bound by."[38]

In addition to wearing military and police uniforms, the rebels imitated British "courtly" attire and stole British equipment for use in their own courts.[39] In July, armed men carried off the typewriters from the offices of the governor of Jerusalem.[40] The high commissioner reported in October:

The rebels conduct a continuous and largely successful propaganda to show that their courts are more just, and above all more speedy, than the King's courts. Incidentally, it is no doubt for this quasi-administrative business that the gangs require typewriters: a considerable number of these machines have been stolen, chiefly from Government offices.[41]

"Propaganda" understated the case. A British physician in Hebron sat in on a rebel court, and wrote of his experience, "Their justice and common sense does not appear to me inferior, and their expedition is demonstrably many degrees superior to that of [the mandatory courts]."[42] A British schoolteacher observed a rebel court outside Ramallah, and "watched the judge producing news sheets on typewriters and duplicators, aimed at publicizing the alternative rebel regime."[43] British troops in the Acre-Safed area "succeeded in capturing a Headquarters Group, complete with its banner and documents; and a Court of Justice, with wig, warders, and witnesses."[44]

While Porath and others are right to note that the rebel courts became imperative in light of Palestinian Arabs' avoidance of the mandatory courts, they fail to appreciate the symbolic import of these institutions. The rebel courts were a manifest rebuke to the British self-identification with law and order. The British practice of placing all references to the courts in scare quotes betrayed the government's discernment of this fact.

It was no doubt aided in this discernment by His Majesty's experience with the Republican rebel courts, which started spreading across Ireland in 1920, displacing and thus discrediting the crown courts.[45] Of all the forms of rebel protest, arguably none was more compelling than such institution-building. Should rebel "courts" have become anything like courts—or rebel "armies" anything like armies—their power to thereby draw the legitimacy of British imperialism into question was immense. Put another way, so long as "law and order" were a British preserve, the *raison d'être* of British imperialism was self-evident; once Palestinian or Irish armies and courts materialized, the British role in tutoring Palestinians and Irishmen in state-building became, to all appearances, superfluous. Francis Costello's anecdote of a British raid on a Republican court well illustrates this point:

> An account by [the Republican judge Conor] Maguire of a British military raid on a private session of a Republican court at Mullingar . . . is useful in demonstrating the awkward position in which the Government found itself: "Suddenly the door at the end of the hall was flung open. A young officer appeared brandishing a revolver. 'What's going on here?' he demanded. 'This,' said Kevin O'Shiel, 'is a court of the Irish Republic. Who are you?' 'You had better get out of this quickly, or you will be removed by force,' came the reply. Turning to us, Kevin O'Shiel said quite calmly, 'Gentlemen, we must yield to

superior force. It can now be judged, who wish to maintain law and order, and who are the disturbers of the peace!'"[46]

Courts, like uniforms, were an attack on British sovereignty. It is no accident that in the period when the Palestinian rebel courts flourished, the British not only sought to repress them, but also took to marching the British flag through areas inclined to support them.[47]

Given the full record of High Commissioner MacMichael's statements in the summer of 1938, it is reasonable to infer that his characterization of the revolt as the work of "a few groups of brigands," although privately expressed, was in fact a suggested public response to the pro-rebel reports of the Syrian press. Either this, or MacMichael was a man truly at odds with himself. By mid-July 1938, as Tom Bowden notes, the high commissioner would observe:

> It is notable that during the last three months the tactical skill of the armed bands has developed. They now operate according to plan and under leaders whose instructions they understand, trust and obey; they have, as is only natural, excellent "intelligence" and many of their schemes owe such local success as they have achieved to a discipline and sense of tactics which are, I am afraid, more marked today than they were, for instance, in the concluding stages of the disturbances of 1936.[48]

In September 1938, the colonial secretary put the point more bluntly: "I use the word 'rebels' advisedly because . . . we have now passed the stage at which we can reasonably talk of brigands or bandits."[49] H. Grattan-Bushe, the legal adviser to the Colonial Office, had said the same two months earlier. As Rendel had cautioned MacKereth in late 1937, so Grattan-Bushe then warned Lord Dufferin, the undersecretary of state for the colonies:

> I do not think that we have faced . . . the realities of the situation. We invented a soothing phraseology to describe those who were fighting against us. They were bandits, or terrorists, or gunmen. That was comforting to the public, and it was adopted with alacrity by the press. The danger is lest we begin to believe it ourselves.[50]

THE SUDDEN EROSION OF *HAVLAGAH*

Whether or not it was causally correlated with this new conviction among the top tier of Colonial Office personnel, the sudden erosion of *havlagah* within the Yishuv could not have been better timed by the Arab rebels themselves. In the month of July, the number of Arabs killed by Jews was over three times that of Jews killed by Arabs.[51] In retaliation for the first British execution of a Jew during the revolt, revisionists hanged an Arab in Haifa. And on 25 July, they detonated a bomb in a bustling Haifa marketplace, slaughtering thirty-five Arabs.[52] Although his own brother-in-law had been killed by Arab rioters two days prior, Weizmann wrote his family on 8 July, "... [A]t this terrible critical moment the Revisionists are our cruelest enemies."[53] Their actions, moaned Ben Gurion, were hacking away at the all-important Zionist link with the mandatory government.[54]

As if in compensation for the revisionist tarnishing of the Jewish reputation for self-restraint, the mainstream Zionist leadership stepped up their efforts to impress upon the British the imprudence of regarding Arab nationalism as akin to its civilized Western counterparts. Rebel actions in the course of July buttressed the Jewish case in this connection, but not as much as they might have. A few days before the revisionist bombing in Haifa, for example, Arab attackers shot and stabbed to death two Jewish families in the village of Kiryat Haroshet, located along the Haifa-Nazareth road, including an eleven-year-old boy and a two-year-old girl.[55] But the disparity in the July body count between the two communities—not to mention the revisionist attacks in and of themselves—limited the extent to which these atrocities could redound to the Zionists' advantage.

Weizmann therefore began pushing the strategic case for British support of the Zionists. He disparaged the broader Arab commitment to Palestine, suggesting to MacDonald in a 12 July letter that some of Amin al-Husayni's closest collaborators in Syria were up for sale.[56] "Arab nationalism," he wrote the colonial secretary, "is totalitarian in nature, shallow, aggressive and arrogant ... In quality it is inferior even to National-Socialism." He then came to the critical point:

> Sooner or later the British Government will have to ask themselves whether they are going to rely on backward Arab populations, which are an easy prey to any political adventurers ... or whether they would rather rely on a progressive Jewish population, bound in loyalty to Great Britain, and depending for its security, and perhaps even for its existence, upon the strength and welfare of the British Empire.[57]

Testifying before the Woodhead Commission in the capacity of a "Zionist apologist," Orde Wingate pressed the case more forcefully. The Arabs, he claimed, were "ruled by either fanatical or cynical factions." Their expulsion from Galilee was a necessity, and just the kind of "arbitrary procedure in the interests of those concerned" on which the British presence in Palestine was rightly predicated.[58] The fierce Zionist advocate and renegade Labour MP Josiah Wedgwood wrote *The Times of London* on 21 July complaining of the government's pigheaded policy of impartiality "between murderers and murdered" and failure to distinguish between "gangsters and their victims." But even as this effort to discredit Palestinian nationalism proceeded, the Arab construction of a Palestinian state advanced.

THE EMERGENCE OF A REBEL PARASTATE

A time-lapse view of events across Palestine in August–September 1938 would display something more than repeated skirmishes between British and Arab forces. The Arabs were laying siege not only to British persons, but to every institutional ramification of the mandatory. They were systematically dismantling the infrastructure of the British state in Palestine, and attempting to supplant it with their own. By late August, the rebels' destruction of government property—including the telecommunications system, the postal service, police posts, banks, and prisons—was, as *The Times* reported, "of such common occurrence that it has almost ceased to be noted in the daily news."[59] In a letter to GOC Haining, Shertok referred to the "creeping paralysis of [government] services."[60] In mid-September, for example, in the face of relentless attacks, the government simply shut down the post offices in Beersheba, Bayt Jala, Bethlehem, Jericho, Khan Yunis, Ramallah, and several other locations.[61] It did the same to a number of police stations and police posts.[62] The rebel courts had rendered the mandatory courts superfluous in many areas, but the authorities actually shuttered the mandatory courts in Nablus, where the insurgents walked the streets "fully armed . . . without any hindrance."[63] The high commissioner reported in October, ". . . [A]ll the law courts except those at Jerusalem, Jaffa, Tel Aviv and Haifa had . . . to be closed."[64] Humphrey Bowman recorded in his diary, "Palestine is worse than ever: the Arab 'rebels' now show great daring, and they attack police posts, and post offices and banks, robbing and killing and [illegible] up the work of the Govt. in a variety of ways."[65]

The insurgents also laid waste to much of the transportation infrastructure. A Jewish engine driver with the Palestine Railways related to the Jewish Agency his experience of being held up at Battir station, en route to Jaffa from Jerusalem. An armed Arab group numbering fourteen had stopped the train. They all wore the same khaki uniform, although one bore also a red stripe across his chest, which signified his status as a bomb expert. On his eventual return journey to Jerusalem, the driver glimpsed one of the many infrastructural chess matches playing out all across the country:

> ... [H]e saw at Kilo fourteen a number of Arabs cutting telephone wires. At Kilos 15 and 16 a party of Post and Telegraph workers, guarded by troops, were repairing telephone wires. At Kilo 17 a band of Arabs was dismantling rails. This party of saboteurs, numbering ten to fifteen, were dressed in the uniform of railwaymen, presumably to avert suspicion of chance patrols.[66]

By the end of September, the trains had stopped running entirely.[67] In October, a visiting military official observed, "[C]ivil government has completely broken down, and civil administration is only in operation to a limited extent in certain towns."[68]

While they could hardly supplant the country's transportation infrastructure, the rebels did partially displace the official postal system with a rudimentary system of their own, which operated through the rebel courts.[69] In his history of the Palestine police, Edward Horne notes of this period: "In some evacuated areas, so called provisional Arab governments claimed control and these imposed their own taxes and even issued their own stamps."[70] In some cases, the stamps functioned as receipts for villagers' tax payments to the nascent parastate.[71] But they also served a more pedestrian purpose. A November 1938 Jewish Agency intelligence report included a stamp which, the writer indicated, "the Arab masses have begun using in their exchanges of letters." The stamp was, he continued, "being distributed secretly by the people, who are in direct contact with the terrorists in every part of the country."[72] Its surface displayed an Arab woman gripping an inverted dagger, from the quillion of which hung the scales of justice. In the background stood the Dome of the Rock, into which "Filastin" was inscribed. Along the bottom of the stamp were written the words (in Arabic), "Justice is the foundation of peace." Another stamp read simply (in both English and Arabic), "Palestine for the Arabs," and also featured an image of the Dome of the Rock.[73] Such aesthetic particulars explained the need for the stamps to be "distributed secretly" through the rebels' postal system, for no letter bearing them could have passed through the tightly monitored official postal system.

While the various rebel factions were not of a piece—and although their members often menaced the Arab population—the level of operational inte-

FIGURE 8. A rebel stamp from 1938. On the left stands the Church of the Holy Sepulcher; on the right, the Dome of the Rock. Note the presence of English print. The rebels targeted not only Palestine's Arabs, but also an international audience, with such tokens of national autonomy. (Library of Congress)

gration to which they had ascended by September 1938 impressed even the most skeptical British observers. GOC Haining insisted that "the damage and dislocation caused to government property and communications forbids their dismissal as trivial," and were, he continued directly, "symptomatic of what is now a deep seated rebellious spirit throughout the whole Arab population."[74] MacMichael explained to MacDonald that while the insurgent movement was "not fully co-ordinated," it was nevertheless "essential to realise its essential unity."[75] A CID report indicated, "[T]he machinery for cooperation between the gangs is more efficient than it was and gives the rebel movement certain claims to the dignity and power of a national cause."[76] *The Times* made reference to a rebel "Government by night."[77] A trusted Jewish informant (whose "accuracy" had "been proved by events," in the view of the War Office) produced an intelligence report suggesting that the newspaper's evocative description was apt. The situation as of September, according to this "most secret source," was as follows:

1. . . . [E]xcept for the coastal strip of Jewish colonies there is no longer any British Government in Palestine. A state of war now exists . . . 80–85 percent of so called Government officials are Arab and are now wholeheartedly in the service of the Mufti and pass all information to his agents. This applies to Post Office and Bank officials, who inform the terrorists of cash in transit, etc; to interpreters and to the Police who now, when engaged with Terrorists, only fire in the air and will soon cease even to do this.

2. The Mufti has now formed his own Government and a complete list of officials has been prepared. These are all ready to take their posts as soon as the time comes, and real prestige has already passed to this Government which gives direct orders that no Arab dare disobey. Seven important Arabs who tried to oppose this Government have already been put out of the way. Taxes are no longer collected nor may any demands be made for the payment of debts for which a moratorium has been declared.[78]

The report went on to concede that "present acts of violence . . . may also be due sometimes to the independent action of local leaders actuated by jealousy of each other," but its thrust was that a shadow rebel government, headed by Amin al-Husayni, now controlled Palestine. Significantly, the report also revealed: "The Terrorists are leaving telegraph lines standing as they intend to use them themselves later. They are well provided with field telephones."

By September 1938, the rebels had put in place the components of a rudimentary Palestinian state. These included an army, courts, systems of tax collection and telecommunication, and a postal service. British and Zionist primary sources, and the bulk of the scholarship on the revolt, tend to denigrate these entities, typically via ironic reference to "courts," "armies," and "governments." Shai Lachman, for example, characterizes this period as one in which "lawless rebels" visited "absolute anarchy . . . upon the Arab community."[79] The implication is that rebel "infrastructure" was, to quote John Marlowe, little more than a "thin but strong web of violence and terror which the rebels had spread all over Arab Palestine."[80] Yet, it is remarkable that these and related institutions emerged on the scale that they did. One must recall that this country-wide institution-building occurred in the shadow of the world's premiere counterinsurgency machine: the British empire. The rebel courts did struggle to maintain legitimacy, and ultimately lost it. No less could be said of the British courts, however. Likewise, rebel discipline frequently faltered, and unscrupulous elements—often operating in defiance of orders—resorted to robbery and brutality.[81] The same, however, was true of British police and soldiers. What distinguished British officials and combatants from their rebel counterparts was neither their discipline nor their tactics. It was, rather, their objectives. The British sought to defy the demands of the Arab Palestinian public, the rebels to meet them.

Leading Zionists were naturally determined to deny any such equivalence. Blanche Dugdale described the condition of Palestine in September 1938 as an "utter breakdown of law and order."[82] Weizmann deemed it "tyranny and anarchy."[83] Such assessments followed inevitably from the Zionist certainty, widely expressed in the mainstream Jewish press in Palestine, as to the "emptiness and superficiality of Arab nationalism."[84] They followed just as inevitably from the British tendency noted throughout this book: the habit of excluding the British state from basic causal calculations regarding the course of events in the mandate. Thus, in summarizing the state of affairs for MacDonald in September, MacMichael wrote:

> The position is deteriorating rapidly and has reached a stage at which rebel leaders are more feared and respected than we are. The movement is definitely a national one, though financed in part by blackmail levied on a large scale in the country.[85]

Absent from this description was the fact that the rebel resort to "blackmail" and extortion was animated in substantial measure by the successful British effort to cut off sources of rebel income. When the second phase of the rebellion began, for example, the rebels could no longer rely on the funds raised by the national committees, because the government had dismantled them.[86] In September 1938, the British shifted control of an important fund—hitherto critical to sustaining the rebels—to a Nashashibi partisan.[87] As Swedenburg notes, they likewise "worked diligently to ensure that the flow of [foreign] monies, as well as the funds of sympathy, were choked off," to the point that by May 1939, these revenue streams had run dry.[88] What is more, as Porath details, the British were actively hiring Arabs to engage in extortionist practices while "pretend[ing] to be true rebels."[89] Such impostors were the targets of notices from the Headquarters of the Arab Revolt in Palestine, which condemned the fraudulent solicitation of money from villagers and townspeople in the Headquarters' name.[90] Matthew Hughes details a case in which "the Nashashibis and Palestinians from the village of Abu Ghosh produced leaflets purporting to come from the rebels but which subtly undermined the insurgents' cause."[91]

Porath thinks such British mischief only "marginally contributed" to rebel disunity, which resulted primarily from "political, family and regional dissensions, personal jealousies and criminal abuse." And yet, it is hard to understand how a movement as utterly riven as Porath and many others claim could have achieved the level of coordination detailed above. As Zeina Ghandour argues, the organizational integration of the revolt in late 1938 suggests that "the feral farmer [and] the barely armed, myopic rebels were presumably operating with some sort of cohesion, *savoir faire* and discipline." And yet "it is familial and clan lines of rebel (dis)organization, their localized and microcosmic understanding of politics, which is focused on."[92]

CONCLUSION

A final episode illustrates with almost poetic force the mandatory's causal implication in the course of events in Palestine, particularly vis-à-vis the incipient Palestinian parastate. The incident occurred in September 1938, and its elucidation requires some background.

The report of the War Office's "most secret source" proved accurate in numerous details, but it overestimated—as the British tended to—Amin al-Husayni's influence over the Palestinian rebels. The ex-mufti and other members of the exiled AHC—including Muhammad ʿIzzat Darwaza, Jamal al-Husayni, and Akram Zuʿaytir—had attempted since late 1937 to exert control over the rebellion, initially creating a "Central War Committee" for this purpose.[93] But the Committee proved incapable of coordinating the different rebel commanders from its base in Damascus, a liability several of the commanders—the most prominent of whom were ʿAbd al-Rahim al-Hajj Muhammad, ʿArif ʿAbd al-Raziq, Yusuf Saʿid Abu Durra, and Hasan Salama—attempted to redress by establishing a "Bureau of the Arab Revolt in Palestine."[94] In the end, the Bureau would fare little better than the Committee in fully unifying the different rebel commanders. In the beginning, however, it appeared promising, a fact which drew the attention of the British.

The formative meeting of the Bureau took place at Dayr Ghassaneh, outside Ramallah, in mid-September 1938. It lasted several days, and hundreds of rebels attended. The meeting reached its summit when ʿAbd al-Rahim al-Hajj Muhammad and ʿArif ʿAbd al-Raziq—the most influential regional commanders and rival claimants to the title of "commander-in-chief of the rebellion"—made peace, sealing their reconciliation with a kiss before the assembled village leaders.[95]

Aside from their vying with each other for the leadership of the rebel movement, ʿAbd al-Rahim al-Hajj Muhammad and ʿArif ʿAbd al-Raziq had a contentious history, which included feuding between their extended families.[96] Both men were merchant farmers. Both hailed from villages in the vicinity of Tulkarm. And both had fought alongside Fawzi al-Qawuqji in 1936. Yet, rather than facilitating cooperation, these similarities bred competition for status and territory.[97] In consequence, the two commanders' reconciliation at Dayr Ghassaneh required an especially trusted mediator, Muhammad al-Salih. Al-Salih, reports Sonia Nimr, was the "most prominent [rebel] leader" in Silat al-Zahir, near Nablus. And as Yehoshua Porath relates, the "Qassamite veteran" was a man "renowned for his honesty and his complete devotion to the national cause."[98]

Al-Salih appears to have been one of those figures whose reputation for integrity positions them to mediate between adversaries, a type critical to the success of any social movement. Alas for the rebels, this esteemed negotiator would die within hours of making peace between ʿAbd al-Rahim al-Hajj Muhammad and ʿArif ʿAbd al-Raziq. British intelligence learned of the gathering at Dayr Ghassaneh, security forces closed in on the village, and the RAF decimated the assembled rebels.[99] Al-Salih and several comrades managed to fight their way out of Dayr Ghassaneh and flee to the village of Sirta in the Nablus mountains, where British forces again encircled them. According to an obituary written by Akram Zuʿaytir, al-Salih was wounded in the hand in the subsequent battle. He nevertheless fought on, and to the death.[100]

Even some of the best scholarship on the revolt neglects to consider the possibility that when the British killed al-Salih, they directly contributed to the Bureau of the Arab Revolt's failure to generate greater cooperation between the various rebel commanders. Yehoshua Porath, for example, writes: ". . . Muhammad al-Salih, and many others were killed and tragically this was the only real result of the [Dayr Ghassaneh] meeting, since no peace was brought about between the rivals." Porath details other factors that aggravated relations between ʿAbd al-Rahim al-Hajj Muhammad and ʿArif ʿAbd al-Raziq in particular, including the social rivalry between their extended families and the Central War Committee's favoring ʿArif ʿAbd al-Raziq. He refers in passing to the possibility that the British stirred up enmity between ʿAbd al-Rahim al-Hajj Muhammad and ʿArif ʿAbd al-Raziq through the deft circulation of invidious misinformation.[101] Yet, Porath overlooks the causal implications of the British bombing of the two leaders' peace summit and killing of the men's chosen mediator, whose continued existence might have enabled their ongoing cooperation. Charles Anderson, to mention a more recent example, writes that at Dayr Ghassaneh, the "rivalry" between 'Abd al-Rahim al-Hajj Muhammad and 'Arif 'Abd al-Raziq "dealt the rebels their single most costly loss."[102] It would be more accurate to say that the two commanders' reconciliation cost the rebels, for that—and not their rivalry—is what the British sought to undermine.

It is worth pausing to appreciate the extent to which the rebels' effort to unify their respective commands conformed to the state-making template of the modern period. The rebel infighting that occasioned this effort replicated the conditions under which the British and other European states had forged their own professional military and police forces from the sixteenth to the eighteenth century. In those cases, too, violent tension between the various groups competing for control of the means of violence paved the path to the state's final commandeering of the means of violence. Moreover, the impetus for the unification of these groups was the same in Palestine as it had been in Europe: namely, the threat of external conquest.[103] Of course, one must see the British as Palestine's Arabs saw them—as outsiders and an external threat—to appreciate the analogy. And neither the British nor the Zionists did. We need not repeat their error.

At Dayr Ghassaneh as elsewhere, the British were implicated in the collapse of the nascent Palestinian state. As Zeina Ghandour has written, "The rebellion did not unavoidably self-implode, it was crushed."[104]

SEVEN

New Policy, New Crime

THE ABORTION OF THE BALFOUR DECLARATION

IN OCTOBER 1938, the revolt reached its apex. Although rebel factions jockeyed for influence and prestige, their differences no longer hobbled their ability to coordinate action on a broad scale. Indeed, as chapter six showed, the rebels managed to put in place the rudiments of a Palestinian state, including countrywide systems of justice, communication, and defense. Needless to say, this circumstance was an affront to British sovereignty in the mandate.

On 24 October, High Commissioner Harold MacMichael sent Colonial Secretary Malcolm MacDonald a summary of events covering the previous month. It was, he wrote, "in every way, the worst since the disturbances broke out in 1936." The number of deaths was the highest for any month of the rebellion (188, not counting rebels). More distressing still, the insurgency had reached an unprecedented scale, such that it had "unquestionably become a national revolt involving all classes of the Arab community in Palestine."[1]

Rebel propagandists availed themselves of the popular mood. Their leaflets appealed in the broadest terms to the Arab youth of the country, drawing freely and fluently upon both national and religious modes of expression. One read: "Rise up . . . young men of Mohammad and followers of Christ . . . youth of Palestine, the flower of the nation . . . under the Arab flag, you will be immortal martyrs in the gardens of Paradise."[2] In addition to fostering the rebellious spirit of the Arab public, such exhortations reflected that spirit's breadth. Entire villages turned out to support the militants in their engagements with British troops.[3] The Times of London reported:

> Military control has taken its place in Samaria and in large sections of
> Galilee, but in the rest of the country, and especially in parts of the southern

and Jerusalem districts, the rebel "government" is in control. The effectiveness and prestige of the British administration are steadily falling, while the prestige and power of the revolutionists are rising.[4]

The New Statesman and Nation similarly observed that the rebels were "establishing themselves in the eyes of the general population as the genuine champions of Arab nationalism and an army of liberation."[5] The rebels had taken over.

LONDON'S TWO-PRONGED APPROACH TO
REGAINING CONTROL OF PALESTINE

The colonial secretary put forward a two-pronged strategy for dealing with this situation. The first order of business was to intensify the repression of Arabs. Prime Minister Neville Chamberlain's 30 September agreement with Hitler having ostensibly secured the European peace, more British battalions were available for deployment in the mandate. The government would send four of them to Palestine, raising their number to seventeen and returning the troop tally to nearly 20,000. MacDonald planned to flood the country with British forces, who would bring the battle to the militants and impose order upon the rest of the population. The latter task would be facilitated by a new system of travel permits and identification cards, designed to curtail the free movement of Arabs in particular.[6] The second prong of the colonial secretary's strategy for regaining control of Palestine was to officially abort the partition proposal and to significantly limit Jewish immigration. Both measures would undermine popular support for the rebels by modulating Arab hostility towards British policy.[7] At an opportune moment, therefore, the government would invite the Arab and Jewish leaders to London to discuss the future of the mandate. While conducted under the pretense of good faith negotiations, this conference would in fact provide the occasion for the government's predetermined reversals on partition and Jewish immigration.

The mode of MacDonald's proposed increase in repression was a matter of dispute within the British government. As in September 1936, the primary point of contention was martial law. A number of top officials advocated it, including the general officer commanding and the secretary of state for war, as well as a pro-Zionist parliamentary faction styling itself the Palestine

Parliamentary Committee.[8] The high commissioner and colonial secretary, however, opposed declaring martial law. MacMichael reasoned that doing so would grant the military "unrestricted power to wage war on the Arab population of Palestine," a scenario amounting to "the negation of all law."[9] Echoing the concerns of 1936, MacDonald worried that martial law would call the legality of the military courts into question, a sentiment seconded by the legal adviser to the Colonial Office.[10] Moreover, the colonial secretary argued, "The actions of a purely military government in Palestine ... might well be disastrous in the wider [international] view."[11] Charles Baxter, the head of the eastern department at the Foreign Office, likewise warned that declaring martial law "would be interpreted in Iraq and Egypt as initiating a new regime of unchecked military 'frightfulness'."[12]

This preoccupation with the international ramifications of martial law was, in fact, the primary obstacle to openly declaring it. But even as they emphasized the negative publicity it was likely to elicit, the opponents of martial law minimized the gravity of its legal implications. Thus, while the colonial secretary stated that military courts would become "illegal" under martial law, he also claimed that this legal status was "the only difference between these courts as constituted at the present time, and similar courts under martial law."[13] "In practice," MacDonald acknowledged, "the military authorities are already in control, though in theory the civil authorities still [retain] that position." For the sake of appearances, he was "most anxious" to keep it that way.[14] The chancellor of the exchequer, Sir John Simon, expressed the same view, with the endorsements of the minister for co-ordination of defence, the foreign secretary, and the secretary of state for air.[15] Perhaps the most candid articulation of the argument against martial law came from Lacy Baggallay at the Foreign Office, who remarked:

> ... [I]t is largely the names of things that count ... what we want to avoid at all costs in view of our relations with the Arab States etc. is saying that we have chosen the moment when we call those States into conference to institute a more rigorous offensive than ever before upon the Arabs of Palestine.

> ... [T]here is no question of declaring martial law as such. Under the Palestine Order-in-Council, the High Commissioner has powers literally to do anything and may delegate these powers at any time he wishes to the G.O.C.[16]

The attorney general agreed: "... [A] proclamation of Martial Law gives the Government no powers which it did not possess before, but operates merely as a notice to the public."[17] The problem was not martial law per se, for the mandatory was already legally unrestrained in its "internal security" prerogatives. The problem was what a martial law declaration would communicate to an international audience: namely, that the British had lost all legitimacy in Palestine and remained there by virtue of force alone.

For a second time, the opponents of martial law won the day. As the debate surrounding the topic revealed, however, the British decision not to declare martial law was more a public relations exercise than a constraint on violent coercion in the mandate. Indeed, unfettered force had become all the more imperative in light of two realities. First, as the high commissioner's summary of events for September indicated, the rebels had taken over large swathes of the country, with the support of the Arab population. As MacMichael put it to MacDonald: ". . . [T]he national hero is [now] the gang leader."[18] A British intelligence report covering August–October 1938 cautioned that the "pot of insurrection was liable to boil over in any or every district separately or simultaneously."[19]

In August, the insurgents seized Hebron, overtaking the police station with ease.[20] The following month, they entered Beersheba and Khan Yunis to the cheers of the women and the sprinklings of rose water from the windows of the people.[21] And on 14 October, the rebels converged on Jerusalem. Within twenty-four hours, they had captured the Old City, locked its entrances, set fire to the police station and the post office, and hoisted their flag over the Damascus gate. The action—which the high commissioner called a "major . . . crime"—gave the newly augmented British forces their "first opportunity to display their heavy hand."[22] Working in coordination with the RAF, British soldiers blasted through the city gates, removed inhabitants from their homes for use as human shields, and retook the Old City on 18 October.[23] It was a pattern they would repeat from one end of the country to the other.[24] In November, for example, the British reconquered Jaffa. According to Akram Zu'aytir, the troops took 15,000 men prisoner, including youths. They rampaged through the houses, trampling children underfoot and causing pregnant women to miscarry. They behaved similarly in the surrounding villages.[25]

The second reality making British force all the more necessary in October 1938 was something the British and Zionists had long sought publicly to conflate with the Arab rebellion: namely, Arab criminality. Events dramatically confirmed the British and Zionist case in this regard when a Qassamite commander named Abu Ibrahim al-Kabir led a barbaric raid on Tiberias early in the month, murdering nineteen Jews.[26] Al-Kabir sat on the Damascus-based Central War Committee, established by the mufti and other members of the exiled AHC to coordinate rebel activities in Palestine. While the Committee failed in this capacity, the fact that a member of a body claiming command of the rebellion was implicated in an episode as disgraceful as that in Tiberius dealt a blow to the nationalist pretensions of the revolt at large.[27] At approximately 8:45 on the evening of 2 October, al-Kabir, after setting up roadblocks outside the city to impede rescuers, led his men into Tiberias, where they proceeded to butcher Jews in their houses.[28] The invaders explicitly targeted children, slaughtering ten. According to one witness, among the nineteen corpses were women whose "naked bodies . . . exposed the evidence that the knives had been used in the most ghastly way."[29]

While the massacre in Tiberias seemed scripted to tarnish the nationalist character of the revolt, it occurred at an inopportune moment for the British. The first prong of the government's scheme for stabilizing the mandate involved a massive, unbridled assault on the rebels. The second prong, however, was an attempted rapprochement with Arab Palestinians at large, a strategy requiring concessions to Arab demands vis-à-vis partition and Jewish immigration. This rapprochement necessitated a degree of British amnesia, especially after the release of the Woodhead report on 9 November. Not only did the government endorse the report's finding that partition was unviable, but MacDonald made a startling disclosure in the House of Commons on 23 November. He announced that the high commissioner would shortly commence negotiations with leading Palestinian Arabs, with the object of selecting an Arab delegation to London. The government having long equated this same leadership with a criminal syndicate, some explanation was in order. On 24 November, the colonial secretary offered one to the House of Commons:

> I know that a great many people regard this Arab agitation as the mere protest of a gang of bandits. Of course it is true that many of these Arabs who have taken part most eagerly in the troubles are cut-throats of the worst type. Their massacres of the innocents at Tiberias, and on a score of other miserable battlefields, have disgraced their cause. It is true also that many of those who are associated with them have been terrorised into that association. But there is much more than that in the Arab movement. I think that this House, which is so capable of a generous understanding of other peoples, ought to recognise that many in the Palestinian Arab movement are moved by a

genuine patriotism. However wrong they may be, however misguided they may be, however disastrous their policy may be, many of them have felt compelled to take the risk of laying down their lives for their country.[30]

The irony was hard to miss: among those who regarded the rebellion as "the mere protest of a gang of bandits" was none other than the colonial secretary himself. Only a few months earlier, he had firmly concluded that the revolt was not "a spontaneous national movement of Palestinian Arabs" but rather "the result of strenuous agitation by political leaders accompanied by intimidation of bands of bandits who had no genuine political significance."[31] His far subtler public statement of November 1938 betrayed an ambivalence that had emerged a month prior during inter-departmental discussions regarding the matter of an Arab delegation to London.

In a meeting of high officials on 8 October, MacMichael insisted that whoever else might be included in such a deputation, the mufti was *persona non grata*. But the undersecretary of state for the colonies, Lord Dufferin, suggested that this precondition was misguided. For the mufti was "the one man who can, on his side, guarantee peace." And London had, after all, come to terms with the Sinn Fein leader Eamon De Valera and other rebel leaders in the past.[32] The subsequent exchange is worth recording:

MACMICHAEL: But His Majesty's Government cannot treat with instigators of murder.

SIR GRATTAN BUSHE (CO): On the contrary, peace in Ireland was made by a treaty between Cabinet Ministers and "murderers".

MACDONALD: [I] appreciate the force of these arguments: but in my view the analogy with Ireland or Egypt is not complete. In all these other cases our object has been to instate the "murderers" as the new Government of the Territory: in Palestine this is not so, as we intend to continue ruling ourselves. Hence to treat with the Mufti would be practically equivalent to recognizing his "Provisional National Government" and make the subsequent administration of the Mandatory authorities impossible.[33]

The colonial secretary's remarkably frank analysis pinpointed the paradox of post-Woodhead policy. If the Arab leaders were mere criminals, the government could not confer with them (certainly not publicly). Yet, if they were statesmen, British sovereignty in Palestine was a sham. The British had thus traded one dilemma (partition) for two: they had somehow to negotiate with a partner they dared not name; and they had simultaneously to repress a population with whom they hoped to reconcile.

The second order was tall indeed. It required, first and foremost, the public denial of British brutality in the mandate. The colonial secretary's first substantive remarks in his 24 November presentation to the House of Commons concerned charges against the troops:

> We all know that certain interested propagandists have been leveling many foul charges against the conduct of our troops. I see a good many things in the Colonial Office, but I have never seen any evidence in support of these charges.[34]

While his claim regarding the troops was ludicrous, MacDonald did not even bother to deny the accusations against the Palestine police. Less than a week after his 24 November presentation, he admitted to the cabinet that he had "received reports of atrocities by members of the Police Force" but chose to "deliberately [omit] any reference" to them before the House of Commons.[35]

There were, as before, many such reports. In October, for example, a merchant from Jaffa sent the high commissioner an eloquent and impassioned letter decrying an official statement concerning the killing of an Arab prisoner. According to the government's version of the incident, British police shot the man when he attempted to escape their custody. But the merchant, one A. Andrawus, claimed that he and twenty others witnessed a much different event. It began when a police car pulled off the road in the vicinity of Andrawus' auto repair shop in Jaffa. As Andrawus and his employees looked on, the driver and other officers extracted a handcuffed man, coaxed him to the front of the vehicle, and then executed him in the manner of mafioso. Andrawus concluded with the plea:

> I make this report in great fear [for] my own life and that of my wife and my family. Murder by the Police is not uncommon ... I ask Your Excellency's personal security for myself and [that] my family be protected against police vengeance.[36]

In December, the high commissioner and the attorney general would both concede that the evidence in the case made "a formal charge of murder ... inevitable."[37] It was one of several such incidents in Jaffa alone.[38]

Other modes of repression either persisted or were intensified. Having already effectively shut down much of the Arab press in Palestine, the mandatory stepped up censorship in the second half of 1938. As Giora Goodman notes, the new measures "helped to conceal the more brutal methods used by the security forces."[39] In August, the rebels started circulating their own newspaper (al-Jihad) in northern Palestine. In the paper's debut edition, the editor-in-chief told his readers that he intended to subvert the British effort to "prevent the outside world from knowing about" the "torture and abuse" of innocent Palestinian villagers.[40] The British considerably increased the number of village searches in the last quarter of the year, and began placing Arab men in cages while conducting them.[41] Given the poverty of British intelligence on insurgent activities, the authorities resorted to mass arrests to locate "the true rebels."[42] Bowden notes that "anything non-military which moved at night, or moved by day without a pass, was fair game for arrest."[43] It was fair game period, in fact. Even before the November 1938 imposition of a countrywide curfew, Arab collaborators traveling after dark shouted special code words to avoid being shot by police and soldiers.[44] Constable Sydney Burr wrote his parents in late 1938, "The greatest menace nowadays is the army, with their indiscriminate firing." The police, too, were "not particular who they shoot."[45] One British resident in Palestine related in a letter home, "On Saturday, here in Jaffa, the troops were merely shooting at sight anyone they had a mind to aim at." Among their victims was a seven-year-old girl.[46] The private journal of the assistant superintendent of police in Jenin, Geoffrey Morton, recorded similar instances of British forces shooting and sometimes killing Arab children.[47]

The British press continued to touch lightly, if at all, upon charges of "Tommy" terrorism, which were appearing more frequently in German and other foreign newspapers.[48] As *The Times* reported, "The German Press . . . devotes much space today to events in Palestine, presenting its news in such a fashion as to give the impression that the action of the British Army is directed at suppressing a justified struggle for freedom on the part of the Arabs."[49] While not so prostrate as *The Times*, *The New Statesman and Nation* was equally firm in rejecting reports of British atrocities in Palestine, stating: "Nobody believes the German newspaper stories that [the British army] is engaged in pillaging, murdering, raping and deliberately starving the Arabs. On the other hand, there is plenty of evidence . . . that Nazi propaganda and money are actively fomenting the rebellion in Palestine."[50] In January 1939, the magazine reported approvingly: "The War Office has been driven to issue a statement to refute the charges of murder, robbery and starvation leveled at the British troops and their officers, and to show that the

FIGURE 9. Bombing of a Palestinian village by the British army, 1938. (adoc-photos/Corbis via Getty Images)

measures, regrettable as they may be, are both necessary and conducted with all the humanity possible."[51]

Even such sympathetic accounts, however, acknowledged that British forces were blowing up entire villages.[52] One article quoted an officer saying, "We must make the population fear us more than they do the rebels."[53] While British repression did frighten the Arabs, it also infuriated them. When government forces attempted to hand out milk and bread to assuage the population of Jaffa after a three-day search of the city in early November, the people refused the food.[54] Anglican missionary efforts to distribute meals to Arabs were also often rebuffed, and this at a time when many Arabs were destitute.[55]

The British could hardly hope to conceal from Palestinians the harsh reality of repression, which they sought instead to blunt with policy concessions. The British public, however, could be fooled. As noted, the colonial secretary, with the support of the domestic press, adamantly denied charges of military wrongdoing. Moreover, it so happened that two of the most assiduous chroniclers of British malfeasance in the mandate were absent from

Palestine at the peak of the counterinsurgency in late 1938. In neither case was this an accident.

The persons in question were a Haifa resident and Anglican missionary named Frances Newton, and the Anglican bishop in Jerusalem, George Francis Graham Brown. Scholars have challenged the credibility of both. Newton in particular has come in for opprobrium. Rory Miller, for example, writes of her unrepentant fidelity to the mufti, and cites testimony to the effect that she was untrustworthy when it came to claims against the Zionists.[56] He neglects, however, to make the same case with respect to her charges against British troops and soldiers, although Newton's reputation suffers so dearly under his scrutiny that the unsuspecting reader would be inclined to dismiss her in this connection as well. The truth, however, is that Newton's reports regarding British atrocities were corroborated by internal government documents as well as the testimony of British police and soldiers. As a correspondent for *The Times of London* wrote privately of her, although Newton was a "strong anti-Zionist," she was also "truthful" and "not to be lightly dismissed."[57]

Despite their unwelcome revelations regarding the actions of British security forces, Newton and the bishop were, in fact, particularly reliable sources of information. The case for their special credibility turns on several points. First, the testimony of both meets the historical criterion of embarrassment; that is, they testified to facts which they were otherwise motivated not to acknowledge. This is clear from the fact that both Newton and the bishop made a point of bringing the evidence in their possession to the British authorities in an off-the-record capacity. That their reason for doing so was chagrin on behalf of the British government is a matter of record.[58] Second, both Newton and the bishop were well positioned to gather evidence. Newton spoke Arabic, and she and the bishop visited villages in the hours after troops had been in them, as well as areas of major cities where violent incidents involving the police occurred. They photographed damaged property, interviewed witnesses, and otherwise carefully documented their conclusions about what had transpired.[59] Third, while Newton and the bishop's detractors regarded them as hopelessly pro-Arab, the two in fact had few illusions about the frequent savagery of rebel tactics. Newton referred to the more bloodthirsty elements of the insurgency as "criminals" and "murderers." The bishop, too, described rebel actions as "wicked brigandage and murders." His and Miss Newton's sympathies lay not with the rebels, but with the Arab noncombatants who suffered unjustly.[60]

By 1938, the authorities' favored tactic of alternately humoring, ignoring, and rejecting the bishop and Miss Newton's reports had begun to backfire. In a 26 February meeting with the chief secretary, the bishop stated exasperatedly, "We have protested since June 1936 and these things are still going on."[61] A day prior, he wrote the secretary, "For many reasons I am loathe to bring these facts forward in Great Britain, but this matter cannot be hushed up indefinitely."[62] Newton lacked the bishop's patience; she went public with her claims. In response, on 4 October 1938, the high commissioner officially forbade her return to Palestine from England, where she was visiting.[63]

The evidence for high officials' intentional diversion of the bishop is more circumstantial, but nevertheless difficult to dispute. The bishop's stock in London mysteriously rose between the Peel hearings—when he sought unsuccessfully to testify before the commission regarding the theological shortcomings of the Jewish claim on Palestine—and the latter months of 1938. By then, his input on Palestinian affairs had apparently become indispensable. The bishop left Jerusalem for London in August 1938, planning to return by December. But his clerical superior, the archbishop of Canterbury, as well as the colonial secretary himself, made every effort to detain him.[64] As the bishop wrote the archdeacon, his surrogate in Jerusalem, on 29 November:

> ... [T]he Archbishop has advised me to remain in [England] for the time being ... in my interview with Mr. Malcolm MacDonald this morning—it only lasted eight minutes, for he was very busy—he definitely said that he would like me to remain in this country so as to be available for consultation during the preliminary discussions before as well as during the proposed Conference, and even if the Conference did not take place he would wish to discuss with me some of the aspects of the Government's policy for Palestine.[65]

It is curious that the colonial secretary made so little time for so important a man. The bishop had nevertheless prepared for this eventuality. He carried into his meeting with MacDonald a letter containing his thoughts on the Palestine situation, for the secretary's later perusal. The interview was so rushed, however, that he had no opportunity to pass it to him. This somewhat undermines the notion that MacDonald was eager for the bishop's input. As does the fact that the bishop seemed in a panic to fill his unexpected role as Palestine expert. He asked the archdeacon to furnish him "the list of books that should be read" in order to "fill in the gaps of my knowledge about the Holy Land, [and] especially about the history of its peoples."[66]

By January 1939, the bishop's absence from Jerusalem had become conspicuous to the point of generating controversy within the Anglican community in Palestine.[67] Under pressure, he inquired of the Colonial Office and the archbishop when he might return. While neither could coerce him, both urged that he "would be well advised to stay."[68] Dufferin counseled the bishop, ". . . I think that unless there is anything urgent to call you back I should remain here if I were you."[69] The bishop informed the archdeacon on 12 January that he had taken "lunch with the Archbishop, who was even more insistent than before that I should remain."[70] The colonial secretary finally granted him permission to leave London in March.[71]

All of these facts must be placed in the context of British intentions vis-à-vis the 1939 conference. London did not anticipate that the conference would result in an agreement between the British, the Jews, and the Arabs regarding the future of the mandate.[72] Indeed, this purported objective was a fiction, as the Palestinian and Zionist leadership understood.[73] British officials had already decided on the fundamentals of their revised Palestine policy; consultations with Jews and Arabs were diplomatic window dressing. The notion that the bishop's presence in London was critical to any government decision related to the conference was therefore intrinsically implausible. The Colonial Office wanted him out of Palestine for the same reason it wanted Newton out of Palestine—to cover the eyes and ears of the British public at the height of British brutality in the mandate.

Such brutality achieved its aim. The commander of the eighth division—and the military official in charge of northern Palestine—Major General Bernard Montgomery, reported confidently that as of 1 February 1939, "The backbone of the armed opposition has been smashed . . . The leaders are being so harried that they are losing their prestige."[74] One telling index of this fact was the government tax yield in Jenin, Nablus, and Tulkarm (the dreaded "triangle of terror") for February 1939, which was four to five times the figure for February 1938.[75] MacDonald had commented several months earlier on the troubling popular identification of the "gang leader" with the "national hero."[76] That equation was now all but undone. Montgomery confirmed that the rebels were "ceasing to be public heroes and are becoming hunted outlaws."[77] The military had made it so.

This was only half the story, however. Even as a *Times* headline highlighted "Faked Palestinian 'Atrocities'" (13 February), troops and police wreaked havoc throughout the country. They killed fourteen Arabs in Jerusalem on 8 February, and nineteen more in Nahf, in Galilee, on 27 February.[78] According to the report of the high commissioner, the dead were mostly militants.[79] But there was every reason to be skeptical of this and other such claims. The high commissioner's report failed, for example, to mention the killing of an Arab boy on 19 February in the village of Jabaʿ, located in the Jenin-Nablus-Tulkarm triangle. In his diary entry for that date, the assistant superintendent of police in Jenin wrote: "0900: Reported that during last night, a detachment of Border Regt. entered Jaba village to arrest gangsters alleged to be holding a meeting. A figure seen running away, was shot and found to be a boy who died later."[80] Other sources painted a grim picture of the effect of British repression on Arab civilians. On 28 February, the Anglican chaplain in Haifa sent the bishop in Jerusalem (who was still in London) an update on events in Palestine. Among other things, he noted:

> We have had some anxiety in regard to Kafr Yasif [in the upper Galilee]. A landmine exploded near the village and one British Soldier was killed and others wounded. The village was searched and seventy houses set on fire; forty houses were totally destroyed. About 250 people were homeless. I do not think the circumstances differ from those with which we are familiar. I have not heard that there is any evidence that the village was responsible for placing the landmine. At the same time nine men from Kwaycat village were shot dead. It is reported from Kafr Yasif that they were ordered to run before the troops and then fired on. I cannot confirm this.[81]

Constable Burr, who was then working out of the Acre police station, gave an account of the same episode in a letter to his parents. Along with the district commissioner, he was summoned to the scene while events were still unfolding. According to Burr, men from the village of Yasif did, in fact, plant the first of two land mines. But this was in response to British troops pursuing an interloper into their village and then brazenly shooting four bystanders. The soldiers were leaving the village when this first land mine detonated, killing two of them, Burr claimed. They then re-entered Yasif and "destroyed the whole village." There were no killings, but there was also no one to kill; the villagers had fled to the hills before the troops came back. Having laid waste to Yasif, the soldiers were again en route to their base when they rolled over a second land mine. This prompted them to attack another village in the vicinity, Kuwaykat, whose inhabitants had no time to evacuate. Burr put the minimum figure of Arab dead at Kuwaykat at twenty-five.[82]

Here is how the high commissioner referred to this incident: "Two villages adjacent to the scene of this crime [the land mines] were subsequently searched by troops. In one of them eight Arabs were killed and in the other about 50 houses were burnt down owing to the ignition of a quantity of gun powder or similar material in a house which was being demolished."[83] At least some in the Colonial Office found this account suspect. One reader of MacMichael's report scribbled in the margin, "This sounds as though the troops went wild and 'savaged' the villages—a not unknown procedure, one hears." Another commented, "I agree."[84]

An Anglican missionary who visited Yasif in May 1939 wrote of his experience there in a letter. For fear of giving the "wrong impressions," he declined the villagers' offer to show him the charred husks of the houses. Nevertheless, he recorded: "I was deeply moved by the obvious needs of these people, and also by their telling me that they considered themselves fortunate as compared with other villages where men had been killed during the searches by the Troops."[85]

The supine British newspapers, the muzzled Palestinian press, and the missing bishop and Miss Newton all but ensured that the piteous stories of Yasif and Kuwaykat, not to mention those of "other villages," would go untold. For some time, in any case. Decades later, the anthropologist Ted Swedenburg and the historian Sonia Nimr met with a former rebel from Kuwaykat. The man, 'Ali Husayn Baytam, began the interview by removing a sheet of paper from his pocket. It contained the names of the men from his village whom the British had killed in 1939. Swedenburg later recalled, "He had kept the list with him for about forty years, hoping to meet someone who would record the names in a book."[86] He also noted, "It was this massacre, typical of peasant experiences during the revolt, that 'Ali insisted that we preserve for posterity before he would discuss anything else."[87] Swedenburg and Nimr's encounter with 'Ali gives some indication of the extent to which the British succeeded in smothering Palestinian voices—to say nothing of Palestinian lives—in the course of retaking the mandate in late 1938, and finally crushing the revolt in 1939.

EIGHT

—————

The End of the Revolt, 1939

INTRODUCTION: THE ARAB DESCENT (WITH BRITISH HELP) INTO CIVIL WAR

Apart from a pliable press and the removal from Palestine of gadflies such as the bishop and Miss Newton, the British also benefitted in 1939 from an emerging civil war within the Arab Palestinian community. On the one hand, this Arab infighting resulted from longstanding rivalries (that between the Husaynis and the Nashashibis, above all) and more recent blood feuds born of rebel ruthlessness. Arab commentators had been voicing concerns over this ruthlessness for some time. *Al-Jami'a al-Islamiyya*, for example, warned its readers in December 1937: "Who ensures that the spirit of revenge will not awaken among the injured and the animosity will not encounter counter-animosity, and only Allah knows what these actions will lead to."[1] This concern was well-founded. In November 1938, Zionist intelligence learned that the number of Palestinians spying on the bands for the British had significantly increased, and that the informants came "mainly from those bereaved families whose sons and property the terrorists have attacked."[2] Likewise, among the so-called "peace bands" that began operating against the rebels in 1938 were the relatives of Arabs put to death by the rebel courts.[3]

On the other hand, the efforts of these anti-rebel factions would have achieved little without the considerable patronage of the British. Consider the case of Farid Irshid of Jenin. His brothers, Ahmad and Muhammad, had been killed in the wave of rebel executions of supposed traitors in May 1938. Seeking to avenge their deaths, Farid went on to lead one of the "peace bands."[4] Yet, his group was part of a larger network of "peace bands" of which Fakhri Bey al-Nashashibi—the nephew of NDP head Raghib al-Nashashibi—was the chief architect. And, as Amnon Cohen observes, "A central source of [Fakhri] Nashashibi's strength was his links to the British military, especially in air force intelligence, which had been assigned the task of gathering information that could be used in repressing the revolt."[5]

Regarding these intra-Arab conflicts, there were two historical scenarios into which the British might have insinuated themselves: one in which the Arab Palestinian political community was evenly divided, with comparable degrees of popular support on either side; and the other in which one of the sides held a sizable popular mandate, while its adversary did not. British intervention in the second circumstance would be of greater consequence than it would in the first. That is, London might exacerbate a civil war between evenly matched partisans, but it might help generate a civil war between unevenly matched partisans by throwing its ample weight behind the weaker party. And this is in fact what occurred.

After dining with cabinet member Walter Elliot on 18 January 1939, Blanche Dugdale recorded in her diary: "The Cabinet is divided into 'Husseinis' and 'Nashashibis'—that is to say those who think peace with the Mufti the most important, and those who say that it is impolitic to ignore the moderate party."[6] The "Nashashibis" at the cabinet level, however, harbored no illusions about the political stock of their namesake. Fakhri Bey had some support among lower level officials, such as the district commissioner of Galilee, Alec Kirkbride.[7] But MacMichael himself regarded Raghib Bey, Fakhri Bey, and the NDP as marginal political players, whose popular base was insignificant compared to that of the mufti.

The high commissioner considered Fakhri Bey in particular to be "rather a disreputable individual with nothing like the following he suggests."[8] He juxtaposed an anti-mufti memorandum that Fakhri Bey sent him (as well as *The Times* and *The Palestine Post*) in November 1938 with the approximately 200 pro-mufti letters he received in response to the memo. The letters came "from all parts of Palestine and [bore] the names of persons in different walks of life ranging from Mayors, Municipal Councillors, [and] Christian and Moslem religious dignitaries to shopkeepers."[9] When Fakhri Bey staged a demonstration in the village of Yatta, south of Hebron, British officials and military men attended and a local shaykh pledged his support for the government. But the CID deemed the meeting a "show" that "obviously lacked spontaneity."[10]

GOC Haining expressed a similarly low estimation of Nashashibi credibility.[11] As did Major General Bernard Montgomery, who reported: "It should be clearly understood that the Defence Party (the Nashashibi faction) has little or no following in northern Palestine. The bulk of the population looks to the Mufti and would do whatever he said."[12] The *Times* correspondent in Jerusalem reported in January 1939 that the Palestinians themselves were "bewildered by the reports that the British Government may not be content with the Mufti's delegates [to the proposed conference in London] and that Arabs abroad are taking the claims to representation of the Nashashibi Party of National Defence quite seriously."[13] The British strongly suspected that the Jewish Agency was financing Fakhri Bey's efforts in late 1938. While this was not true, Fakhri Bey did solicit money from the Agency.[14] And he was apparently in the pay of Pinhas Rutenberg, the former president of the Va'ad Leumi and the founder of the Palestine Electric Company.[15]

The British themselves were meanwhile subsidizing the activities of Fakhri 'Abd al-Hadi, another prominent "peace band" leader and former insurgent.[16] 'Abd al-Hadi hailed from the village of 'Arraba, southwest of Jenin. Before Fawzi al-Qawuqji reached Palestine in August 1936, some had considered 'Abd al-Hadi the "commander-in-chief of the revolt."[17] When Qawuqji organized his command into Iraqi, Syrian, Druze, and Palestinian companies, he placed 'Abd al-Hadi at the head of the last.[18] And when Qawuqji departed Palestine in October 1936, 'Abd al-Hadi was at his side.[19] But by 1938, the former rebel luminary had been exiled to Damascus and become the quarry of assassins linked to Amin al-Husayni. And so, when the British consul in Damascus, Gilbert MacKereth, arranged for him to return to Palestine in exchange for his cooperation with the British, 'Abd al-Hadi seized the day.[20]

According to both Zionist intelligence and the testimony of fellow rebels, 'Abd al-Hadi was "cruel" and "merciless" toward his enemies, and he stole from friend and foe alike.[21] Significantly, the rebel leader Muhammad 'Izzat Darwaza disavowed 'Abd al-Hadi in crimino-national terms. According to Darwaza, 'Abd al-Hadi "was and remains a gang leader and was never a nationalist activist, even when he took part in the rebellion."[22] As with Fakhri al-Nashashibi, the esteem in which British officials held 'Abd al-Hadi was notably low. As GOC Haining would later recount of the government's dealings with him: ". . . [I]t was not long before Abdul Hadi was found to be reverting to his old habits and playing for both sides."[23]

Beyond the government's underwriting of the "peace bands," British forces actually fought alongside them, as did Jewish forces.[24] That the primary organizers of the "peace bands" depended on the material aid of the Zionists and the British government indicated their paltry support among the Palestinians. While vendettas against the rebels were common, they were hardly sufficient to undermine the popularity of the revolt. Only by co-opting the "peace bands" into the larger counterinsurgency effort could the British hope for these groups to play a significant role in defeating the rebellion.[25]

The insurgent groups did, nevertheless, suffer from structural deficiencies that undermined their ability to maintain large-scale coordination. According to Subhi Yasin, four factors in particular afflicted the rebels: the lack of protective mountain ranges to shelter their major bases of operation; the bands' distance from Damascus, where the Central War Committee was located; a paucity of the Qassamites who had helped to found the rebel movement; and the disputes between the different rebel factions. Of course, the first two were weaknesses vis-à-vis British military pressure. Protective mountain ranges might have shielded the rebels against the RAF, and the bands' distance from Damascus was a consequence of the British having driven the Arab Higher Committee out of Palestine in the first place.[26]

As GOC Haining emphasized in January 1939: "... [The] disorganisation of the [rebel] machinery [is] due solely to intensive military activity. Any slacking off of this activity ... would in the circumstances that now exist inevitably lead to a reorganisation of [the] rebel ranks."[27] Montgomery concurred, writing, "... [O]ur intensive operations have split up the large gangs ... But until we have collected the last remnants the rebellion cannot be said to have been stamped out. We have therefore got to keep at it and not relax the pressure."[28] As late as April 1939, Haining was adamant that although "rebel activity has been small and there has been no major encounter," it was nevertheless "essential that there should be no relaxation of military pressure after [the] publication of Government's proposals."[29]

THE COLLAPSE OF THE PALESTINIAN PARASTATE

By 1939, the majority of Palestinians had lost faith in the institutions of the revolt. Those abandoning the rebels included both combatants and civilians, even in insurgent strongholds. According to the assistant superintendent of police for Jenin, for example, among that city's militants in 1938 were "a growing band" of "ex-gangsters" who collaborated with British officials.[30] In January 1939, Arab civilians abandoned the rebel courts *en masse* and began flocking back to the mandatory courts.[31]

As the assessments of Haining and Montgomery intimated, the disintegration of the rebel courts, and the civil war itself, resulted in significant measure from the British counterinsurgency campaign. In late 1938, the absence from Palestine of the supreme judge 'Abd al-Qadir al-Yusuf and of the rebel commander 'Abd al-Rahim al-Hajj Muhammad—whom even the British regarded as a man of virtue—accelerated the breakdown of the rebel courts' legal integrity.[32] As one British judge put it, "When the legal system of the revolt disappeared, the public reverted to the government courts."[33] Of course, the rebel courts did not simply "disappear." In addition to their deterioration from within, they were crushed from without. Numerous cases of British troops physically breaking up the rebel courts, arresting their participants, and confiscating their property appear in the record.[34]

In addition to their relentless disruption of the revolt's most salient institution, the British ceaselessly harried the revolt's most promising and principled leader, 'Abd al-Rahim al-Hajj Muhammad. Security forces searched the rebel commander's home on an almost daily basis, often threatening his children.[35] The harassment finally ended on 23 March 1939, when British troops killed 'Abd al-Rahim al-Hajj Muhammad at Sanur, in Samaria. They had tracked him down using intelligence drawn from the "peace bands" the military had shrewdly chosen to underwrite.[36] This was just after the Central War Committee at last recognized 'Abd al-Rahim al-Hajj Muhammad as the commander-in-chief of the revolt, for whatever that was worth, and he had re-entered Palestine from Syria.[37] More important than the Damascus-based committee's recognition was 'Abd al-Rahim's position within Palestine itself, where, according to British intelligence, he "probably [controlled] the largest number of armed men in the country" and was "regarded by himself and by most Arabs as the supreme commander" of the revolt.[38] The most exhaustive account of the revolt in Arabic reaches the same conclusion.[39]

The effect of 'Abd al-Rahim al-Hajj Muhammad's assassination on rebel discipline may be gleaned from the letter of an Anglican missionary who visited the village of Shifa 'Amr, outside Haifa, a month after the insurgent leader's death. Along with the bishop in Jerusalem, the missionary and his wife stayed in the village for several days in late April 1939. While noting that "the insurgents visited the Mission House simply to see that the Bishop and his wife were safe," he also indicated that the rest of the population were laboring under the still heavy yoke of the waning rebellion. The rebels were forcing the villagers to attend their courts, to fix their weapons, and even to entertain them. They had also executed four residents of Shifa 'Amr, one

Christian and three Druzes. The missionary lamented that such behavior was proliferating in the vacuum left by the death of 'Abd al-Rahim al-Hajj Muhammad. "'Abd ul Rahim, the leader who was opposed to assassination and other barbaric deeds, was killed nearby, and armed Moslems now gain the ascendancy," he wrote.[40]

Akram Zu'aytir comments that the death 'Abd al-Rahim al-Hajj Muhammad, coupled with 'Arif 'Abd al-Raziq's capture the following month by French authorities at the Syrian border, undermined the rebels' morale, despite their issuing statements to the contrary.[41] In the aftermath of 'Abd al-Rahim's death and 'Abd al-Raziq's capture, Zu'aytir received a letter from his longtime Nabulsi comrade, Mamduh al-Sukhn. It read in part:

> I'll describe the situation to you in a few lines. The movement around Nablus has begun to dwindle. All the effort to avert the danger has come to naught ... The paralysis in this area has had an effect on all the other fronts as well. [The rebels] have begun to make their calculations. They haven't left the field, but they've weakened. The movement shows signs of stagnating. For that reason, an initiative was sent to that area to revive activity. I hope it succeeds.[42]

The political scientist Wendy Pearlman argues that the efficacy of British repression in 1936–39 turned in large measure on its being "mediated by the [fragmented] organizational structure of the Palestinian movement." She then acknowledges:

> Beyond this, repression directly attacked the mechanisms through which any movement regenerates command and control. The government undercut leadership structures when it stripped [Amin al-] Husayni of the presidency of the SMC, outlawed the AHC, deported those members it was able to arrest, and prevented those who were abroad from returning to Palestine.[43]

To this list should be added the government's targeting for destruction the rebel courts and commanders. British repression did not merely benefit from the fragmentation of the revolt, it helped to bring that fragmentation about. The mandatory's part in crushing the infrastructure required to maintain rebel discipline and thereby the revolt's popular legitimacy was substantial.

None of this is to deny the agency of those rebels who abused and exploited their fellow Arabs and who terrorized the Zionists. It is rather, as Jacob Norris has advocated, to "add greater historical balance" to the literature on the revolt by reinserting the mandatory, alongside the Arab and Jewish communities in Palestine, into the basic causal calculus of the rebellion. In stressing rebel fragmentation and indiscipline, much of the scholarship has obscured the British implication in both.[44]

GOC Haining's depiction of the military's reassertion of control in Palestine well summarizes the vital role of the mandatory in dissolving the revolt:

> The whole country, from Dan to Beersheba, from the Jordan to the Plain of Sharon and the sea coast, was now in the hands of, and occupied by, British troops and the Trans-Jordan Frontier Force. From this time on it became increasingly difficult for the remnants of the rebel gangs to find any security or rest. Constant searches of villages and areas harried them by Day and Night. Their Rebel Courts of Justice were gradually discovered and broken up. One by one the leaders and financial organisers began to disappear, to lose influence, or to squabble among themselves.[45]

Yet, even as he foregrounds the role of the British military in crushing the rebellion, Haining retreats into passive and oblique language at critical points. The rebels' courts "were ... broken up." Their leaders and financiers "began to disappear." A more accurate summary would state openly that the British killed the most promising and popular rebel leader, actively cut off sources of rebel financing, and subsidized and fought alongside anti-rebel factions whose support within the Palestinian community was negligible.

THE CONFERENCE AT SAINT JAMES

Even as it escalated the counterinsurgency and conscripted disaffected Arabs into the effort, London pursued the diplomatic side of its two-pronged strategy for retaking Palestine. On 7 February 1939, the long-awaited conference opened in London at St. James Palace. It was ostensibly a forum in which the British government would negotiate its way to an understanding with the Zionists and the Palestinians regarding the future of the mandate. As noted, however, London had already settled upon a new policy in Palestine and had no intention of being diverted from it. His Majesty would jettison the Balfour Declaration by at last agreeing to a limit on Jewish immigration. London would retain control of Palestine, but it would lock in the demographic balance between Arabs and Jews, and thus alleviate Arab fears of Jewish domination. The colonial secretary laid out the strategic considerations underlying this policy shift:

(a) Palestine gives us a footing in the Eastern Mediterranean; without it we should be limited to Cyprus only in this area.

(b) Palestine is of great importance as a "buffer" state between our vital interests on the [Suez] Canal and possible enemies to the northward.

(c) In twenty years' time the Anglo-Egyptian Treaty will be due for revision, and it might well be that, after that time, we should no longer be able to maintain troops in Egypt. In that case it would be of the greatest value for us to be able to keep troops in Palestine as an Imperial reserve for the Near and Middle East.

(d) Owing to the alteration in conditions in the Mediterranean and Italy's position in the Red Sea, Palestine has increased in importance as a link in our Lines of Communication to and from the East. There still remains the necessity for the protection of our interests in Iraq, which include the important Royal Air Force Base at Dhibban. The overlap [illegible] via Iraq and Palestine might also prove essential [illegible] for the reinforcement of Egypt, in the event [illegible] passage through the Mediterranean and Red Sea [illegible] too hazardous.

(e) The protection of the pipeline to Haifa depends upon the maintenance of internal security in Palestine.[46]

This strategic framework made "internal security" the paramount British priority in Palestine. Hence the two-pronged policy of crushing the rebels and eliminating the Arab grievances that had occasioned—and might re-occasion—a rebellion. Neither Arab nor Jewish recalcitrance at St. James would thwart these objectives. British officials were nevertheless concerned to temper Arab and Jewish demands, so as to shorten the distance between those demands and the new policy that would override them (to soften the blow, in other words) and to enable the British to say yes to some demands of marginal significance (to appear balanced, in other words).

Of course Jewish demands were, in a sense, irrelevant. London's snubbing the Zionists was unlikely to cause them to turn against the British empire, certainly not when it appeared to be on a collision course with the Third Reich.[47] The real risk, as the previous three years had made plain, lay in thwarting Arab demands, not Jewish ones. The British thus encouraged, as they had in 1936, Arab leaders from the surrounding states—whom they regarded as more moderate than the Palestinians—to involve themselves in the government's negotiations with the Palestinian leadership. The idea was to dilute Palestinian ultimatums to the point that ceding to them would cost the British nothing. When Arab statesmen persuaded Amin al-Husayni (still in exile and forbidden to enter the United Kingdom) to permit Nashashibi representatives to attend the conference, this "Arab states" strategy seemed to have borne fruit.[48] The Arab statesmen also eventually agreed to meet privately (and unofficially) with the Jewish delegates, thus circumventing the Palestinians' refusal to do the same.

The first such meeting took place on 23 February 1939, with mixed results. Among the Arabs present were Nuri al-Saʻid and Tawfiq al-Suwaydi, the Iraqi prime and foreign ministers, respectively. The main Zionist spokesmen were Weizmann and Ben Gurion. MacDonald, Foreign Secretary Halifax, eastern department head Charles Baxter, and several other British high officials were also in attendance. A Foreign Office summary of the meeting stated that it "started well," only to deteriorate into a "strained atmosphere" due to "two rather ill-advised speeches by Mr. Ben Gurion and [the American Jewish Congress's] Dr. [Stephen] Wise."[49]

The occasion for the informal gathering was supposed to have been a discussion regarding the constitution of the future Palestinian state. But the Arabs believed that no such discussion could proceed until the matter of Jewish immigration had been settled. Tawfiq al-Suwaydi argued that "the admission of the right of Palestine to independence was incompatible with the conception of further [Jewish] immigration," which would only facilitate the Zionist plan to create "a majority and a government in Palestine."[50] Neither al-Suwaydi nor ʻAli Mahir, the head of the Egyptian delegation, was able to say much more before Wise and Ben Gurion broke in with their "ill-advised" remarks. Among these was Ben Gurion's statement that while "it was legitimate for the Government and people of Egypt to say whether or not they would accept further [Jewish] 'guests' within their frontiers . . . this was not the case with Palestine." In any case, added Wise, there was no need for the Arabs to worry. Ignoring the surging Jewish population in Palestine, Wise claimed that he "could not understand what had happened since the [First World] War to have excited [the Arab] fear of domination." This despite the fact that only minutes before, ʻAli Mahir had observed, "At the end of the War Palestine's population was about ninety-two percent Arab and eight percent Jew."[51] By 1939, these figures stood at approximately seventy and thirty, respectively.[52] If it had not been clear previously, it was now: a "great gulf fixed" lay between the Arab and the Jewish sides. The meeting adjourned with no agreement other than to reconvene.

It was not until early March that one of these informal gatherings generated a fleeting ray of diplomatic hope. When ʻAli Mahir suggested (again) that the foundation of future Jewish-Arab cooperation was a halt to Jewish immigration, Weizmann replied in a surprisingly favorable manner, stating:

"We can reach an understanding in this spirit . . . If we are told that an agreement can be reached by slowing down immigration a little, we will find common ground for negotiations."[53] Although an autonomous Arab state in Palestine remained unacceptable to MacDonald, he expected that granting the Arabs "the form rather than the substance" of political autonomy might elicit concessions from them on the matter of Jewish immigration.[54] He was therefore thrilled at Weizmann and Mahir's apparent breakthrough, rejoicing, "This meeting has achieved something."[55] Alas, even as Weizmann extended the olive branch, Ben Gurion withdrew it, telling MacDonald, ". . . [T]here can be no question of slowing down immigration." On the contrary, he suggested, immigration should be accelerated.[56] Weizmann fell back in line. Ben Gurion, meanwhile, advanced the idea of joining a Jewish Palestine to an Arab federation. This proposal sat poorly with the Arabs.[57]

The formal meetings of the Zionist delegation with British officials proved equally unproductive. In the fourth such forum on 13 February, Weizmann declared that High Commissioner Wauchope ought not to have coddled the Arabs in 1936, that the Balfour Declaration had a divine warrant, and that the British should force it upon the Arabs—with bayonets, if necessary.[58] (The same sentiments were widely expressed among Jews generally in Palestine.[59]) Ben Gurion chided MacDonald that if British force was not employed in support of the Zionist program, it would have to be employed against it. "Only British bayonets can prevent the immigration of Jews," he announced.[60]

Weizmann also brazenly tossed the issue of democracy—which MacDonald had raised with the Zionists when explaining his proposal to limit Jewish immigration—back into the lap of the colonial secretary. According to MacDonald's notes from the 13 February meeting:

> Government by consent, as [Weizmann] had said before, was an ideal. Few countries today approximated to it, and he thought it was somewhat rash for the Secretary of State to expect it of Palestine. But were the British themselves in Palestine by the consent, or even the acquiescence of the Arab population?[61]

Weizmann may have elected to reprise the theme of British hypocrisy based on the rhetorical success it had yielded him a few days before. Blanche Dugdale wrote of that earlier St. James meeting in her diary on 11 February: "MacDonald . . . talked a lot about the 'natural right' of the Arabs, and how the Jews had been let in without their consent . . . Chaim, listening, became inspired . . . He asked, à propos of 'consent'—by whose consent are we [the

British] in India—or Egypt?" This and an immediately subsequent remark rendered the secretary speechless. Dugdale exulted, "All the dialectical honours fall, so far, to the Jews." She added, however, that the Jews themselves considered such verbal victories hollow.[62]

On 15 February, MacDonald at last laid before the Zionist delegation the government's plan for future immigration into Palestine. Not surprisingly, the delegation rejected his proposal that a limit be placed on Jewish immigration going forward, and that the Arabs be given a veto over Jewish immigration above that quota. Any such plan, the delegation reasoned, would surely be the death of the Zionist dream: that is, of a Jewish Palestine.[63]

As Weizmann had cast aspersions on the British empire's democratic credentials, so Ben Gurion now questioned its vaunted association with law and order. Arguing that the colonial secretary's proposal amounted to a "law by which the Mufti would have the right to exclude the Jews from Palestine," Ben Gurion declared himself bound to "something . . . higher than the law."[64] While this statement had celestial connotations, Ben Gurion put the point in more earthly terms to his wife Paula. The Zionists' dispute, he wrote her, was not so much with "the British government" as it was with "the holder of the Mandate given to it by fifty nations."[65] Given the legitimacy of the international legal order, he implied, any unqualified identification of the British empire with law and order was facile.

This was a new tack for the Zionists, but the Arabs had been pressing the same point for years. And Ben Gurion no doubt appreciated this fact. In the 23 February meeting, his exchange with 'Ali Mahir had touched on the matter of laws international and "higher":

> ALY MAHER PASHA intervened to ask what Mr. Ben-Gurion meant in calling Palestine the Jews' "own country".
> MR. BEN-GURION said that the world admitted the historical connection of the Jews with Palestine dating back over 3,000 years.
> ALY MAHER PASHA enquired whether they held that this was a valid claim under international law.
> MR. BEN-GURION replied that it was so recognised in the Mandate, which was an international instrument.
> ALY MAHER PASHA remarked that the Arabs at one time in history achieved wonders in Spain, but that they laid no "historical claim" to that country.[66]

'Ali Mahir was playing the same game as Ben Gurion. He was drawing the legitimacy of the legal order into question. And like Ben Gurion, he was doing so in two registers: international law and "higher law." When Ben Gurion appealed to international law both to fend off the Arab claim on Palestine and to insist that the British fulfill their duty as described in the mandate instrument, 'Ali Mahir invoked a still higher law, subtly suggesting that any "law" violating it was itself suspect. In reply to Ben Gurion's reference to the mandate instrument, 'Ali Mahir suggested that the principle contained therein—"legal" or not—was absurd, as demonstrated by the corresponding Spanish case. But 'Ali Mahir himself invoked international law on behalf of the Arabs, both in questioning Ben Gurion and earlier in the meeting, when he averred:

> Great Britain never had the right to dispose of Palestine. There was no right of conquest, as the Arabs had been on the side of Great Britain in the War. There had been no notification on the British side that Palestine would be annexed. On the contrary, there was the Mandate which made it clear that Great Britain was not the owner of Palestine. Not having rights of ownership, she could not transfer such rights to the Jews.[67]

Unfortunately for Ben Gurion, 'Ali Mahir's argument from international law was now that of His Majesty's Government. By February 1939, as N. A. Rose observes, "It required considerable semantic skill to differentiate between the Arab and the government case."[68] Weizmann, Ben Gurion, Shertok and Brodetsky had, by then, privately acknowledged amongst themselves that "the colonial secretary . . . although clothing [his statements] in the form of arguments as advanced by the Arabs, conveyed the impression that in reality he was speaking the government's own mind."[69]

The conditions of the conference were hardly propitious. Indeed, the three-way negotiations were so delicate that a single indiscretion was sufficient to cause their collapse. MacDonald had proposed that a second conference be convened in August 1939, during which the Arab and Jewish delegates could hammer out a constitution for the future Palestinian state. In the period preceding the completion of the constitution, the high commissioner would bring select Arab and Jewish leaders onto his executive council in an advisory capacity. MacDonald originally planned for equal numbers of Arabs and Jews to sit on the council. But the Jewish delegation soon learned that he had privately conceded to the Arab demand for a three-to-two ratio of Arabs to Jews. Simultaneously, the delegation mistakenly received a copy of MacDonald's most recent proposal to the Arabs. It offered to shorten the period of Jewish immigration preceding the Arab veto from ten to five years, after which Palestine would gain independence. For the Zionists, this was the last straw.[70] On 1 March, they formally withdrew from the conference, although they continued to participate informally.[71]

Two weeks later, on 15 March, the German army invaded Czechoslovakia. The same day, MacDonald tabled the final British proposals for Palestine at St. James. For the British, the day's events in central Europe confirmed the wisdom of His Majesty's new policy in the mandate. But for the Arabs and the Jews, MacDonald's proposals formed a Gordian knot, which neither delegation could untie. These proposals made Jewish immigration above 75,000—spread out over the next five years—contingent upon Arab approval. At the same time, the proposals made Palestinian independence in the form of an Arab-majority state—to be granted ten years hence—contingent upon Jewish approval.[72] Of course, neither party would assent to both conditions. Ben Gurion wrote his wife:

> ... [T]he Arab countries were inclined to accept the proposals, but the Palestinian Arabs were vehemently opposed to them, and in my opinion rightly. Although these proposals take almost everything away from us, they give the Arabs nothing, and it is obvious that the Arabs will also turn them down.[73]

The remaining members of the Jewish delegation departed London on 16 March.

THE SHIFTING CRIMINO-NATIONAL MOSAIC OF THE REVOLT

From this point forward, the shifting crimino-national mosaic of the revolt settled into a new pattern. For their part, leading Zionists came decisively to regard the British government's touted commitment to law as a ruse. In the aftermath of the conference, Weizmann accused MacDonald of "betraying the Jews ... under a semblance of legality."[74] To Leopold Amery, the conservative imperialist and former colonial secretary, Weizmann wrote bitterly:

> I wonder whom an enlightened judge would charge with illegal behaviour—the unfortunate Jews who are fleeing from the hell which is Central Europe, to the country where a National Home was promised to them, or the

Government which, despite its solemn pledges and international obligations, is imposing arbitrary restrictions on Jewish immigration and is driving the wretched victims of its policy into the open seas.[75]

As far as Weizman was concerned, the government's actions deprived it of "every basis [of] legality," rendering it a "purely coercive agency." The Jews were "bound," he declaimed, "[to] resist with every resource at their disposal."[76]

Without calling for violent action, the Histadrut issued a manifesto in late April calling on Jews everywhere to "aid in a campaign of resistance to any limitation on the National Home."[77] Ben Gurion meanwhile spoke to the Haganah leadership, telling them: "Until now, we have acted according to the spirit of the law. From now on, some of our activities will be directed against the law and with the aim of making that law powerless."[78] He did not mean strikes or demonstrations, as a 6 March letter to his wife made clear. Rather, he intended for the Jews to adopt the same strategy the Arabs had in the period leading up to 1936: first, non-participation in the political institutions that would eventually constitute the Palestinian state; and second, violent resistance.[79]

Of course, revisionist Zionists were out in front of Ben Gurion with regard to violent resistance, at least as it pertained to Arabs. While the Haganah braced itself for future armed conflict, its revisionist competitor, the Irgun, launched attacks.[80] Jewish militants killed thirty-two Arabs in a single day in late February.[81] The coordinated offensive shocked even the jaundiced Burr, who wrote his parents, "I have been out here some time now but have never seen such a holocaust and slaughter as happened that day."[82] In March, the Irgun began broadcasting from a clandestine radio station, boasting of its assaults on the Arabs.[83] "Radio Liberated Zion" also featured accounts of the Irgun's executions of Jewish "traitors" and sabotage of government property. A broadcast from early June 1939 rattled off the prior month's exploits. The text of the transmission gives a sense of the organization's grim determination:

Hallo, Hallo. This is Radio Liberated Zion! The National Military Organization ... JERUSALEM DISTRICT. 29.5.39. Two bombs were hidden in an Arab cinema in Jerusalem—the fragments of which caused injury to eighteen persons (thirteen Arabs, three British Constables, and two Jewish youths—a boy and a girl—who went there to enjoy themselves in the company of Arabs) ... Damage estimated at over £P2,000 was done. Simultaneously, Corporal Polanski was shot at and he died later. He was a

trickster in the pay of the Jewish Agency and the C.I.D. His was a death
sentence. He was the second traitor to be done away with . . . At 0900 hours
[30 May] a bomb exploded beyond the Tower [of] David and 9 Arabs were
killed, 40 were injured, of whom only five died. We regret having disturbed
the High Commissioner while he was spending his time at the King David
Hotel during these explosions.[84]

As the attack near the Tower of David indicated, the Zionists' charge of
British criminality had by no means eclipsed their charge of Arab criminality. While MacDonald broke bread with the same Palestinians he had, only
months before, deemed "agitators" (whose "bandit" minions were of "no
genuine political significance"), Zionist leaders unequivocally condemned
the government's volte-face. The Jewish Agency's Leo Kohn spoke for many
when he declared:

> If the British Government accepts as the representatives of the Arabs those
> who, under the cloak of a "national revolt" have let loose on the country
> bands of gangsters and adventurers, hired with the money of foreign pow-
> ers, who, by murder, torture and blackmail have terrorised the peaceful Arab
> population into silence and turned the country into a shambles, then it will
> not be very long before similar "national revolts" flare up in other corners of
> the empire.[85]

While leading Zionists increasingly accused the British, along with the
Arabs, of lawlessness in Palestine, the British responded in kind. "Extremist,"
a term hitherto reserved for revisionists, now featured in officials' descrip-
tions of mainstream Zionists. In an early March cabinet briefing, for instance,
the colonial secretary contrasted Weizmann with "Mr. Ben-Gurion and Mr.
Shertok, and other extreme Zionists."[86] Hints of this change of tone vis-à-vis
official Zionism were already surfacing in late 1938. In a December summary
of events, MacMichael remarked that "in some respects His Majesty's
Government has to face extremism in Jewry as fully developed as it is among
the Arabs."[87] By June 1939, he was warning MacDonald that "the more
thoughtful and decent elements" of the Yishuv were "definitely outweighed
. . . by the more ardent political Zionists and extremists."[88] Of course, official
Zionism had not changed, British policy had. The Jews simply found themselves on the wrong side of a labile law.

On 17 May 1939, the government made its policy reversal in Palestine
official. It published a white paper that limited the Jewish population of
Palestine to one third of the total. This translated to a cap of 75,000 Jewish

FIGURE 10. Jewish residents of Jerusalem flood the streets to protest the White Paper, 18 May 1939. (Library of Congress)

immigrants over the next ten years, after which Palestine would be granted independence and any further immigration would be subject to Arab approval. Jewish protest marches took place throughout the country on 18 May. In Jerusalem, there were riots.

If the Zionist leadership were at all uncertain of the new crimino-national state of affairs, GOC Haining now clarified it for them. He summoned Ben Gurion, Bernard Joseph, Va'ad Leumi chair Yitzhak Ben Zvi, and several other leading Zionists to seventh division headquarters on the morning of 19 May. Referring to the death of a British policeman in the course of the previous day's disorders, Haining sternly warned the men:

> If murder takes place like this there can be no forbearance again. I am responsible for law and order and I carry it out impartially for both Jew and Arab . . . Impartiality is my motto, force is my weapon where force is needed; the maintenance of law and order is the objective . . . there must be no more rioting in Jerusalem. But if blood is shed that blood will be on the head of the Jews.[89]

Haining's remarks embodied the implicit British response to Ben Gurion and Weizmann's claims vis-à-vis a "higher law": there was no law higher than the British. The lawbreaker might change, but never the lawmaker.

And yet, the British self-identification with law and order was not a mere tautology. It entailed a certain conception of British behavior, to which Haining referred when he assured Ben Gurion and the others that the British police in Jerusalem had "not fire[d] a shot" and had exercised "the utmost restraint." But as the Arabs had before them, the Jews came quickly to appreciate the peculiar nature of British "forbearance" and "impartiality." Contrary to Haining's claims regarding the "restraint" the police had shown in the course of the riots in Jerusalem, the executive committee of the Magen David Adom (the Red Shield of David, or First Aid Society) reported numerous instances of policemen beating up and otherwise interfering with the emergency workers who were tending to wounded Jews.[90] Other sources testified to similar police behavior.[91]

The British intensification of repression in the mandate from late 1938 forward was accompanied by a general deterioration of police discipline. Evidence of this development appeared in the writings of Constable Burr, who referred routinely to police unruliness. In an undated letter from March or April 1939, Burr noted in passing, "The police menace out here is still very critical and about twenty a week are getting the sack and being sent home."[92] The uppermost officials in the mandate were aware of the problem. Major General Bernard Montgomery, the commander of the eighth division in Palestine, disclosed in a letter to the deputy chief of the imperial general staff:

> The [police] are badly looked after and badly housed. Their officers take no interest in them. They (the men) are drinking very heavily. The real trouble is that the senior officers in the Palestine Police are utterly and completely useless. Furthermore the organization is basically unsound; there is no proper chain of command which enables responsibility to be fixed when things go wrong . . . The matter is urgent. Strong action requires to be taken <u>at once</u> . . . I gave my views as above, with [GOC Haining's] full agreement, to the High Commissioner when he was last in Haifa . . . We do not want it said later that when we had the Police under our orders we never told the civil government what was wrong with its Police Force.[93]

In his response to Haining's concerns regarding the Palestine police, MacMichael, before quibbling over certain details, conceded: ". . . [N]either Sir Charles Tegart nor I query the general tenor of the General Officer Commanding's remarks." The high commissioner observed that, prior to their disarmament, the Arab members of the police force had been its "backbone." Their replacements, he admitted, were "in effect ex-soldiers dressed in Police uniforms," who had been "hastily selected in London and despatched in large numbers to Jerusalem." In a remarkably candid passage, MacMichael confessed, "In Sir Charles Tegart's view, from which I have no reason to differ, the senior personnel in charge of police districts, with few exceptions, are unsuited for their duties."[94]

Given these conditions, the police were bound to misbehave. But while the high commissioner and the general officer commanding pondered how to address that problem, their immediate concern was less the misbehavior than it was the reports of the misbehavior. The government was eager to counter "the 'atrocity campaign' which certain Continental countries are endeavouring to hang upon the search for illicit arms in Palestine."[95] Rushbrook Williams at the Colonial Office, for example, drafted a retort to the accounts of British terrorism appearing in German and other hostile newspapers. Williams derided the "new crop of atrocity-stories invented about the conduct of British troops and police."[96] In keeping with this policy of denial, London elected not to appoint a commission of inquiry to investigate the charges of police and military misconduct in the mandate, and made a point of communicating this decision to the Permanent Mandates Commission.[97]

Many of the charges were true, however. As in 1936, the village searches that troops and police were conducting throughout the country were, in reality, something more than searches. Military leaders again emphasized the searches' "moral effect," suggesting that among their unspoken objectives was the terrorization of the population into obedience.[98] German and other newspapers' pictorial evidence of British forces' destructive escapades in the villages led the government, in March 1939, to enforce more strictly the prohibition against the filming and photographing of the searches.[99] But even this measure could not prevent the spread of information regarding some of the more egregious incidents that occurred during the searches.

After reading reports in the German press of British atrocities in the village of Halhoul, in the Hebron district, Nevile Henderson, the British ambassador to Germany, cabled London from Berlin asking for the facts. In its top-secret reply, the Foreign Office acknowledged, "Although the German press accounts of this affair are exaggerated, there is unfortunately some basis of truth behind [their] assertions."[100] While searching Halhoul for arms, British troops, as they had many times before, placed the men of the village in an outdoor cage. On this occasion, however, the inmates languished in the sun-drenched enclosure for nearly a week, during which they were denied sufficient food and water. The thirst of some prisoners became so intense that they drank their own urine. In the end, between eight and ten men, most of them elderly, died of heat exhaustion.[101]

Elliot Forster, a British doctor who worked at St. Luke's Hospital at Hebron, wrote in some detail about the Halhoul incident in his May 1939 diary entries. This particular debacle was one of several that he mentioned that month. On 14 May, for example, he recorded:

> Up in Jerusalem this morning we were talking to Ballard about Halhoul. There seems to have been a good deal of upset about it (not really!) but even more about a village in the Jerusalem area called Beit Rima, where even more lurid things are said to have happened ... Ballard says a man at Beit Rima died after a beating up by an officer. "He's a known sadist" is the explanation. Then he oughtn't to be let loose.[102]

Forster also noted on 4 May that two Arabs, one a young boy and the other an adult male, were brought to his hospital with gunshot wounds. Both, it appeared, had violated the curfew announced that day in Haifa. The boy had been shot through the stomach. He died three days later. Although the army attempted to blame the usual police indiscipline for his death, subsequent investigation determined definitively that both shootings were the work of the same military patrol. Forster, who by then had ample experience reporting such incidents to the authorities, concluded: "... [I]t is to be presumed that some action will be taken against [the culprit]. Or will it redound to his glory?"[103]

In light of such realities, the Arab case against both the British and the Zionists was the one stationary tessera of the above-mentioned crimino-national mosaic. As they had throughout the revolt, the rebels continued to draw attention to the causal correlation between British repression and the allegedly criminal rebellion. In April 1939, insurgents in Jerusalem calling themselves the "Central Committee of the Arab Revolt" posted a communication to British troops. It read in part:

> To the British Police and the civilian-clothed among them: Acts which you are perpetrating on Arabs in the Old City and outside, surprising and mal-treating the innocent, unwarrantedly hurting their feelings, are driving us unwillingly to meet your conduct with similar action ... if you still continue your ways of using harsh force, your persecution tactics will be met by equal force. Should you, however, revert to the honest way of executing your orders, the Arabs will resume their former attitude then ... You should always remember that we are freedom-seekers and want Palestine to remain Arab

as you would want England to remain English and Eire to remain Irish. That is what you openly declare, so, why not admit the Arabs' right to what they claim?[104]

As Haining had cautioned the Jews, so the rebels now effectively warned Haining: force is our weapon where force is needed.

While insurgents on the ground implored the British to forego coercion in the mandate, their ostensible representatives at St. James publicly set forth the case against the policy actuating the British resort to violence. In its official reply to the May white paper, the exiled Higher Committee deplored that while "the British were induced [at St. James] to recognize in principle the rights of the Arabs," they nevertheless "could not be persuaded to submit practical proposals such as would lead to an agreement."[105]

The Arab leadership thus drew public attention to the form/substance distinction that the colonial secretary had hoped to smuggle past them (recall MacDonald's plan to grant the Arabs "the form rather than the substance" of sovereignty). With regard to the form specifically, MacDonald had proposed a phasing in of Arab and Jewish control over the political institutions that would compose the future Palestinian state. Yet, as the AHC rightly pointed out vis-à-vis the substance, "the Jews will abstain from participating in any government which is not Jewish in order to obstruct the realization of independence."[106] Again, as Haining had assured the Jews that any future bloodshed would be "on the head of the Jews," so the AHC proclaimed to the British: "The Government insists on continuing to administer by force . . . The Government therefore will be responsible for all the tragedies, atrocities and ruin which will result from their insistence."[107]

THE END OF THE REVOLT

While both the rebels and the AHC blamed the British for the disorder in the mandate, they were not otherwise united. On 10 April 1939, a new rebel manifesto appeared. It insisted on amnesty for the insurgents and complete independence for Palestine. These demands dovetailed entirely with those of the AHC. But the declaration also made explicit that the rebels regarded themselves as independent of the Nashashibis, the Husaynis, and the Arab states.[108]

The fractured Palestinian front, however, did not merely separate the rebels from their ostensible spokesmen on the AHC and among the Arab states. Especially after the publication of the white paper in May 1939, the rebels themselves began to fragment along ideological, not merely territorial, lines. Many denounced the white paper and called for a reinvigorated rebellion.[109] Their numbers were sufficient to make defying them politically inconvenient, if not impossible, for Amin al-Husayni.[110] On the other hand, other high-ranking rebels, including former intimates of the mufti, issued a statement denouncing those who pressed for a renewed revolt and condemning the AHC. The Higher Committee's rejection of the white paper, this statement claimed, was motivated by the mufti's thwarted political ambitions, not by its concern for the long-suffering people of Palestine.[111] Yet, the same was true of many rebels.

For that reason, as the last remnants of the insurgency scattered across the country, ordinary Palestinians began openly defying the more predatory armed bands. In June, they apprehended Mahfuz ʿAli ʿAbd al-Majid and ten members of his band near Nablus, and handed them over to British troops.[112] A similar incident occurred in Samaria three weeks later.[113] In July, villagers near Mt. Carmel captured Muhammad Said Zaudik, another rebel leader.[114] Days later, more villagers in Samaria seized a rebel and transferred him to British custody.[115]

But even as Arabs captured men they regarded as bandits and offered them to the British authorities, they rejected the "crime wave" framing of the revolt. The NDP accepted the white paper, and yet felt compelled to address and implicitly rebut the criminal charge. While readily assenting to the criminality of those against whom the Nashashibi-led "peace bands" continued to wage war, Raghib al-Nashashibi pled with the high commissioner:

> . . . [T]he Party ask for amnesty to be granted to those who have not committed crimes, or those who have not participated in plotting against the lives of the Arabs and in destroying their belongings. Such amnesty, the Party is convinced, will include a large majority of detainees and abscondees.[116]

The NDP thus denied what the British affirmed: that the majority of those whom the government identified as rebels were in fact criminals worthy of incarceration or exile. Indeed, Raghib al-Nashashibi's basis for distinguishing between criminal and non-criminal elements in Palestine was not violence against the British security forces—which he neglected even to mention—but rather violence against fellow Arabs.

On the matter of amnesty for the rebels, then, there was little daylight between the NDP, the AHC, and the Arab states, all of whom called for the release of political prisoners, notwithstanding the NDP's qualifications. Inasmuch as it implied the non-criminality of those rebelling against British rule in Palestine, this general plea answered the formative and enduring question of the revolt: who were the criminals in Palestine? If the rebels whom the British incarcerated, exiled, and killed were not in fact criminals, then such incarcerations were kidnappings, such expulsions thefts, and such killings murders. The British, in that case, were the criminals.

At last the Jews and the Arabs agreed upon something, although for different reasons. Regardless, both would have preferred that the British be held to a higher law in 1939. Alas, the only higher law on earth was international law. And that law's fledgling guardians at the League of Nations would prove unable, in the end, to call the British to account.

The terms of the mandate required the British government to submit the May 1939 white paper to the League of Nations for approval, which it did. The preliminary finding of the League's Permanent Mandates Commission was that the new British policy announced in the white paper failed to meet the legal requirements of the mandatory power. But, in a final indignity to both the Zionists and the Palestinians, the onset of the Second World War preempted the League's official declaration that London had violated the law in Palestine. Only years later would the criminal charge be forced upon the British, when another violent rebellion—that of the founders of Israel—finally drove the self-proclaimed guardians of "law and order" out of Palestine in the name of a higher law.

Conclusion

THIS BOOK HAS ESTABLISHED SEVERAL FACTS. First, the British were causally implicated in the events of 1936–39 in Palestine. This proposition might seem to be true almost by definition. The above argument, however, suggests that where the empirically obvious is politically problematic, politics wins. The second fact this book has established is that the British were afflicted in Palestine by far more than rebelling Arabs. They suffered as well from the limits of their own imperial discourse, particularly in its crimino-national dimensions. These limits were perceptual. Many Britons simply could not see themselves contributing to the "lawlessness" of the mandate, because their association of London with "law and order" was intimate to the point of equation. The limits were also political. Even those Britons who appreciated the possibility that the British were behaving criminally in Palestine considered it inadvisable to acknowledge as much publicly. Of course, these perceptual and political limitations marked two ends of a discursive spectrum, and a great many Britons fell somewhere in between them.

The third fact that this book has established is that much of the contemporary scholarship on the Great Revolt has reproduced the crimino-national perspective of the British, along with its Zionist corollary. A more critical and deconstructive approach to the archives unearths not only the contents of official and popular British and Zionist thought, but also the discursive limitations within which those contents arose historically. Palestinian voices falling outside these limitations were thereby largely silenced at the time of the revolt. In the interest of accuracy, it behooves the historian to recover them.

To review our findings, we began by charting the institutional trajectory of the British criminalization of Palestinian nationalism. This criminalization was not initially explicit. The British made it legally impossible for Arab Palestinians to advance an agenda of national autonomy. Once the inevitable Arab resort to force transpired, the British deemed it criminal, and thereby underplayed its national implications. There were two versions of this crimino-national claim, one strong and one weak. The strong claim was that neither the Arab strike launched in April 1936 nor the violent rebellion of subsequent months had the support of the Arab public. Rather, insofar as either enterprise endured, it did so because the Arab leadership employed thugs to coerce the masses into supporting it. The weak crimino-national claim affirmed that both the strike and the armed Arab attacks on the British and the Zionists were illegal, but it denied that the strike was coerced.

In April and May 1936, the Zionists endorsed the strong claim, while the British affirmed the weak claim. But as the months passed, the British drifted toward the strong crimino-national claim. Finally, in September 1936, they publicly endorsed it by holding the Arab Higher Committee directly responsible for the rebellion. The cause of this drift was discursive. British imperial discourse had traditionally downgraded to the status of "criminal" (and specifically, "terrorist") the national movements that impinged on London's imperial prerogatives. But whereas in the nineteenth century the equation of national movements with criminal enterprises was common, by the 1930s it jarred with the prevailing conception of nationalism as a fundamentally moral phenomenon. Nations were not criminal; nations named the criminal. For this reason, the British were compelled to restrict the criminal charge in Palestine to the Arab leadership, and simultaneously to deny this leadership's national credentials. In this way, the British portrayed a national revolt as a crime wave. Privately, however, British officials acknowledged that the Arab Higher Committee did not control the rebels, and that the revolt reflected the national aspirations of the Arab Palestinian public. A number of leading Zionists conceded the same in private. Nevertheless, the strong crimino-national claim was the operative British and Zionist framing of the revolt from September 1936 until the termination of the revolt's first phase in October 1936. And the majority of British and Zionist observers sincerely regarded the rebellion as a criminal affair.

Well before the British publicly adopted the strong crimino-national claim regarding the strike and the rebellion, they adopted strong punitive measures against Palestine's Arabs. They did so on the pretext of "searches" ostensibly designed to recover weapons and wanted men. In fact, as revealed in classified government reports, the point of the "searches" was to frighten the urban and especially the rural population of the country, whom the British sought to discourage from joining the rebel bands then organizing in the hills. Unfortunately for the British, the "village search" policy failed to achieve its objective. Indeed, it backfired by lending credibility to the basic Arab critique of the mandate, which held that it was superior force that had paved the British path to Palestine in the first place. The acts of violence required to sustain the British presence there only manifested what had been latent all along. The British, on this understanding, were the criminals.

The sharpest articulation of the contrary claim contended that the Palestinian rebels were members of known criminal networks. While dating to the period of the rebellion, this argument has recurred in scholarship. Our analysis of the "criminal network" claim revealed it to be a function of narrative themes endemic to the British and Zionist archives, not an empirically sustainable explanation of the revolt. For their part, Palestinian narratives of the revolt have often erred in the opposite direction. They have tended to purify the rebellion of any criminal taint by ignoring the criminal affiliations of some of its leaders.

Beneath the misconceptions on both sides of the debate about the revolt's legality lay a more intriguing reality. The rebels took their crimino-national cues from the British. In addition to their violent attacks on British forces and institutions, the insurgents were alert to the theatrical significance of their activities vis-à-vis an international audience. They therefore tended to this significance with a good deal of intelligence and discipline. Like the British, they wore uniforms, formed military chains of command, and convened their own courts of justice. In response, the British insisted all the more adamantly on the criminality of the rebellion. In so doing, they gave evidence of a rising imperial anxiety regarding the revolt's national credentials, especially as outside observers might perceive them.

The consequent "war on the discursive frontier" was a central feature of the 1936 rebellion. The British had one option with regard to the public waging of this war, namely the strong crimino-national claim. But the imperial anxiety to which the rebel effort gave rise led to passionate debates within the government regarding the legal implications of British repression in Palestine. These debates culminated in the British decision to reach a cease-fire with the rebels, rather than declaring martial law in Palestine.

Part two of the book began by discussing the interlude between the end of the revolt's first phase in October 1936 and its recommencement a year later. As they had in April and May 1936, British and Zionist views regarding Arab crime in Palestine diverged in the early months of 1937. The Zionists continued to insist that the Arab leaders were a criminal cabal, who cynically employed nationalist rhetoric to agitate an otherwise passive Arab population. The British, by contrast, reverted to the weak crimino-national claim in early 1937, which denied the link between the Arab Higher Committee and the violent elements of the Arab population. Then, in a repeat of 1936, the British began moving in the direction of the Zionist view, eventually reverting to the strong crimino-national claim.

In scrutinizing this drift, we noticed an important and—so far as the scholarship is concerned—underappreciated fact. The limited reach of the mandatory into the lives of Arab Palestinians in 1937 prevented the authorities from acquiring detailed knowledge of developments in the Arab community. British officials were therefore left, once again, with no option other than blunt force in the face of Arab challenges to their authority. They thus overreacted to the moderate uptick in intercommunal violence that occurred after the July 1937 publication of the Peel Report. Indeed, the government adopted a policy of "vicarious punishment" that willfully incarcerated innocent Arabs. In so doing, London once again created a problem with which it then had to contend: in this case, a renewed rebellion. The Arab Higher Committee warned British officials that this would be the likely outcome of the government's indiscriminate use of force in July and August 1937, and repeated the warning after the 26 September assassination of Lewis Andrews, the assistant district commissioner in Galilee. The Committee's prediction proved prescient when the revolt began anew in mid-October 1937.

Whereas most histories of the revolt date its second phase to the Andrews assassination, we saw that in fact this event did not reignite the rebellion. On the contrary, it was followed by a period of quiet, during which the British nevertheless stepped up repressive measures, outlawing the Arab Higher Committee and the regional national committees and imprisoning persons against whom the government had no evidence of wrongdoing. Only then did the rebellion recommence.

Although British and Zionist discourses regarding Arab crime reconverged in the latter half of 1937, before long, British officials were again divided regarding the root cause of the political instability in the mandate. There was a bureaucratic struggle over this issue between the Foreign Office, on one side, and the Colonial and War Offices, on the other. While the Foreign Office pressed for a more nuanced understanding of the rebellion, its opponents moved in the opposite direction. They framed as criminals not merely the rebels, but the entire Arab population of Palestine.

By late 1938, however, the weight of events impressed upon many top officials the imprudence of continuing to regard the rebellion as a criminal affair. The rebels had, by then, put in place the rudiments of a Palestinian state, including an army, a justice system, and even a postal service. While the British continued publicly to characterize the revolt as a crime wave, they resolved privately to engage the rebels as they would an opposing army. They therefore refrained from declaring martial law even as they effectively implemented it. London chose to crush the revolt by whatever means proved necessary, knowing that many innocents would be killed in the process.

Of course, by late 1938, the British had bigger problems than the rebellion in Palestine. Although Hitler agreed in September 1938 to refrain from further aggression in Europe, British planners remained alert to the possibility of a new war on the continent in the near future. They re-calibrated their regional ambitions accordingly, and decided that pressing forward with the Zionist project was no longer strategically viable. The need for Arab allies in the event of a German invasion of the Middle East would be too great to risk alienating the Arab world any further in the name of the Balfour Declaration.

Unburdening themselves of Balfour, however, created new problems for the British. Above all, they had somehow to rehabilitate an Arab leadership they had hitherto deemed criminals, for these were the only legitimate representatives of the Arab Palestinian community with whom they could reach a binding understanding. At the same time, the British could not crush the rebellion without inflicting enormous harm on the same Arab population that London's new, post-Zionist policy was intended to win over. In fact, both of these objectives could not be met vis-à-vis the Arab public of Palestine. The British therefore pursued them instead with an eye to the British public, and hoped for the best with regard to the Palestinians. As the British press was largely cooperative with the government, this effort consisted chiefly of ensuring that Anglican missionaries in Palestine—who had previously related the gruesome details of British repression to interested outsiders—be silenced, along with the Arab Palestinian press. The result was that at the height of British repression in the mandate, Palestinian voices fell beyond the boundary of mainstream British political discourse.

Meanwhile, the British capitalized upon Arab grievances born of rebel excesses by financially and militarily backing the Nashashibi-led "peace bands" with the aim of collapsing the revolt from within. The belligerent endeavors of the "peace bands," in conjunction with the relentless British pursuit of the rebels and a thoroughgoing British attempt to crush the rebel courts, defeated the rebellion. These British efforts marked another instance of the causal implication of the mandatory in events Palestine. Our highlighting of this and other such examples throughout the book has served to balance the emphasis in the scholarship on the Arab factional quarrels and internal divisions that contributed to the revolt's demise.

THE SYNCHRONIC AND DIACHRONIC IMPLICATIONS OF THE CRIMINO-NATIONAL FRAMEWORK

Our exploration of the overlap between the criminological and nationalist dimensions of British imperial discourse in Palestine has generated a historical picture of the Great Revolt that is significantly different from that of the existing literature. A crimino-national critique of the archival materials relating to 1936–39 turns the prevailing historical depiction of virtually every pivotal point of the revolt on its head. By re-narrating the history in a manner that returns the British to their proper place in the causal matrix constituting the rebellion, we learn that the British were implicated in both the revolt's outbreak and its recommencement. It is not at all clear whether the revolt would even have occurred, or recurred, had London not reacted to modest upticks in Palestinian violence with outsized doses of repression. Similarly, the crimino-national perspective has undermined the traditional historical rendering of the rebellion's collapse, which underestimates both the extent of rebel institutional organization and the critical role of the British in disrupting and finally destroying the rebel institutions. Unless we adopt the implausible view that Palestinian history is *sui generis*, it stands to reason that crimino-national analyses of other episodes in the history of interwar imperialism will result in similarly significant revisions of the existing historical understandings of those episodes.

To these synchronic revisions of imperial episodes from the interwar period may be added diachronic revisions of existing Palestinian histories addressing the decades after the rebellion. In the broadest terms, a crimino-national framework of the history of the Israel-Palestine conflict would emphasize the following. From the founding of the mandate to the present day, Palestine's Arabs have lacked democratic representation in any form, including that of a state. This lack of democracy was the precondition of the Jewish settlement of Palestine, which the British promoted in plain opposition to the wishes of the Palestinian majority population. They managed this feat through force of arms. The Zionist program in Palestine proceeded by virtue of British violence—usually latent, occasionally manifest. When the Palestinians at last resorted to violent rebellion in an effort to force their demands upon an imperial power unafraid to impose its will by brute force, they were killed, incarcerated, and expelled—and, critically, their violent actions were framed by their violent oppressors as crimes. It is the nation, and specifically the nation-state, that names the criminal. The British had such a state, the Palestinians did not, and do not. It is important to appreciate that, as Benny Morris observes, most of the violent measures that Israel adopted in the face of Palestinian protest from 1967 forward "had been introduced by the British during their suppression of the Arab rebellion of 1936–39 and were still on the statute books in the form of 'emergency regulations.'"[1]

The Israel-Palestine conflict has been a bloody and at times murderous business. As with the rebel atrocities that occurred during the Great Revolt, we rightly lay responsibility for the murder of Israeli children and other crimes of violence at the feet of their authors. But we must simultaneously recognize that much of the modern discussion concerning the Israel-Palestine conflict—particularly as that discussion unfolds in the United States—proceeds from a theoretical perspective that is anything but neutral. On the contrary, it is the perspective from which the colonizer has traditionally gazed upon the colonized. The Palestinians have no state, and therefore no means of legitimating their violence—of framing it as retaliation, or as a last resort in the service of a just end. Too many commentators ignore this fact, and thereby relate the story of the Palestinians' conflict with the Israelis from the perspective of the Israeli state, with its arsenal of legal and rhetorical devices that are denied to the stateless. They thus highlight Palestinian violence, while ignoring or justifying Israeli violence. The first is, in essence, criminal behavior; the second is merely a response to criminal behavior. By discarding this traditional understanding in favor of a crimino-national understanding, we gain a more empirically credible, and therefore more just, understanding of the conflict.

A WORD ON THE ENDURANCE OF THE CRIMINOLOGICAL CATEGORY OF "TERRORISM" AND ITS IMPLICATIONS FOR SCHOLARS

Finally, we noted in chapter four the emergence and endurance of the category of "terrorism" as a link between crime and nationalism. We also observed that this term's potency as a means of discrediting national movements declined in the age of nationalism. Today, well into that age, "terrorism" persists as a rhetorical device. It has, for example, frequently been used to frame as criminal enterprises transnational threats to the security and interests of various states. The barbarism of movements like al-Qaʿida has, of course, done much to validate this framing. This is perhaps nowhere as evident as in the frequently heard left-wing critique of the U.S. response to the attacks of 9/11, which holds that the attacks should have been treated as a "police matter" rather than as an act of war; that is, as a "crime" in the traditional sense.

The strategy of framing as terrorist criminals those threatening the state thus remains a salient phenomenon. This suggests that terrorism's linking of nationalism and crime has not only become more tenuous as the decades have passed (witness Israel's international isolation on the matter of its policy towards the Palestinians), but that it remains a protean category, which might link any threat to state power to criminality, while simultaneously and preemptively removing the state itself from the ensemble of terrorist actors.

It is interesting to note, in this connection, that the term "terrorism" was coined in reference to the Jacobin government of late eighteenth-century France—a state power. Its usage in relation to non-state actors began with the mid-nineteenth century Fenian movement against British rule in Ireland. Then, as now, those fighting against a given state often attempted to reintegrate the state into the ensemble of terrorist actors. They thus spoke of "state terrorism" and its role in prompting what they regarded as their own retaliation against that terrorism.

All of this points to the fact that while the discursive relationships between crime, nationalism, and terrorism have proven historically unstable, the use of criminalization to seal insurgent groups within a causal frame that excludes the state has endured. The abiding link, therefore, is between crime and causation. Insofar as a state actor succeeds in criminalizing those that threaten it, it also succeeds in silencing their critique of the state's behavior by preemptively withdrawing the state from causal consideration. It is therefore incumbent upon analysts of insurgencies to make explicit their critique of given governments' employment of a crimino-national vocabulary in describing those actors that threaten their sovereignty or security, whether this critique amounts to agreement, disagreement, or something in between. This book has been an attempt to provide such a critique of the British and Zionist framing of the Palestinian Great Revolt of 1936–39, and the scholarship which has too often reproduced it.

NOTES

INTRODUCTION

1. George Salah (attorney for prisoners) to high commissioner (HC), 21 November 1936, ISA 275/22–מ.

2. Chief justice to HC, 25 November 1936, ISA 275/22–מ.

3. Gellner, *Nations and Nationalism*, 4.

4. Examples include: Bowden, "The Politics of the Arab Rebellion in Palestine"; Cohen, *Army of Shadows*; Cohen, "Sir Arthur Wauchope, the Army, and the Rebellion in Palestine, 1936"; Gelber, *Sorshe ha-Havatzelet*; Habas, *Sefer Meʾoraʿot TRZ"V*; Hanna, *British Policy in Palestine*; Lachman, "Arab Rebellion and Terrorism"; Marlowe, *Rebellion in Palestine*; Segev, *One Palestine, Complete*.

5. Examples include: Abu Gharbiyya, *Fi khidamm al-nidal al-ʿarabi al-filastini*; ʿAllush, a*l-Muqawama al-ʿarabiyya fi Filastin*; Darwaza, *Hawla al-haraka al-ʿarabiyya al-haditha*; al-Sakakini, *Kadha ana ya dunya*; Yasin, *al-Thawra al-ʿArabiyya al-kubra (fi Filastin)*; Zuʿaytir, *Wathaʾiq al-haraka al-wataniyya al-Filastiniyya*.

6. Those works nearer to the top-down end of the spectrum include: al-Hut, *al-Qiyadat wa-al-muʾassasat al-siyasiyyah fi Filastin*; Porath, *From Riots to Rebellion*. Those nearer to the bottom-up end include: Anderson, *From Petition to Confrontation*; Kanafani, *The 1936–39 Revolt in Palestine*; Swedenburg, *Memories of Revolt*.

7. "Despatch by Air Vice-Marshal R. E. C. Peirse, D.S.O. A.F.C., on Disturbances in Palestine, 19th April to 14th September, 1936," WO 32/4177.

8. This logic was occasionally spelled out in classified correspondence. For example, the head of the eastern department at the Foreign Office, George Rendel, noted in late 1937 that the purpose of British "reprisals" against "the innocent" was "to cow the population into some kind of acquiescence." The British intelligence officer Orde Wingate made the same point in 1938. With regard to the Arab villagers, he wrote, "It can be pointed out to them that terror by night will in future be exercised, where necessary, by Government"—or, as he put it in the same report, by "Government gangs." See: "Palestine: question of martial law," 20 October 1937, FO

371/20817; Private Papers of Major General H E N Bredin CB DSO MC, IWM, 81/33/1.

9. "Periodical Appreciation Summary No. 11/36," 23 June 1936, ISA 1058/21–ב.

CHAPTER ONE

1. Testimony of Naftali Barukh, CZA S25/4239.

2. Segev, *One Palestine, Complete,* 323–25. Many more Arabs, it should be noted, hid Jews in their homes.

3. Zuʿaytir, *Yawmiyyat,* 56.

4. CZA S25/6324.

5. Ibid.; Gelber, *Sorshe ha-Havatzelet,* 146.

6. HC to CS, 6 August 1936, CO 733/314/5.

7. Ibid.

8. Interim report on Jaffa riots, April 1936, CO 733/314/5.

9. Ibid.

10. Ibid.

11. CZA S25/4428.

12. Interim report on Jaffa riots, April 1936, CO 733/314/5.

13. Ibid.

14. Palestine: The Disturbances of 1936 Statistical Tables, Jewish Agency for Palestine, December 1936, ISA; Kalkas, "The Revolt," 240.

15. The Jewish Agency's institutional history is complicated. It began as the Palestinian branch of the World Zionist Organization (WZO), which received legal recognition as an international body with the establishment of the British mandate for Palestine in 1923. By 1935, the WZO had offices in close to fifty countries. The Jewish Agency's authority structure paralleled that of the WZO, consisting of a council, an administrative committee, and an executive. In 1929, it was expanded such that its council came to consist of Zionists and non-Zionists (many of whom did not reside in Palestine) in equal proportions. The council, in turn, elected the administrative committee's forty members (also equal parts Zionist and non-Zionist). The council also elected half of the members of the Jewish Agency executive (effectively the Agency's cabinet), while the Zionist Congress (the core legislative body of the WZO, which staffed its various institutions) elected the other half, drawing from the WZO's own executive (the Zionist Executive). The members of the Agency's executive headed its various departments. In 1930, the expanded Jewish Agency officially supplanted the WZO in Palestine, although these institutional links remained. It is important to note that by 1935, Zionists outnumbered non-Zionists on the Agency executive two to one, and were by far the more influential party. See: Burstein, *Self-Government of the Jews in Palestine since 1900,* 33–39; Hurewitz, *The Struggle for Palestine,* 40–41.

16. Black, *Zionism and the Arabs, 1936–1939,* 12; Lockman, *Comrades and Enemies,* 76–108.

17. For early examples, see: McTague, *British Policy in Palestine, 1917–1922*. For a detailing of various Arab conferences and delegations, see: Porath, *The Emergence of the Palestinian-Arab National Movement, 1918–1929*. Arabs staged numerous protests and demonstrations against British policy in the 1920s and 1930s. They held conferences protesting the same in 1920, 1921, 1922, 1923, 1928, etc. They sent three delegations to London between 1921 and 1923 and another after the 1929 Wailing Wall riots, and were in contact with British officials regarding the establishment of a legislative council between 1925 and 1927, and again prior to the 1936 revolt.

18. The British sent three such commissions to Palestine prior to the revolt, in 1920, 1921, and 1929. See: Verdery, "Arab 'Disturbances' and the Commissions of Inquiry," 275–303.

19. Lesch, *Arab Politics in Palestine, 1917–1939*, 81.

20. The British granted Iraq independence in 1932, and officially agreed to withdraw from Egypt in May 1936. The French government began negotiating with the Syrian opposition in March 1936, a process which would culminate in Syrian independence that September.

21. Kolinsky, *Law, Order and Riots in Mandatory Palestine, 1928-35*, 79.

22. Ibid., 80, 92-93, 104; Eshed, *Reuven Shiloah, The Man Behind the Mossad*, 22–23.

23. Bowden, *The Breakdown of Public Security*, 157.

24. Kolinsky, *Law, Order and Riots*, 102-103. Steven Wagner argues that Dowbiggin erred in insisting that "the police and CID [were] the only appropriate source[s] for security intelligence, and enforcement" in Palestine. According to Wagner, Air Staff Intelligence (ASI) produced more reliable and actionable intelligence on Palestine than the CID, but ASI's reports had little influence over the British officials responsible for Palestine. See: Wagner, *British Intelligence*, 196.

25. As David French writes, among the "five functions" of "an effective intelligence system" was "a parallel organization . . . to prevent the enemy from gathering intelligence about British activities." See: French, *The British Way in Counter-Insurgency*, 19.

26. *Official Gazette of the Government of Palestine*, 25 October 1929; Kolinsky, *Law, Order and Riots*, 110.

27. Kolinsky, *Law, Order and Riots*, 111.

28. Biger, *An Empire in the Holy Land*, 35–36, 96–97, 115, 123–27, 132–33, 178–87, 246–48, 252–65.

29. Ibid., 275.

30. Ibid., 244, 274.

31. Meiton, "Electrifying Jaffa: boundary-work and the origins of the Arab-Israeli conflict," 7–8.

32. Norris, *Land of Progress*, 9.

33. Meiton, "Electrifying Jaffa," 8.

34. Shepherd, *Ploughing Sand*, 184–85.

35. It can be argued that this analysis mistakes cause for effect, since the mandatory refused to recognize the Arab political institutions only because they had

refused to recognize its authority. But it is actually this argument that mistakes cause for effect. The mandate's very terms of reference were prejudicial toward Palestine's Arabs, and indeed preempted the Arabs' core political concerns. To begin with, Article 4 of the mandate charter specifically called for the creation of a Jewish Agency that would serve as a consultative body for the government. It made no mention of an equivalent Arab body. Furthermore, the Balfour Declaration was incorporated into the mandate charter. Consequently, for the Arabs, any formal participation in the mandatory was tantamount to formal acceptance of the Jewish National Home policy.

36. Shepherd, *Ploughing Sand*, 197, 200–201.

37. Notes Amos Nadan, in this connection: ". . . [T]he lack of capital, imperfect information about the *fallahin*, and the dishonesty of some of the *mukhtars* created a syndrome in which the main beneficiaries of government assistance were well-off *fallahin* or the associates of *mukhtars* and were not the poor *fallahin* whom the government originally intended to help on grounds that they had the greatest potential to rebel. In time of crisis, the government was especially interested in assisting these *fallahin* and provided loans to 'villages in need' via their *mukhtars*. However, the *mukhtar* was also the guarantor for loans (and feared defaults) and usually had an interest in obtaining them for himself and his associates. Consequently, many loans intended for the poorest *fallahin* did not reach their destination." See: Nadan, *The Palestinian Peasant Economy*, 329–30.

38. Norris, "Repression and Rebellion," 32.

39. Townshend, "Defence of Palestine," 942.

40. The government's recourse to juridical and finally military repression of the Arabs was of a piece with its failure to engage Arab ideological production at its points of origin. This failure precluded what Raymond Williams has deemed the "true condition of hegemony": that is, the individual's internalization of the hegemonic worldview, as signified by his or her resignation to the naturalness (or, at a minimum, necessity) of the hegemonic order. The imposition of the natural is a critical thread of disciplinary power (Foucault). The punitive measures attendant on the latter entail a "double juridico-natural reference," which redirects the offender to (and, ideally, reincorporates the offender into) the ontology s/he has transgressed. Such punishment, however, exists within a wider regime of largely non-punitive disciplinary mechanisms, which visually arrays and temporally coordinates its subjects (human bodies) in a manner so fastidious as to culminate in their uninterrupted coercion-supervision. The British failure to approximate this disciplinary ideal in the mandate nourished Arab Palestinians' disaffection and anger regarding the government's indifference to their demands. Instead of internalizing the inevitability of their political exclusion via the British educational and medical institutions acting upon their bodies, Arabs drew on their increased literacy and longevity to mobilize and to agitate against it. While the British met these efforts with interdiction and force, this response was not continuous with the disciplinary ensemble required to seamlessly merge punishment with inculcation. Repression was, rather, a graceless last resort, and both a symptom and a

symbol of the government's tenuous connection with its Arab subjects. Instead of smothering the revolt, British violence nurtured it. See: Williams, *Marxism and Literature*, 118; Foucault, *Discipline and Punish: The Birth of the Prison*, 180-82, 200-209, 216-17, 227-28; Ransom, *Foucault's Discipline: The Politics of Subjectivity*, 52–53; Foucault, *Power/Knowledge: Selected interviews and other writings*, 98; Foucault, *The History of Sexuality, Volume 1: An Introduction*, 60; McNay, *Foucault*, 90–100; Rabinow, *French Modern: Norms and Forms of the Social Environment*, 82.

41. As noted, the Jewish Agency was the institutional hub of the Yishuv, as well as the "sounding board of Official Zionist policy." The "official" Zionists embodied the mainstream of political discourse in the Yishuv, and had ambivalent relations with their two primary competitors, the right-wing revisionists and the left-wing bi-nationalists. Although important differences marked these groups off from one another, they had become negligible by late May 1936, by which time all three were agreed that British repression of the burgeoning revolt was the only feasible course forward. See: Haim, *Abandonment of Illusions: Zionists Political Attitudes Toward Palestinian Arab Nationalism, 1936–1939*, 3–8, 41.

42. Testimony of Naftali Barukh, CZA S25/4239.

43. Testimony of Yisrael Ligal, CZA S25/4239.

44. Testimony of H. Eden, CZA S25/4239.

45. Burstein, *Self-Government*, 47.

46. "Note of an interview with the chief secretary on Sunday, April 19th, 1936," CZA S25/6324.

47. Ibid.

48. Ibid.

49. "Note of an interview between His Excellency the High Commissioner and Dr. Chaim Weizmann on April 21, 1936," CZA S25/6324.

50. Wauchope to Shertok, 24 April 1936, CZA S25/6324.

51. Gelber, *Sorshe ha-Havatzelet*, 146.

52. JA executive (Shertok), 7 May 1936, CZA S25/6325.

53. Ibid.

54. "Note of conversation with the Rt. Hon. J. H. Thomas," 18 May 1936, CZA S25/7559.

55. HC to CS, 18 April 1936, CO 733/297/2.

56. HC to CS, 5 May 1936, CO 733/297/2.

57. Goodman, "British Press Control," 704.

58. HC to CS, 5 May 1936, CO 733/297/2.

59. HC to CS, 4 May 1936, CO 733/310/1.

60. Manifesto of 24 April 1936, CO 733/310/1.

61. Extract from cabinet conclusions 36(36), 13 May 1936, FO 371/20020.

62. HC to CS, 16 May 1936, FO 371/20020.

63. "Monthly summary of 'intelligence', Palestine and Transjordan," 29 April 1936, FO 371/20030. As it happens, Wauchope and the RAF were mistaken about the strike's having begun in Jaffa alone. In fact, organizing committees were formed

virtually simultaneously in Nablus and Jaffa on 19-20 April 1936. See: Anderson, *From Petition to Confrontation*, 616.

64. The Jewish portion of the population of Palestine shortly approached thirty percent. See: Waines, "The Failure of the Nationalist Resistance," 232.

65. Matthews, *Confronting an Empire, Constructing a Nation*, 236.

66. Lesch, *Arab Politics in Palestine*, 68.

67. Ibid., 70.

68. Matthews, *Confronting an Empire*, 2.

69. Ibid., 237–38.

70. Ibid., 240. The press itself provides another index of the expanding Arab public sphere in Palestine. While three potential Arab publishers applied to the government for newspaper licenses in 1934, nine applied in the last few months of 1935 alone. See: Kabha, "The Palestinian Press," 171–72. At the same time, the Arab papers were adopting a sharper tone, one that increasingly targeted the government for criticism. See: Kabha, *The Palestinian Press*, 173.

71. Porath, *Riots to Rebellion*, 165.

72. Mattar, *The Mufti of Jerusalem*, 1.

73. Ibid., 8–10.

74. HC to CS, 21 April 1936, CO 733/310/1.

75. HC to CS, 23 May 1936, CO 733/310/2.

76. "Minutes of a meeting held at government house on the 5th May, 1936, at 5 p.m.," 13 May 1936, CO 733/310/2.

77. Kayyali, *Palestine*, 191; Mattar, *Encyclopedia of the Palestinians*, 4–5; Nimr, *The Arab Revolt*, 56, 191.

78. "Minutes of a meeting held at government house on the 5th May, 1936, at 5 p.m.," 13 May 1936, CO 733/310/2.

79. "Minutes of a meeting held at Government Offices on the 30th May, 1936, at 12 noon," 6 June 1936, CO 733/310/3.

80. Ibid.

81. First Arab Rural Congress to high commissioner, 24 May 1936, FO 371/20028.

82. al-Sakakini, *Kadha ana ya dunya*, 286.

83. Darwaza, *Hawla al-haraka al-ʿarabiyya al-haditha*, 124; al-Sakakini, *Kadha ana ya dunya*, 284–85.

84. ʿAbd al-Wahhab Kayyali claims, for example, that by late May 1936, "In almost all . . . towns and villages there was sniping at the Police and the troops." See: Kayyali, *Palestine*, 196.

85. "Periodical Appreciation Summary No. 11/36," 23 June 1936, ISA 1058/21–2.

86. "Monthly summary of 'intelligence', Palestine and Transjordan," 3 June 1936, FO 371/20030.

87. Government of Palestine Office of Statistics, General Monthly Bulletin of Current Statistics of Palestine, October–November, 1936, FO 371/20036. In the interest of numerical perspective, it should be noted that the total population of

Palestine at this time was approximately 1.2 million, of which Jews numbered roughly 340,000.

88. "Monthly summary of 'intelligence', Palestine and Transjordan," 3 June 1936, FO 371/20030.

89. Ibid.; Pearlman, *Violence, Nonviolence*, 45.

90. Kabha, "The Palestinian Press," 170, 174.

91. Ibid., 178–79.

92. Mattar, *The Mufti of Jerusalem*, 76.

93. "Minutes of a meeting held at Government Offices on the 30th May, 1936, at 12 noon," 6 June 1936, CO 733/310/3.

94. Kabha, *Thawrat 1936 al-kubra*, 64–65.

95. Meeting of high commissioner with 'ulema of Jerusalem, 1 June 1936, CO 733/310/3.

96. "Minutes of an interview granted by His Excellency to Arab leaders at Government Offices on the 21st April, 1936, at 12 noon," CO 733/310/1.

97. Archdeacon to chief secretary, 2 June 1936, Jerusalem and the East Mission (JEM) GB165–0161, Box 61, Middle East Centre Archives (MECA), St. Anthony's College, Oxford.

98. Cahill, "'Going Beserk': 'Black and Tans' in Palestine," 64.

99. "A Heavy Writer," 13 May 1936, *Palestine Post*; "D. V. Duff in Jerusalem," 15 May 1936, *Palestine Post*.

100. Duff, *Palestine Picture*, 156–57.

101. Abu Gharbiyya, *Fi khidamm al-nidal*, 72.

102. "Passersby searched and harassed," 1 June 1936, *al-Difaʿ*.

103. Kabha, *Thawrat 1936 al-kubra*, 65.

104. Archdeacon to chief secretary, 2 June 1936, JEM GB165–0161, Box 61, MECA. "Every side" included "constables themselves."

105. W.H.S. to J.G.M., 9 June 1936, JEM GB165–0161, Box 61, MECA.

106. Archdeacon to chief secretary, 2 June 1936, JEM GB165–0161, Box 61, MECA.

107. Horne B.E.M., *A Job Well Done*, 211–12.

108. Abu Gharbiyya, *Fi khidamm al-nidal*, 72; Hughes, "Assassination in Jerusalem," 9.

109. "Military lessons," WO 191/70.

110. "Despatch by Air Vice-Marshal R. E. C. Peirse, D.S.O. A.F.C., on Disturbances in Palestine, 19th April to 14th September, 1936," WO 32/4177.

111. *Ibn Saʿud: The Puritan King of Arabia* (London: Jonathan Cape, 1933).

112. "Note conversation with Mr. Kenneth Williams," 5 June 1936, CO 733/297/2.

113. Smith, "Communal conflict and insurrection in Palestine, 1936–48," 66–67.

114. "Despatch," WO 32/4177.

115. Hodgkin (ed.), *Thomas Hodgkin*, 164–65, 171.

116. "Despatch," WO 32/4177.

117. "Murder of an Arab policeman," 26 May 1936, *al-Difaʿ*.

118. "Arab policemen's reaction to the murder," 26 May 1936, *al-Difaʿ*.

119. "The nobility and honor of the Arab police," 1 June 1936, *al-Difaʿ*.

120. CZA S25/6325. Protests against the stationing of British police inside (and at the expense of) Arab villages begin appearing in the notes of local national committee meetings in the first half of May 1936. The high commissioner also noted the establishment of "punitive posts" in "seven villages in the northern district" in a 5 May memorandum. Our information about the conduct of the police attached to these punitive posts is scant, but evidence available from other parts of the British empire offers some context for the claim that the posts were "most effective" in "teaching turbulent villages wisdom." One British security official who served in India, for example, claimed, "[A]fter some of my punitive police have been stationed in a village for a few days the spirit of the toughest of the political agitators is broken." See: Kayyali, *Wathaʾiq al-muqawama al-Filastiniyya al-ʿArabiyya*, 398–99; HC to CS, 5 May 1936, CO 733/310/1; Newsinger, "Hearts and Minds."

121. *Sefer Toldot ha-Haganah*, Vol. 2, 1318.

122. One humorous index of this fact crops up in a 2010 article by Matthew Hughes, in which the author modestly states the article's intention to "[complement] recent academic studies on Britain's use of force in Palestine" during the revolt. Checking his footnote, one learns that the two "recent academic studies" to which Hughes refers were authored by him! See: Hughes, "Assassination in Jerusalem," 6, 12. Charles Anderson is another example of a contemporary scholar whose treatment of the 1936 revolt corrects for the British blind spot vis-à-vis the role of colonial violence in triggering the rebellion. See footnote 134 below. Finally, ʿAbd al-Wahhab Kayyali may be the earliest example of a scholar pointing to the causal primacy of British violence in 1936. In his 1978 English-language volume, Kayyali wrote that the village searches were "instrumental in bringing about a greater degree of cohesion and identification between the villagers and the rebels." See: Kayyali, *Palestine*, 195.

123. Hughes, "From Law and Order to Pacification," 10. My emphasis.

124. Norris, "Repression and Rebellion," 27; Sinclair, "'Get into a Crack Force . . . ,'" 60.

125. Haim, *Abandonment of Illusions*, 38.

126. Gelber, *Sorshe ha-Havatzelet*, 144.

127. Cohen, "Sir Arthur Wauchope," 21, 29.

128. Porath, *Riots to Rebellion*, 195.

129. Ibid., 196–97.

130. Bowden, "The Politics of the Arab Rebellion in Palestine, 1936–39," 160–61.

131. "Precis of General Dill's dispatch No. C.R./Pal./1026/G dated 30th October, 1936," WO 32/9401.

132. GOC to the undersecretary of state (WO), 30 October 1936, WO 32/9401.

133. There was, of course, some degree of overlap between strikers and rebels from the first. Within days of organizing the national committee in Nablus on 19 April 1936, for example, Akram Zuʿaytir and two fellow committee members, Mam-

duh al-Sukhn and Wasif Kamal, began plotting violent attacks against the local government in Nablus. But, as Weldon Matthews observes, Zu'aytir and his co-conspirators made their plans "secretly and apart from the other Nablus national committee members." See: Matthews, *Confronting an Empire*, 252–53. Charles Anderson notes that national committee members in Tulkarm and Jaffa were coordinating with rural rebels as early as the second half of May, when the armed bands first appeared. See: Anderson, *From Petition to Confrontation*, 690–91. Such cases notwithstanding, in April and May 1936, the strike was thriving in a largely nonviolent capacity. It converged with the revolt only with the passage of time. And even then, as Anderson details, "some rebel fighters [came] to see the [national committees] and urban youth as cowards" who would have to be bullied into taking up arms. As late as October 1936, with the rebellion having already crested, Akram Zu'aytir was lamenting the strike's "relative disconnection from the revolt." See: Anderson, *From Petition to Confrontation*, 693, 752.

134. Charles Anderson deserves credit for expanding the causal frame, and thereby drawing British violence back into the picture. Of the four factors Anderson claims "catalyzed the strike's transformation into an armed uprising," two (and arguably three) involved British repression. The four were: Palestinians' conviction that only force would win them national independence; British security forces' "use of firearms against demonstrators"; London's refusal to suspend Jewish immigration; and the British mass incarceration of Palestinian activists such as Akram Zu'aytir. See: Anderson, *From Petition to Confrontation*, 663.

135. "Despatch by Air Vice-Marshal R. E. C. Peirse, D.S.O. A.F.C., on Disturbances in Palestine, 19th April to 14th September, 1936," WO 32/4177.

136. Kayyali, *Palestine*, 195.

137. Cohen, *Palestine: Retreat from the Mandate*, 18.

138. Arab Orthodox Priests Congress for Palestine and Transjordan to high commissioner, 18 July 1936, ISA 5076/4–12.

139. Darwaza, *Hawla al-haraka al-'arabiyya al-haditha*, 124.

140. Archdeacon in Palestine to Stanley Baldwin, 16 July 1936, Jerusalem and the East Mission papers (JEM), GB165–0161, Box 62, Files 1–2, MECA.

141. Quoted in French, *The British Way in Counter-Insurgency*, 33.

142. In a 2016 essay, Ari Kerkkanen disputes my claim (first articulated in a 2015 *Journal of Palestine Studies* article) that "British violence was a basic cause of the [1936] revolt," contending on the contrary that "while the violence was certainly one of the aggravating factors, it can hardly be defined as a basic cause of the revolt." He goes on to enumerate what he claims Wauchope correctly identified as the rebellion's causes: Arab Palestinians' thwarted desire for national independence; the Balfour Declaration; and London's neglect of "its duty to encourage local autonomy." The last two of these points were species of the first, which, as noted above, Palestinian leaders consistently raised in their meetings with British officials from May 1936 forward—alongside a second grievance, which concerned the British maltreatment of Arabs. The qualitative distinction between Palestinians' resentment of the British frustration of their national aspirations and their chafing under

British repression is flagged in the *JPS* article by the word "proximate": "The evidence suggests . . . that British repression during the 1936 revolt . . . was . . . among the proximate causes of the Arab community's ultimate resort to violence on a large scale." Proximate causes should here be contrasted with efficient causes. The most basic of the latter, as no competent analyst of the rebellion denies, was Arab Palestinians' thwarted national independence. Nevertheless, in assessing why the rebellion broke out when it did, the historian must address both proximate and efficient causes, and it is the contention of the *JPS* article (and of this book) that British violence was a basic proximate cause of the rebellion. Arab political leaders and activists contended as much at the time of the revolt's outbreak, and the evidence indicates that they were right to do so.

It must be added that this analytic distinction between proximate and efficient causes is not so clean in reality, since London's neglect of Palestinians' national aspirations depended all along upon British violence, albeit usually latent. It was therefore not so much violence as it was manifest violence that triggered the Arab revolt. In an expanded sense, then, British violence *was* among the basic efficient causes of the rebellion, for there was no thwarting Arab national aspirations without the threat of British violence. It was British officials' inability to register this very fact that blinded them to their own causal implication in the revolt. In light of that fact, it is not surprising to find that Kerkkanen's primary sources consist exclusively of British officials' correspondence. These sources include not only data, but also an implicit causal framework for construing that data. British violence lies outside that framework.

Wauchope and other officials naturally understood that Arab resentment of British policy in Palestine animated the rebellion. What they overlooked was the Arab apprehension of the British violence that underwrote that policy. What they overlooked, in other words, was the rebellion's underlying logic. See: Kerkkanen, "A Struggle Between Different Approaches," 75–77; Kelly, "The Revolt of 1936," 29, 35.

143. HC to CS, 19 December 1936, CO 733/311/1.

144. CO 733/341/20.

145. George Salah (attorney for prisoners) to HC, 21 November 1936, and chief justice to HC, 25 November 1936, ISA 275/22-ב.

146. The British brought the same self-oblivion to bear in Iraq, where they projected fictive social hierarchies onto the rural political landscape. British fetishization of the rural as uncorrupted by capitalist modernity placed it at the center of the state building project in the Iraqi mandate. Yet, the British simplification of rural Iraqi society did violence to its "complex and ambiguous social, political, religious and cultural reality," writes historian Toby Dodge, who concludes: "The clash between this sociological romance and the problems of trying to rule Iraq through its categories led the British to adopt policies that can only be described as contradictory. Ultimately this clash sabotaged any successful realization of liberal modernity for the newly constructed Iraqi state." Thus, as in Palestine, British misrule in Iraq created many of the problems with which the British had then to contend. And, as in Palestine, the British failed to apprehend this fact. See Dodge, *Inventing Iraq*, 75–81.

CHAPTER TWO

1. CZA S25/4525.

2. In fact, Zionist leaders had long promoted this claim. As Zachary Lockman details, in the early 1910s, Poale-Tsiyon leader Yitzhak Ben Zvi argued that Arab opposition to Zionism resulted not from an authentic national movement but rather from from the outside agitation of a "reactionary and anti-Semitic elite." This theme persisted into the 1920s, when David Ben Gurion promoted Zionist solidarity with the Arab working class and opposition to the elite elements trying to stir up a false national consciousness among the Arabs. See: Lockman, *Comrades and Enemies*, 51–76.

3. HC to Weizmann, 3 May 1936, CZA S25/6324.

4. JA to HC, 17 May 1936, CZA S25/6324.

5. JA to HC, 14 May 1936, CZA S25/6324.

6. JA to HC, 17 May 1936, CZA S25/6324.

7. "Short note of telephone conversation with His Excellency the High Commissioner of Palestine, Sunday, May 17th, 1936, at 5 p.m.," CZA S25/6325.

8. Shertok to Wauchope, 6 June 1936, CZA S25/6330.

9. Gelber, *Sorshe ha-Havatzelet*, 148.

10. JA to HC, 14 May 1936, CZA S25/6324.

11. "Lourie Zioniburo London," 7 June 1936, CZA S25/6326.

12. Ben Gurion to Lourie, 10 June 1936, CZA S25/6326.

13. Teveth, *Ben-Gurion and the Palestinian Arabs*, 135.

14. Ibid., 136. The quotation is from Ben Gurion.

15. Ben Gurion to Lourie, 10 June 1936, CZA S25/6326.

16. Humphrey Ernest Bowman, GB165–0034, Box 4B, MECA.

17. Ibid.

18. Ibid.

19. HC to CS, 2 June 1936, CO 733/297/2.

20. "Precautions in Palestine: convoys on the roads," *Times of London*, 24 April 1936; "Palestine Arabs' demands: continued disorders in the north," *Times of London*, 26 April 1936.

21. "Palestine Arabs' demands: continued disorders in the north," *Times of London*, 26 April 1936.

22. "Another Palestine inquiry," *Times of London*, 19 May 1936.

23. "Race-hatred in Palestine, daily outrages (Arabs and Royal Commission)," *Times of London*, 20 May 1936.

24. "New disorder in Palestine: police stoned by women; ship attacked at Jaffa; Gaza rioting," *Times of London*, 26 May 1936; "A firm hand for Palestine," *Times of London*, 26 May 1936; "A quiet day in Palestine," *Times of London*, 27 May 1936.

25. "More shooting in Palestine," *Times of London*, 30 May 1936.

26. "More troops in Palestine," *Times of London*, 3 June 1936.

27. "Peace move in Palestine: Arab conference at Amman; Cameron Highlanders in sharp fight," *Times of London*, 8 June 1936.

28. "News of the Week," *Spectator*, 29 May 1936; "The Palestine Turmoil," *Spectator*, 22 May 1936.

29. "News of the Week," *Spectator*, 29 May 1936.

30. "Strikes in Palestine," *Spectator*, 5 June 1936.

31. Letters to editor, *Spectator*, 12 June 1936.

32. Jankowski, "The Palestinian Arab Revolt," 224–25.

33. CZA S25/4510.

34. HC to CS, 2 June 1936, CO 733/297/2.

35. "Despatch by Air Vice-Marshal R. E. C. Peirse, D.S.O. A.F.C., on Disturbances in Palestine, 19th April to 14th September, 1936," WO 32/4177.

36. HC to CS, 18 June 1936, FO 371/20021.

37. Wauchope to Ben Zvi, 20 June 1936, CZA S25/6330.

38. "Weekly summary of intelligence," 17 June 1936, FO 371/20030.

39. "Periodical Appreciation Summary No. 11/36," 23 June 1936, ISA 1058/21–ר.

40. "Despatch," WO 32/4177.

41. "Weekly Summary of Intelligence, Palestine and Transjordan," 24 June 1936, FO 371/20030.

42. HC to CS, 11 July 1936, CO 733/297/4.

43. HC to CS, 12 July 1936, CO 733/310/4.

44. Gelber, *Sorshe ha-Havatzelet*, 156. The Haganah (Defense) was the underground Jewish army in Palestine. Though technically illegal, the organization collaborated extensively with the British military during the revolt years.

45. ISA 3221/18– פ.

46. "Note of a conversation with Hassan Khalid Pasha Abdul-Huda: 22 August 1936," CO 733/297/4.

47. "Military Lessons of the Arab Rebellion in Palestine, 1936," General Staff, Headquarters, The British Forces, Palestine & Transjordan, February 1938, WO 191/70. See pp. 31–32.

48. Mustafa Bey al-Khalidi and 136 others to the high commissioner, 30 June 1936, FO 371/20804.

49. Daniel Sirkis to the high commissioner, 6 August 1936, FO 371/20804. The Jewish bodies endorsing the memorandum included "the Association of Sepharadi Jews, Yemenite Jews Associations, Jewish Artisans Union, Retail Merchants Union, Mizrachi Organisation, Mirahi Workers Organisation, World League of General Zionists, World Union of General Zionists, Zionist Revisionist Organisation, and representatives of Local Councils in the Tel-Aviv District."

50. Ibid. The memo also listed cases in which Arab officials (including policemen) had allegedly actively collaborated with the rebels, but these included none of the signatories to the statement.

51. "The Strike Goes On," CZA S25/4510.

52. Ormsby-Gore to Weizmann, 19 June 1936, CZA S25/6326.

53. Kabha, *The Palestinian Press*, 176.

54. Black, *Zionism and the Arabs*, 186–87.

55. The *Post*'s columns on Arab affairs frequently issued from the pen of the department's Leo Kohn. Along with Eliyahu Epstein, Kohn "exercised an incalculable influence on the formation of the dominant Zionist view on Near Eastern affairs." See: Ibid., 191.

56. "Probing the disorder," *Palestine Post*, 20 May 1936.

57. "What price resistance?" *Palestine Post*, 26 May 1936.

58. Both from the 31 May 1936 edition.

59. "The new emergency measures," *Palestine Post*, 4 June 1936.

60. Government of Palestine Office of Statistics, General Monthly Bulletin of Current Statistics of Palestine, October–November, 1936, FO 371/20036.

61. "Weekly summary of intelligence, Palestine and Transjordan," 17 June 1936, FO 371/20030.

62. "Royal Air Force Intelligence Summary, Palestine and Transjordan," 24 June 1936, FO 371/20030.

63. "Despatch by Air Vice-Marshal R. E. C. Peirse, D.S.O. A.F.C., on Disturbances in Palestine, 19th April to 14th September, 1936," WO 32/4177.

CHAPTER THREE

1. Haim, *Abandonment*, 37–38.

2. "Despatch by Air Vice-Marshal R. E. C. Peirse, D.S.O. A.F.C., on Disturbances in Palestine, 19th April to 14th September, 1936," WO 32/4177.

3. Kabha, *Thawrat 1936 al-kubra*, 63–64.

4. "Despatch by Air Vice-Marshal R. E. C. Peirse, D.S.O. A.F.C., on Disturbances in Palestine, 19th April to 14th September, 1936," WO 32/4177.

5. Swedenburg, *Memories of Revolt*, 155.

6. Testimony of Yisrael Ligal, 10 August 1936, CZA S25/4239.

7. Swedenburg, *Memories of Revolt*, 88–89; Swedenburg, "The Role of the Palestinian Peasantry in the Great Revolt (1936-1939)," 467–68, 481; Matthews, *Confronting an Empire*, 260; Cohen, *Army of Shadows*, 164.

8. Cohen, *Army of Shadows*, 99; The Palestine Police Force Annual Administrative Report, 1936, ISA.

9. HC to CS, 16 June 1936, CO 733/297/3.

10. See, for one of numerous examples, Weizmann to Wauchope, 5 May 1936, CZA S25/6324.

11. Kimmerling and Migdal, *Palestinians: The Making of a People*, 103.

12. ʿAwni ʿAbd al-Hadi to HC, 19 August 1936, ISA 5076/4-מ.

13. "From the Jewish public in Israel to the civilized world," Undated, CZA S25/4518. Although the document contains no date, its content and file placement indicate that it was produced in July 1936.

14. Yasin, *al-Thawra al-ʿArabiyya*, 30. Other sources contradict Subhi Yasin's account. The son of the rebel commander ʿAbd al-Rahim al-Hajj Muhammad told the historian Sonia Nimr that his father led the 15 April attack. Meanwhile, the son

of the rebel leader ʿArif ʿAbd al-Raziq told Nimr that *his* father led the attack. See: Nimr, *The Arab Revolt*, 80–81. Such mutually contradictory claims are typical of national mythologies, which recast chaotic but consequential events as the planned outcomes of patriotic heroes.

15. Zuʿaytir, *Yawmiyyat*, 7.

16. Yasin, *al-Thawra al-ʿArabiyya*, 31; Zuʿaytir, *Yawmiyyat*, 18–19.

17. The best examples come from two excellent researchers: Shai Lachman, "Arab Rebellion and Terrorism in Palestine 1929–39," and Yuval Arnon-Ohanna, "The Bands in the Palestinian Arab Revolt."

Lachman suggests that the rebel bands were the descendants of early 1930s "gangs" such as the Green Hand of Safed and Galilee, a group "mainly composed of rioters and wanted criminals." These groups coalesced around three geographic hubs—Jerusalem-Ramallah, Tulkarm-Qalqilya, and Haifa-Galilee—and were all "connected in one way or another with the Mufti and his camp." It was only the Haifa-Galilee group, however, led by Shaykh ʿIzz al-Din al-Qassam, that "actually resorted to violence" and "put into practice the idea of armed struggle."

Numbering "no more than 50–60 persons," al-Qassam's group clashed with British forces at Yaʿbad, near Jenin, in 1935. In the course of the battle, the shaykh was killed, and was thereby elevated to the status of a national hero. In his wake flourished "a new cult of armed bands in the Arab community," including groups led by the followers who survived him. These became known as Qassamites, and they would go on to become "one of the pillars of the revolt" of 1936–39.

But while the Qassamites would come in the latter years of the rebellion to shed "all sense of responsibility" and resort to "indiscriminate murders," Lachman's analysis does not, in the end, reveal anything like a criminal substructure of the revolt. It suggests, rather, that al-Qassam's willingness to fight the British resonated widely with a public that was increasingly dubious regarding the value of diplomacy for advancing the cause of Palestinian independence.

Like Lachman, Yuval Arnon-Ohanna regards the Green Hand and similar groups as "forerunners of [the armed band] phenomenon," and counts "seasoned rioters," "fugitives from justice," and "a notorious robber" among the founders of the first regular bands—thus advancing again the idea that armed Arab protest in 1936 and after had its origins in criminal networks. See Porath's statistics on the criminal records of the rebels below.

18. See, for example, the RAF intelligence summary of 21 August 1936 in FO 371/20030.

19. Quoted in Wagner, *British Intelligence*, 194.

20. Quotations are taken respectively from: Bowden, "The Politics of the Arab Rebellion," 151; Cohen, "Sir Arthur Wauchope," 24; Gelber, *Sorshe ha-Havatzelet*, 144. Neither does the claim that Amin al-Husayni led the rebel movement from May 1936 forward hold up. Setting aside his ultimate descent into factional gangsterism, the mufti's future course was not fixed as of April-July 1936. Whatever his later role in the revolt, he did not direct the activities of the rebels in its early months. Thus, according to intelligence gathered by the Arab Bureau of the Jewish Agency's politi-

cal department, when bedouin leaders contacted the mufti after the 19 April riots to seek his guidance, he informed them that there was "no unified plan" and that "each person was acting on his own." By August, British intelligence had concluded that the mufti was "the primary instigator ... of the strike movement" and "definitely hand-in-glove with the extremist movement." But while the mufti had begun contributing financially to the rebels in the summer of 1936, the revolt was by no means under his control. On the contrary, his and other Committee members' continued pursuit of a diplomatic solution to the crisis in Palestine won them the ire of such prominent revolutionaries as Akram Zuʻaytir. See: Gelber, *Sorshe ha-Havatzelet*, 146; Weekly Summary of Intelligence, Palestine and Transjordan, 13 August 1936, FO 371/20030; Mattar, *The Mufti of Jerusalem*, 78–79; Zuʻaytir, *Yawmiyyat*, 138–140.

21. Porath, *Riots to Rebellion*, 264.

22. Swedenburg, *Memories of Revolt*, 222 (footnote 18).

23. In a 2015 article, Alex Winder observes that while Abu Jilda "remain[ed] marginal in the Palestinian imagination through the 1980s," his "legend has enjoyed something of a rebirth in recent years." In a manner reminiscent of the recent proliferation of Che Guevara stencils across the American pop-art landscape, Abu Jilda's visage has begun cropping up in Palestinian art shows and his person has become the subject of a sort of Palestinian "fan fiction." See: Winder, "Abu Jilda, anti-imperial antihero: banditry and popular rebellion in Palestine," 317.

24. Swedenburg, *Memories of Revolt*, 95–96.

25. Courtney, *Palestine Policeman*, 75.

26. Ibid. Courtney spells the name "Abu Jildi," likely reflecting the pronunciation of "Abu Jilda" in colloquial Palestinian Arabic.

27. Ibid., 75–76, 80–81. My emphasis.

28. Abu Gharbiyya, *Fi khidamm al-nidal*, 72.

29. Imray, *Policeman in Palestine*, 71–72. One of the police officers actually survived, and it was on the basis of his testimony that Abu Jilda was implicated in the killings of the other three.

30. Ibid., 72.

31. Ibid., 74.

32. Bartels, *Policing Politics*, 97–98.

33. Tamari, "Najati Sidqi (1905–79): The Enigmatic Jerusalem Bolshevik," 92.

34. Haganah Archives (HA) 116/50.

35. Papers of G. J. Morton CPM BEM KPM, Imperial War Museum, London (IWM), PP/MCR/390.

36. CID periodical appreciation summary no. 14/36, 18 August 1936, ISA 1058/21-מ.

37. Memoir of Lieutenant Colonel A. C. Simonds, IWM 08/46/1.

38. Porath, *Riots to Rebellion*, 266.

39. HA 116/50.

40. Hussain, *Jurisprudence of Emergency*, 107, 128.

41. WO 106/5720.

42. Barker, "Policing Palestine."

43. Smith, "Communal conflict and insurrection in Palestine, 1936–48," 79.

44. Cahill, "The Image of 'Black and Tans' in late Mandate Palestine".

45. Ben Gurion, *Letters to Paula*, 99–101.

46. Lourie to Shertok, 6 July 1936, and "Note of conversations between Lord Melchett and certain persons, 7th July 1936," both in CZA S25/6329.

47. HC to CS, 2 July 1936, FO 371/20034.

48. Periodical appreciation summary No. 12/36, 12 July 1936, ISA 1058/21–מ.

49. Ibid.

50. Ibid.

51. Ibid.

52. Porath, *Riots to Rebellion*, 187.

53. ISA 3221/18–פ. There are three Palestinian villages of Jabaʿ, one near Haifa, one near Jenin, and one near Jerusalem. The hand-written document referring to the telegram does not specify from which of the three the message originated.

54. Abboushi, "The Road to Rebellion: Arab Palestine in the 1930s," 37.

55. Kayyali, *Watha'iq al-Muqawama*, 455.

56. Matthew Hughes records a case in which peasants, having been fined £P2,000, simply packed up their belongings and abandoned the village. See: Hughes, "From Law and Order to Pacification," 13.

57. Arab Women of Jaffa to HC, 8 July 1936, ISA 5076/4–מ.

58. Awni Abdul Hadi [*sic*] to HC, from detention camp at Sarafand, 12 July 1936, ISA 5076/4–מ.

59. Ibid.

60. Supreme Arab Committee to HC, 15 July 1936, ISA 5076/4–מ.

61. Arab Orthodox Priests Congress for Palestine and Transjordan, Jerusalem, 18 July 1936, ISA 5076/4–מ.

62. Government welfare inspector to chief secretary, 13 July 1936, Jerusalem and the East Mission papers, GB165–0161, Box 66, File 1, MECA.

63. "Extract from report of Interview of H.E. with Messrs. Shertok and Ben Gurion," 9 July 1936, CO 733/286/10.

64. Percy Cleaver, Jerusalem and the East Mission papers, GB165–0358, MECA.

65. Kabha, *The Palestinian Press*, 187.

66. "Jewish children stay up all night; the Arabs are not the criminals, you criminal!" 24 June 1936, *al-Difa'*.

67. ISA 3060/6–פ.

68. Ibid.

69. Sandy Sufian, "Anatomy of the 1936 Revolt," 23–25.

70. Ibid., 28.

71. From the 23 July 1936 edition of *Filastin*. Noted in Bowden, *The Breakdown of Public Security*, 148.

72. The rebels also set up courts for the purpose of trying petty and other conventional criminals, in addition to cases of treason. See: Kabha, "The Courts of the Palestinian Arab revolt, 1936–39."

73. "Firm hand in Palestine," 20 June 1936, *Times of London.*

74. "The Arab and Zionist Policy," 17 July 1936, *Spectator.*

75. "The Problem of Palestine," 30 May 1936, *The New Statesman and Nation.*

76. "The State of Palestine," 13 June 1936, *The New Statesman and Nation.*

77. "The Palestine revolt: case for impartial tribunal," 7 July 1936, *Times of London.*

78. See, for examples: "Result of drive in Palestine," 8 July 1936, *Times of London*; "More shooting in Palestine," 9 July 1936, *Times of London*; "Arab intimidation in Palestine," 14 July 1936, *Times of London*; "The Army: forces in Palestine," 20 July 1936, *Times of London.*

79. 21 July 1936, *Times of London.*

80. See N. A. Rose, *The Gentile Zionists: A Study in Anglo-Zionist Diplomacy, 1929–1939* (London: Frank Cass, 1973).

81. 3 July 1936, *The Spectator*; "A Jew Recently in Palestine," 10 July 1936, *The Spectator.*

82. 17 July 1936, *The Spectator.*

83. Ibid.

84. 31 July 1936, *The Spectator.*

85. Weekly summary of intelligence, Palestine and Transjordan, 31 July 1936, FO 371/20030.

86. CZA S25/4461.

87. Shertok to Lourie, 24 July 1936, CZA S25/6326. The original document is mistakenly dated 24 June.

88. The Council was an umbrella organization, which counted among its member groups the Zionist Women's Orgnisation in Palestine (WIZO), the Council of Jewish Working Women in Palestine, the Women's Equal Rights Association, and the Palestine Council of Hadassah. See CZA S25/6330.

89. CZA S25/4460.

90. "Does Savagery Pay?" 24 July 1936, *Palestine Post.*

91. *Sefer Toldot ha-Haganah*, Vol. 2, 650.

92. "Jewish Family in Safed Victim of Arab Attack," 14 August 1936, *Palestine Post*; "Murder of Father and His Three Children," 16 August 1936, *Davar.*

93. Shertok to Bengurion and Brodetsky, 16 August 1936, CZA S25/6326; "Murder of Father and Three of His Children," 16 August 1936, *Davar.*

94. Shertok to Lourie, 16 August 1936, CZA S25/6326; Letters to the Editor (Royal Commission on Palestine), 30 July 1936, *Times of London.*

95. CID periodical appreciation summary no. 14/36, 18 August 1936, ISA 1058/21–מ; "Martha Fink, Nehama Tsedek," 18 August 1936, *Davar.*

96. "Telegram from the High Commissioner Palestine [*sic*] to the Secretary of State for the Colonies," 18 August 1936, FO 371/20034.

97. "Statement by the National Committee at Jaffa" (18–22 August 1936) and "[S]tatement given by Asim Bey Al Said" (18 August 1936), CO 733/310/5.

98. Lourie to Shertok, 18 August 1936, CZA S25/6326.

99. Ibid.

100. Ben Gurion to Shertok, 31 August 1936, CZA S25/6326; "Interview at the Colonial Office on August 31st, 1936, at 3 p.m.," CZA S25/6329; Rose (ed.), *Baffy: The Diaries of Blanche Dugdale, 1936–1947*, 27.

101. Ben Gurion to David Lloyd George, 20 August 1936, CZA S25/6326.

102. "After the cabinet decision," Undated, CZA S25/4509.

103. Humphrey Ernest Bowman, 22 August 1936, GB165–0034, Box 4B, MECA.

104. Union of the Jewish Socialist Labour Confederation Poale-Tsiyon (united with Z. S. Federation) and of the Zionist Labour Party, 9 August 1936, CZA S25/4525.

105. Bauer, "From Cooperation to Resistance," 184.

106. Anderson, *From Petition to Confrontation*, 667.

107. "The virtue of self control—those who had it, lost it," 17 August 1936, *al-Jami'a al-Islamiyya*.

108. "An open letter from the Council of Jewish Women's Organisations in Palestine," August 1936, CZA S25/4518.

109. Jacobson,"Writing and Rewriting the Zionist National Narrative," 1–2.

110. Ibid., 5

111. Ibid.

112. Ibid., 9.

113. Ibid., 10.

114. Henrietta Szold for Council of Jewish Women's Organisations in Palestine to high commissioner, 18 August 1936, CZA S25/6330.

115. "Notes of interview granted by the High Commissioner to representatives of the Agudath Israel at Government Offices at 11.30 a.m. on the 31st August, 1936," CO 733/311/1.

116. "Martha Fink, Nehama Tsedek," 18 August 1936, *Davar*.

117. Chairman Jerusalem Jewish Medical Society to high commissioner, 19 August 1936, CZA S25/4462.

CHAPTER FOUR

1. Royal Air Force Summary, Palestine and Transjordan, 7 August 1936, FO 371/20030.

2. Ibid.

3. CID periodical appreciation summary no. 14/36, 18 August 1936, ISA 1058/21-מ.

4. CID periodical appreciation summary no. 15/36, 1 September 1936, ISA 1058/21-מ. It is noteworthy that even when the CID could explicitly exclude traditional banditry from the equation in the case of given rebels, it continued to disparage the idea that they could be patriots.

5. RAF summary, Palestine and Transjordan, 28 August 1936, FO 371/20030.

6. Headquarters, British Forces in Palestine & Transjordan, "Weekly Summary of Intelligence, Palestine and Transjordan," 11 September 1936, FO 371/20030.

7. "Palestine: Statement of Policy," 7 September 1936, CO 733/297/5.

8. HC to CS, 4 September 1936, CO 733/297/5.

9. "Military Lessons of the Arab Rebellion in Palestine, 1936," WO 191/70, pp. 28–29.

10. Cabinet meeting of 2 September 1936, CAB 56 (36).

11. Mattar, *The Mufti of Jerusalem*, 79.

12. Quoted in Kayyali, *Palestine*, 204.

13. "Military Lessons of the Arab Rebellion in Palestine, 1936," General Staff, Headquarters, The British Forces, Palestine & Trans-Jordan, February 1938, WO 191/70, pp. 114–15.

14. Hussain, *The Jurisprudence of Emergency*, 3–4.

15. Harris, *Private Lives, Public Spirit*, 209–210; Wiener, *Reconstructing the Criminal, 1830-1914*, 150–51.

16. Wiener, *Reconstructing the Criminal*, 216.

17. Harris, *Private Lives, Public Spirit*, 210.

18. Wiener, *Reconstructing the Criminal*, 30–33; Cannadine, *Ornamentalism*, 5–6.

19. Ibid., 219–220.

20. Rafter (ed.), *The Origins of Criminology*, 96, 184–85.

21. Martin, *Alter-nations*, 107–111, 126.

22. Bennet, "Legislative Responses to Terrorism: A View from Britain," 947–48; Jenkins, *Fenian Problem*, 39; Jenkins, "1867 All Over Again? Insurgency and Terrorism in a Liberal State," 88.

23. Peatling, "The Savage Wars of Peace," 163.

24. Jenkins, *Fenian Problem*, 34, 82.

25. Article 22 of the Covenant of the League of Nations, which laid out the terms of the mandate system, stated: "Certain communities formerly belonging to the Turkish empire have reached a stage of development where their existence as independent nations can be provisionally recognized subject to the rendering of administrative advice and assistance by a Mandatory until such time as they are able to stand alone." The British affirmed these terms, despite their dilatory tactics in recognizing the national independence of Arabs in either of their two mandates (Iraq and Palestine–Transjordan). By the Great Revolt's commencement in 1936, they had already granted the Arabs of Iraq national independence, and had likewise recognized the national independence of the Arabs of the Arabian Peninsula, although these had not been under mandate. But even as far back as 1921, Colonial Secretary Winston Churchill sought to mollify members of the Arab Executive in Palestine by assuring them that while the British supported a Jewish national home in Palestine, they had no intention of establishing the whole of Palestine as a Jewish national home. As he explained: "We cannot tolerate the expropriation of one set of people by another or the violent trampling down of one set of national ideals for the sake of creating another"; that is, the Arabs of Palestine had national aspirations, and the British were committed to protecting them. See: Porath, *The Emergence of the Palestine-Arab National Movement, 1918-1929, Volume 1*, 128.

26. Antony Anghie, *Imperialism, Sovereignty, and the Making of International Law*, 189–190.

27. Townshend, "The Defence of Palestine: Insurrection and Public Security, 1936–1939," 920.

28. Jenkins, *Fenian Problem*, 67.

29. Ibid., 68.

30. Mann, *Incoherent Empire*, 87–88.

31. "Extract from proceedings of Cabinet," 2 September 1936, CO 733/315/6. The high commissioner approved this recommendation. See: CS to HC, 7 September 1936, in the same file.

32. CS to HC, 4 September 1936, CO 733/315/6; Air officer commanding to Air Ministry, 3 September 1936, CO 733/315/6; Danin, *Te'udot u-demuyot mi-ginze ha-kenufyot ha-'Arviyot bi-me'ora'ot 1936–1939*, 5.

33. CID periodical appreciation summary no. 14/36, 18 August 1936, ISA 1058/21–נ.

34. "Military Lessons of the Arab Rebellion in Palestine, 1936," General Staff, Headquarters, The British Forces, Palestine & Trans-Jordan, February 1938, WO 191/70, pp. 51–52. The fact that the rebels' organizational sophistication entailed counterintelligence of the order described here was strong evidence of what the British were coming, privately, to appreciate: namely, that they faced something other than widespread "banditry" in Palestine. As Eric Hobsbawm writes, "a very high degree of information about top-level national politics . . . removes [an organization] far from the sphere in which social banditry . . . operates." See: Hobsbawm, *Bandits*, 194.

35. CID periodical appreciation summary no. 16/36, 28 September 1936, ISA 1058/21–נ.

36. Laila Parsons, "Soldiering for Arab Nationalism: Fawzi al-Qawuqji in Palestine," 39.

37. al-Qawuqji, *Filastin fi mudhakkirat al-Qawuqji*, 27.

38. Ibid., 28–29.

39. Humphrey Ernest Bowman, 13 September 1936, GB165–0034, Box 4B, MECA.

40. Testimony of John Evetts, IWM, Catalogue No. 4451.

41. Danin, *Te'udot u-demuyot*, 2.

42. "Military Lessons of the Arab Rebellion in Palestine, 1936," February 1938, WO 191/70, p. 160.

43. Headquarters, British Forces in Palestine & Transjordan, "Weekly Summary of Intelligence, Palestine and Transjordan," 4 September 1936, FO 371/20030.

44. Headquarters, British Forces in Palestine & Transjordan, "Weekly Summary of Intelligence, Palestine and Transjordan," 11 September 1936, FO 371/20030.

45. Arnon-Ohanna, "The Bands in the Palestinian Arab Revolt," 235; Gelber, *Sorshe ha-Havatzelet*, 157.

46. Danin, *Te'udot u-demuyot*, 2.

47. Arnon-Ohanna, "The Bands in the Palestinian Arab Revolt," 236; Porath, *Riots to Rebellion*, 191–92.

48. "Military Lessons of the Arab Rebellion in Palestine, 1936," February 1938, WO 191/70, pp. 159–160.

49. Bowman, 13 September 1936, MECA. Emphasis in original.

50. See: Duff, *Palestine Picture*, 205–206; Hodgkin (ed.), *Thomas Hodgkin*, 171; "Military Lessons of the Arab Rebellion in Palestine, 1936," February 1938, WO 191/70, p. 127.

51. "Memorandum by Legal Adviser to the Secretary of State for the Colonies," [i.e. Grattan-Bushe to Ormsby-Gore], 9 September 1936, CO 733/315/2. See also: Attorney general to chief secretary, 1 September 1936, CO 733/315/2.

52. See: Ormsby-Gore's handwritten note on the 5 September memo; Judvocate London to Palforce Jerusalem, Undated (responding to message of 31 August 1936); and handwritten note beginning "Mr. Williams . . .," undated. All are in CO 733/315/2.

53. "Memorandum by the Secretary of State for the Colonies," 15 September 1936, CO 733/315/2.

54. Wauchope to Parkinson, 8 September 1936, CO 733/315/2; Adam to Williams, 10 October 1936, CO 733/315/2.

55. Pirie to Williams, 12 September 1936, CO 733/315/2.

56. Somervell to Bushe, 11 September 1936, CO 733/315/2; Hussain, *Jurisprudence of Emergency*, 21, 103–104.

57. "Note of Conference at the Colonial Office on Saturday the 19th September, 1936, at 10.30 a.m.," CO 733/315/2. See also: "Note on conclusions of legal sub-committee set up by the cabinet to advise of the best methods of vesting emergency powers in the commander-in-chief in Palestine," 21 September 1936, FO 371/20026.

58. Ibid.

59. "Note on conclusions of legal sub-committee set up by the cabinet to advise of the best methods of vesting emergency powers in the commander-in-chief in Palestine," 21 September 1936, FO 371/20026.

60. Ibid. A day prior, the secretary of state for war had made the same point as Shapcott regarding the courts. He sought to ease the colonial secretary's worries over the behavior of the chief justice under conditions of martial law by reassuring him that "Lieutenant-General Dill's powers should be sufficient to enable the closing down of the Civil Courts." See: "Conclusions of a Meeting of Ministers held at No. 10, Downing Street, S.W.1., on Friday, September 18th, 1936, at 10.30 a.m.," FO 371/20025.

61. Schmitt, *Political Theology*, 15.

62. Ibid., 20–35.

63. "Conclusions of a Meeting of Ministers held at No. 10, Downing Street, S.W.1., on Friday, September 18th, 1936, at 10.30 a.m.," FO 371/20025. My emphasis.

64. For the solicitor general's remark, see: "Conclusions of a Meeting of Ministers held at No. 10, Downing Street, S.W.1., on Friday, September 18th, 1936, at 10.30 a.m.," FO 371/20025.

65. Undated, CO 733/315/2.

66. Simson, *British Rule in Palestine*, 99–100.

67. Townshend, "Martial Law: Legal and Administrative Problems of Civil Emergency in Britain and the Empire, 1800–1940," 167–95.

68. CS to HC, 3 June 1936, CO 733/297/2.

69. Fergusson, *Trumpet in the Hall*, 32. My emphasis.

70. CS to HC, 3 June 1936, CO 733/297/2.

71. Simson, *British Rule*, 248.

72. "Address by G.O.C. to 6 Squ R. A. F. Ramleh and 33 Squ Gaza," 5 November 1936, and "Letter from G.O.C. to Gen. Sir Henry Jackson," 26 February 1937, both in WO 282/1.

73. Simson, *British Rule*, 92, 98.

74. Speaking of the communist insurgency in Malaya, for example, High Commissioner Henry Gurney once stated forthrightly, "[I]n order to maintain law and order in present conditions . . . it is necessary for the government itself to break it for a time." He clarified, "[T]he police and the army are breaking the law every day." Quoted in Newsinger, "Hearts and Minds." Julie Evans offers similar evidence from the Australian case. See her "Colonialism and the Rule of Law: The Case of South Australia," 59. See also Nasser Hussain's analysis of the *Indian Minority Report* in the "Martial Law and Massacre" chapter of his *The Jurisprudence of Emergency*.

75. CID periodical appreciation summary no. 16/36, 28 September 1936, ISA 1058/21–2.

76. Arthur Ruppin, for example, recorded in his diary on 7 September, "Apparently, martial law is to be proclaimed." See his *Memoirs, Diaries, Letters*, 281.

77. "Note of Mrs. Dugdale's Interview at the Foreign Office on the 1st September 1936," CZA S25/6327.

78. "Reflections," 29 September 1936, *Palestine Post*.

79. CO 733/297/5.

80. Duff, *Palestine Picture*, 105–106.

81. Ibid., 126.

82. Ibid., 174–78.

83. Ibid., 191.

84. Ibid., 260–61.

85. Ibid., 283.

86. Danin, *Te'udot u-demuyot*, 3.

87. Kayyali, *Watha'iq al-Muqawama*, 442–43.

88. That the legal grounds of their respective challenges differed merely reflected the juridical hybridity of the time, to which the very existence of the mandates system—a perfunctory compromise between competing conceptions of national sovereignty—bore testimony. As Natasha Wheatley details, both Arab and Jewish jurisprudential arguments in the mandate period drew on an ever-shifting hierarchy of legal entitlement, which found its ground first in the mandate instrument, then in historical and religious pedigree; first in a narrow reading of the text, then in the text's spirit, which no literalistic rendering could smother. See: Wheatley, "Manda-

tory Interpretation: Legal Hermeneutics and the New International Order in Arab and Jewish Petitions to the League of Nations."

89. Hussain, *Jurisprudence of Emergency,* 109.

90. Porath, *Riots to Rebellion,* 211–12.

91. Weekly summary of intelligence, Palestine and Transjordan, 16 October 1936, FO 371/20031.

92. CS to HC, 22 September 1936, CO 733/315/2.

93. Private notes of Colonel Fredrick Kisch, 2 October 1936, CZA S25/4391.

94. "Dear Mr. Graves . . .," 12 October 1936, CZA S25/4509.

95. Headquarters, British Forces in Palestine and Transjordan, Jerusalem, Weekly Summary of Intelligence, Palestine and Transjordan, 2 October 1936, FO 371/20030.

96. Yasin, *al-Thawra al-ʿArabiyya,* 37–38.

97. "Note of an interview granted by His Excellency the High Commissioner to the Arab Supreme Committee at Government Offices at 12 noon on the 24th October, 1936," CO 733/311/1.

98. C.P. 272 (36), 22 October 1936, FO 371/20028.

99. Weekly summary of intelligence, Palestine and Transjordan, 16 October 1936, FO 371/20031.

100. HC to CS, December 1936, WO 32/4178.

101. Simonds, IWM, 08/46/1. Pictures of Qawuqji inspecting his own troops emerged shortly thereafter. See Keith-Roach, *Pasha of Jerusalem,* 187.

102. "16 Inf Bde Situation Report No. 30," 28 October 1936, WO 191/62. Emphasis in original.

103. Weekly summary of intelligence, Palestine and Transjordan, 30 October 1936, FO 371/20031.

104. "The Situation of the head of the gangs in Transjordan," 4 November 1936, *Davar.*

105. Royal Air Force summary, Palestine and Transjordan, 6 November 1936, FO 371/20031.

106. Black, *Zionism and the Arabs,* 54–55.

107. "Letter from GOC to Gen Sir Henry Jackson," 26 February 1937, WO 282/1.

108. "Special Order of the Day by Lieutenant-General J. G. Dill, C.B., C.M.G., D.S.O.," 12 October 1936, WO 191/74.

109. Porath, *Riots to Rebellion,* 215.

110. "A Skirmish in Palestine," 26 October 1936, *Times of London.*

111. "The Strong Hand in Palestine," 12 September 1936, *New Statesman and Nation.*

112. Habas, *Sefer Meʾoraʾot TRZ"V,* 312; Black, *Zionism and the Arabs,* 52–53; Waines, "Failure," 232; Hurewitz, *The Struggle for Palestine,* 70. Hurewitz also notes some of the negative economic consequences of the revolt.

113. HC to CS, 18 November 1936, CO 733/311/1.

CHAPTER FIVE

1. "Palestine situation," 1 January 1937, CAB 24/267.

2. Note of a talk with Dr. Brodetsky, 6th January, 1937," CO 733/332/11.

3. HC to CS, 24 January 1937, and 75528/55/36, Part III, Downing Street, January 1937, CO 733/315/4.

4. "The Arab case in Palestine: Auni Bey's evidence," 14 January 1937, *The Times of London.*

5. "For the Press," 9 February 1937, CO 733/311/2.

6. No. CF/72/37, 15 February 1937, CO 733/311/2; "It is reported in *Daily Herald*
. . . ." 19 February 1937, CO 733/311/2; "More shooting in Palestine," 5 February 1937, *Times of London*; "Acts of violence in Palestine," 8 February 1937, *Times of London*; "More shooting in Palestine," 16 February 1937, *Times of London*; "Another murder in Palestine," 27 February 1937, *Times of London.*

7. HC to CS, 27 March 1937, CO 733/333/2.

8. Despatch No. SECRET, Reference No. CF/67/37, 24 March 1937, CO 733/311/2.

9. Chomsky, *Middle East Illusions*, 34.

10. Teveth, *Ben-Gurion and the Palestinian Arabs*, 170.

11. Hall to Parkinson, 11 March 1937, CO 733/316/3.

12. Ibid.

13. HC to CS, 8 April 1937, CO 733/333/2.

14. "Cabinet: maintenance of order in Palestine," CP 109 (37), 2 April 1937, CO 733/333/2.

15. "The Prophet's birthday in Palestine: Arab Nationalist displays," 22 May 1937, *Times of London.* This was not the first display of popular Arab sympathy for the Nazis. As early as 21 April 1936, a man in western attire managed to spare himself a beating (or worse) at the hands of an Arab mob in Tulkarm only by shouting "Heil Hitler" and giving the Nazi salute. Scholars have recorded several such incidents from the revolt era, but they have varied widely in their estimations of the significance of these acts for determining the extent of popular Palestinian affinity with Nazism. See, for examples: Gilbert Achcar, *The Arabs and the Holocaust: The Arab-Israeli War of Narratives*; Fredrik Meiton, "Anti-Semitism and Ignorance," *Dissent* (November 2010).

16. HC to CS, 27 March 1937, CO 733/333/2.

17. Lachman, "Arab Rebellion," 80. On the origins of the Qassamites, see chapter three, endnote 17.

18. Anderson, *From Petition to Confrontation*, 799.

19. Lachman, "Arab Rebellion," 80.

20. Cohen, *Army of Shadows*, 121.

21. Private letters of British constable Sydney Burr, IWM 88/8/1.

22. Ibid.

23. CO 733/328/10.

24. Shepherd, *Ploughing Sand*, 205.

25. "Jewish immigration into Palestine," 13 May 1937, *Times of London.*

26. Bauer, "From Cooperation to Resistance," 187.

27. Shepherd, *Ploughing Sand*, 202.

28. Mosley, *Gideon Goes to War*, 50.

29. The closest that the Arabs came to such institutional imbrication with the government was in their employment in government service. This was an increasingly dangerous business, however. Typical of the predicament faced by Arabs working for the British was the plea of Mursi ʿAli Ibrahim, who wrote Prime Minister Neville Chamberlain from Palestine in June 1937: "During the last strikes and disturbances that took place in Palestine I worked in connection with His Majesty's Forces against the wish of the Palestine Arab Public and I was the main factor in keeping Haifa port working . . . I am at present in a very bad state of poverty and unable to obtain any employment to earn my living as the Arabs will never tolerate me." Indeed, the circumstances of Arab government workers were quite often more dire than penury. On 18 May, for example, Arab assailants attempted to assassinate an Arab police sub-inspector named ʿIsa Ghurani in Jenin. See: Mursi ʿAli Ibrahim to PM Chamberlain, 2 June 1937, ISA 622/1-ב; HC to CS, 1 June 1937, ISA 622/4-ב.

30. *Palestine Royal Commission Report*, vi.

31. *Summary of the Report of the Palestine Royal Commission.*

32. Ibid.

33. Ibid.

34. Bar-Zohar, *Ben-Gurion: A Biography*, 90–91; Rose, *Gentile Zionists*, 135; Cohen, *Retreat from the Mandate*, 37.

35. Litvinoff and Klieman (eds.), *The Letters and Papers of Chaim Weizmann, Volume XVIII, Series A, January 1937–December 1938*, 125–26.

36. Ben Gurion, *Letters to Paula*, 119.

37. Rose, *Baffy*, 48–49.

38. P.T. 65/1, 7 July 1937, ISA 4159/8-ב.

39. C.P. 200 (37), 23 July 1937, FO 371/20811.

40. Numerous near-fatal attacks had been launched on members of Raghib Bey's NDP in June, as Hillel Cohen documents. Cohen concludes, "The message was clear: anyone who leaned toward compromise [vis-à-vis partition] or disputed Hajj Amin's leadership was a traitor whose life was forfeit." See: Cohen, *Army of Shadows*, 122. It is not clear, however, that the attempts on the lives of the NDP members he mentions traced back to supporters of the mufti, as opposed to mere opponents of partition, some of whom had also threatened to assassinate the mufti.

41. Kayyali, *Palestine*, 206–207.

42. Mattar, *Encyclopedia of the Palestinians*, 330–31.

43. C.P. 193 (37), 19 July 1937, FO 371/20811.

44. Headquarters, British Forces, Palestine & Transjordan, Jerusalem, 15 July 1937, WO 191/86.

45. See the two 10 July letters from Gilbert MacKereth under No. (1486/1486/2) in FO 684/10. MacKereth's boast was not idle. *Al-Qabas* and *Alif Baʾ* were the two

most influential papers in Syria, alongside a third, *al-Ayyam*, which the Syrian government had suspended for most of 1937. Email exchange with Professor Sami Moubayed, 5 July 2016.

46. CS to HC, 30 July 1937, FO 371/20811.
47. "Palestine: Royal Commission Report," 19 July 1937, FO 371/20811.
48. Wauchope to Dill, 15 July 1937, WO 191/86.
49. CS to HC, 30 July 1937, FO 371/20811.
50. HC to CS, 31 July 1937, FO 371/20811.
51. Statement of the AHC, 23 July 1937, FO 371/20810.
52. Ruppin, *Memoirs, Diaries, Letters*, 285.
53. Wauchope to Dill, 20 July, WO 191/86.
54. CS to HC, 29 June 1937, WO 191/86.
55. "Future of Palestine," 23 September 1937, *Times of London*.
56. *Palestine Royal Commission Report*, 390.
57. Statement of the AHC, 23 July 1937, FO 371/20810.
58. Litvinoff and Klieman, *Letters and Papers, Volume XVIII*, 185–87.
59. Ibid., 179–180, 206–207. As Nur Masalha points out, "... [A]lthough references to 'compulsory' transfer were studiously avoided [by the Jewish Agency leadership], statements of Ben-Gurion and Shertok showed their awareness that the Palestinian Arabs were unlikely to remove themselves to Transjordan voluntarily." See: Masalha, *Expulsion of the Palestinians*, 54.
60. Ibid., 131–36.
61. Bethell, *The Palestine Triangle*, 32.
62. Teveth, *Ben-Gurion and the Palestinian Arabs*, 188.
63. Ben-Gurion, *Letters to Paula*, 154.
64. See: "A Palestine Dispatch," 5 January 1938, and "The White Paper on Palestine," 6 January 1938, *Times of London*.
65. Morris, "Revisiting the Palestinian exodus of 1948," 48.
66. "Palestine: policy of His Majesty's Government," 14 October 1937, FO 371/20816.
67. Masalha, *Expulsion of the Palestinians*, 67–80; Bar-Zohar, *Ben-Gurion*, 92.
68. OAG to CS, 11 September 1937, and Statement of Arab Higher Committee, 31 August 1937, CO 733/341/20.
69. OAG to CS, 11 September 1937, CO 733/341/20 (emphasis in original); Mattar, *The Mufti of Jerusalem*, 82.
70. CO 733/341/20.
71. Ibid.
72. OAG to CS, 18 December 1937, and Hasan S. Dajani to OAG, 15 November 1937, CO 733/333/7.
73. "Copy of a Telegram received by the Prime Minister, London, on the 19th August, 1937, from the Arab Higher Committee," ISA 622/7–ב.
74. "Complaint about mistreatment of prisoners in ʿAka," 12 August 1937, *al-Jamiʿa al-Islamiyya*.

75. Office of Statistics, general monthly bulletin of current statistics of Palestine, September, 1937, ISA 4908/8–ב.

76. *Report to the League of Nations on Palestine and Transjordan*, 11.

77. "Extract from semi-official letter from Sir Arthur Wauchope to Sir Cosmo Parkinson, dated 2nd September, 1937," CO 733/341/20.

78. "Palestine situation," 28 October 1937, FO 371/20818.

79. From the 13, 31 and 18 August editions of *The Times of London*, respectively.

80. "Lawlessness in Palestine," 18 August, *Times of London*.

81. "Extract from S.O. letter to Sir C. Parkinson from Sir A. Wauchope, dated 25th August, 1937," CO 733/341/20.

82. "Assassination of Mr. L. Y. Andrews, District Commissioner, Galilee, and Mr. P. R. McEwan, British Constable," 9 October 1937, and OAG to CS, 14 October 1937, CO 733/332/10; Segev, *One Palestine*, 6–7. A number of sources, including early newspaper reports, mistakenly state that Andrews was killed while departing the church after the morning service. His assassins in fact intercepted him as he approached the church before the evening service, which he attended weekly.

83. "Note of Conference at the Colonial Office on the 30th September, 1937," CO 733/341/17.

84. Joseph to Weizmann, 22 September 1937, CO 733/332/11. Joseph partially reconciled these two perspectives by suggesting that downgrading Amin al-Husayni's status, while simultaneously keeping him in Palestine, would place him on the level of an "ordinary politician," to whom people would "dare to stand up."

85. CS to OAG, 29 September 1937, CO 733/332/11.

86. 'Allush, *al-Muqawama al-'arabiyya*, 124.

87. Darwaza, *Mudhakkirat Muhammad 'Izzat Darwaza*, 33.

88. Mufti to OAG, 29 September 1937, CO 733/333/7.

89. Anderson, *From Petition to Confrontation*, 851–52; Lachman, "Arab Rebellion," 81–82; Porath, *Riots to Rebellion*, 234. Porath suggests that it remains an open question whether Andrews' assassins were operating according to a decision reached by a minority faction of Syrian and Palestinian delegates to the 8 September "Arab National Conference" in Bludan, Syria, which had been organized to "mobilise Arab public opinion and organisations against partition." That decision was, in a word, to prepare for a violent struggle against the British. Porath does not suggest, however, that members of the AHC were privy to these "behind the scenes" discussions. See: Porath, *Riots to Rebellion*, 231–32. Drawing on multiple sources, Anderson characterizes the Bludan conference as a last Arab "olive branch to the British empire," to which London, in typical fashion, "made no reply." See: Anderson, *From Petition to Confrontation*, 841–42. 'Abd al-Wahhab Kayyali notes that in June 1937 the mufti traveled to Damascus, where he met with "prominent nationalist leaders" from Iraq, Lebanon, Sa'udi Arabia, and Syria to discuss his (and their) opposition to partition. While in Syria, the mufti "had more than one lengthy private meeting with Syrian and Palestinian rebel leaders such as Mohammad al-Ashmar and Shaykh 'Attiyeh

and other persons known for their gun-running activities." The mufti was, Kayyali continues, "reported to have stated on several occasions that he would 'declare war on the British on the 8th July', following the publication of the Royal Commission's report." See: Kayyali, *Palestine*, 206. But despite these militant statements, well into autumn 1937, the mufti's primary approach to resolving the crisis in Palestine remained diplomatic. As noted above, while Wauchope was eager to remove Amin al-Husayni from the Palestinian scene, he admittedly lacked "any evidence" of the mufti's involvement in violent activities. Furthermore, in a replay of April 1936, al-Husayni's moderation was such that he even opposed the Arab strikes that broke out across Palestine in response to the British outlawing of the AHC on 1 October 1937.

90. al-Hut, a*l-Qiyadat*, 375.

91. CS to OAG, 5 October 1937, FO 371/20816.

92. OAG to CS, 8 October 1937, FO 371/20816.

93. Zu'aytir, *Yawmiyyat*, 335.

94. al-Hut, a*l-Qiyadat*, 375.

95. These misconstruals of the outbreaks of the first and second phases of the Great Revolt fall prey to the post hoc fallacy, which is often summarized in the Latin phrase *post hoc ergo propter hoc* ("after this therefore because of this"). From the fact that rebellions arose after the assassinations of 15 April 1936 and 26 September 1937, it does not follow that the rebellions were caused by the assassinations.

96. Porath, *Riots to Rebellion*, 236.

97. Kabha, *The Palestinian Press*, 209.

98. Ibid., 213, 215. In 1933, the British instituted a new press ordinance that required newspapers in Palestine to immediately print any official statement they received from the government. See: Goodman, "British Press Control," 701–702.

99. "Translation of a telegram dated 2nd October, 1937, sent to King Ghazi, King Ibn Saud and King Farouk by a number of Gaza notables," FO 371/20817.

100. "Palestine situation," 28 October 1937, FO 371/20818.

101. "The Murder of Mr. Andrews," 28 September 1937, *Palestine Post*.

102. "The Terrorists in Palestine," 8 October 1937, *Spectator*.

103. Kedourie, *Islam in the Modern World*, 93.

104. Klieman, "The Divisiveness of Palestine," 425.

105. Palestine situation, 9 October 1937, FO 371/20818.

106. "Palestine: question of martial law," 20 October 1937, FO 371/20817.

107. Porath, *Riots to Rebellion*, 238–39.

108. Kabha, *The Palestinian Press*, 232.

109. "Palestine: attitude of the Colonial Office, War Office and Air Ministry," 30 October 1937, FO 371/20818.

110. "Palestine: Colonial Office, War Office and Air Ministry Attitude," 1 November 1937, FO 371/20818.

111. Ibid. He also advanced the curious view that the British government faced, in late 1937, bands of "professional murderers," who were not to be confused with the "bands of Arab nationalist rebels such as had operated in the hills under Fauzi el Kawakji" in 1936.

112. Ibid. To be clear, in stating that "the distinction between criminal and nationalist elements was a very difficult one to establish," Rendel did not mean to insinuate that criminals and nationalists were one and the same in Palestine. Rather, his comment should be taken in the context of the British crimino-national discourse elaborated in the last chapter (and again below), which attempted to dismiss as criminals the leading national figures in Palestine. This discourse accepted that Palestinian nationalism was a real phenomenon, but it rejected the idea that the AHC, the mufti, and the armed bands were its most conspicuous products. Against this prevailing view, Rendel was arguing that the "criminal" Arab leadership were, in reality, not so easy to distinguish from a genuine national leadership.

113. "Local Press Extracts. 'Al Istiqlal' of 13th October, 1937," FO 684/10.

114. "Formation of the Syro-Palestinian Executive Committee," 10 December 1937, FO 371/20823.

115. Ghandour, *A Discourse on Domination in Mandate Palestine*, 105.

116. Rendel to MacKereth, 28 October 1937, FO 684/10.

117. Ibid.

118. Barr, *A Line in the Sand*, 168–69.

119. Rendel to MacKereth, 28 October 1937, FO 684/10.

120. Sheffer, "Appeasement," 389.

121. See Kedourie's chapter "Great Britain and Palestine: The Turning Point" in his *Islam and the Modern World*.

122. "Palestine: suggested alternative policy," 3 November 1937, FO 371/20819.

123. Sheffer, "Appeasement," 389–90.

124. Cohen, *Palestine: Retreat from the Mandate*, 44.

125. Ibid., 46–48; Rose, *Gentile Zionists*, 154–55.

126. Sinanoglou, "British plans for the partition of Palestine," 151.

127. Kayyali, *Watha'iq al-Muqawama*, 400–401.

128. John Marlowe comes close to appreciating this point. He writes: "From a military point of view an evacuation of certain areas followed by systematic reconquest would have had considerable advantages. But politically it was considered undesirable. It would have identified the Palestine Arab population as a whole with the rebellion." Rather than so identifying the Arab population, the civil administration in Palestine, according to Marlowe, "tried to deal with the rebellion as if it were nothing more than an outbreak of crime on rather a large scale." So far so good, but Marlowe then proceeds to misconstrue the implications of this fact. Under the civil administration, he continues: "A man was assumed to be a good citizen unless there was reason to believe that he was a rebel. Under military administration this viewpoint underwent a change. The military assumed that every Arab was an actual or potential rebel, until he showed himself to be otherwise." This analysis reproduces the British archival depiction of the civil administration in the mandate, overlooking, inter alia, the policy of vicarious punishment officials instituted in the summer of 1937. The British move to effective martial law in late 1938 only intensified the already existing trend of willfully afflicting the innocent alongside the "guilty." The mandatory, whether under civilian or military control, did not treat the rebellion as

"an outbreak of crime" in order to refrain from employing draconian measures against the Arabs. Rather, it did so in order to deny that the British were waging war against a popular nationalist movement in Palestine. See: Marlowe, *Rebellion in Palestine*, 228.

129. Battershill to Shuckburgh, private communication, 21 November 1937, CO 733/332/12.

130. "Assassination of Mr. L. Y. Andrews, District Commissioner, Galilee, and Mr. P. R. McEwan, British Constable," 9 October 1937, CO 733/332/10.

131. See the "Rewards" section of the Tegart report in CO 733/383/1.

132. Battershill to Shuckburgh, private communication, 21 November 1937, CO 733/332/12.

133. November 1937, CAB 24/273.

134. 15 November 1937, ISA 5076/4‑מ.

135. 17 November 1937, ISA 5076/4‑מ.

136. Battershill to Shuckburgh, private communication, 21 November 1937, CO 733/332/12.

137. Hughes, "From Law and Order," 12.

138. Private letters of British constable Sydney Burr, IWM 88/8/1.

139. Ibid.

140. Ibid.

141. "Dear Lord Bishop . . .," 29 November 1937, JEM, GB165–0161, Box 65, File 5, MECA.

142. Kabha, *The Palestinian Press*, 231; Hughes, "From Law and Order," 12.

143. *Palestine and Transjordan Administration Reports 1937–1938*, 33–34.

144. Boyd, "Hebrew-language clandestine radio broadcasting during the British Palestine mandate," 104; Sabbagh, *Palestine: A Personal History*, 217–18; "Sabotage in Palestine," 4 January 1938, *Times of London*; Fergusson, *Trumpet in the Hall*, 50.

145. Harvey to Ormsby-Gore, 13 January 1938, CO 733/379/10.

146. CO 733/371/6.

147. Ormsby-Gore to Harvey, 18 January 1938, CO 733/379/10.

148. Office of Statistics, general monthly bulletin of current statistics of Palestine, March, 1938, ISA 4908/7‑מ.

149. "Extracts from Daniel Oliver's letter dated 3rd January to Walter H. Ayles - Re <u>Hanging in Palestine</u>," CO 733/379/10.

150. See Tegart's report in CO 733/383/1.

151. See the "Rural Mounted Police" section of Tegart's report in CO 733/383/1. Reading Tegart's description of "the tough type"—especially in such close proximity to his references to "gangs of banditry" and "know[ing] as much of the game as the other side"—one is reminded of Eric Hobsbawm's description of the political functions to which otherwise politically unconscious bandits are often put to use: "Bandits, except for their willingness or capacity to refuse individual submission, have no ideas other than those of the peasantry . . . of which they form a part. They are activists and not ideologists or prophets from whom novel visions or plans of social and

political organization are to be expected. They are leaders, in so far as tough and self-reliant men often with strong personalities and military talents are likely to play such a role; but even then their function is to hack out the way and not to discover it." See: Hobsbawm, *Bandits*, 29.

152. CO 733/383/1.

153. Sykes, *Orde Wingate*, 128; Testimony of John Evetts, IWM, Catalogue No. 4451.

154. Ibid., 104–125.

155. Ibid., 149.

156. Private Papers of Major General H E N Bredin CB DSO MC, IWM, 81/33/1.

157. Mosley, *Gideon Goes to War*, 58.

158. Simon Anglim makes a strong case that the Wingate of scholarship is, in many ways, a creature of fiction. Much of the writing on Wingate, for example, suggests that, compared with ordinary police and soldiers in Palestine, the captain was especially brutal. In fact, as Anglim observes, Wingate's brutality was consistent with general British practice in Palestine. See: Anglim, *Orde Wingate and the British Army*, 91–93.

159. See, for example: Newton to Pirie-Gordon, 12 March 1938, CO 733/370/8; Bishop in Jerusalem's letters to the archbishop of Canterbury, 26 February 1938, JEM, GB165–0161, Box 61, Files 1–2, MECA.

160. See, for example, the 29 March 1938 memo to John Shuckburgh in CO 733/383/3.

161. HC to CS, 11 March 1938, FO 371/21870.

162. March 1938 letter of British constable Sydney Burr, IWM 88/8/1.

163. "Report on Military Control in Palestine, 1938/39," April 1939, WO 191 /90, p. 43.

164. Margaret Travers to the colonial secretary, 16 March 1938, CO 733/370/8.

165. "NOTES: The Bishop's Visit to the Chief Secretary," 17 February 1938, JEM, GB165–0161, Box 61, File 3, MECA.

166. Barr, *A Line in the Sand*, 174.

167. Keith-Roach, *Pasha of Jerusalem*, 191.

168. Bishop in Jerusalem to chief secretary, 25 February 1938, JEM, GB165–0161, Box 61, File 3, MECA.

169. "Notes by D.W.I. on Interview with the Chief Secretary," 26 February 1938, JEM, GB165–0161, Box 61, File 3, MECA.

170. See report beginning, "The LOCALITY[:] The Village of Igzim [*sic*] on the slopes of Mount Carmel," in JEM, GB165–0161, Box 61, File 3, MECA.

171. See: "A Prisoner's Story," 18 February 1938, JEM, GB 165–0161, Box 65, File 5, MECA. For the Russian precedent of enforced prolonged standing, see: McCoy, *A Question of Torture*, 46.

172. Arab Ladies of Jerusalem to high commissioner, 5 February 1938, and C. W. Baxter to the secretary-general, League of Nations, Geneva, 28 April 1938, FO 371/21875.

173. Miller, "The other side of the coin," 203–204.

174. "Arab propaganda regarding British troops in Palestine," 23 March 1938, FO 371/21871.

CHAPTER SIX

1. Rose, *Baffy*, 90.

2. Rose, *Gentile Zionists*, 160; Litvinoff and Klieman, *Letters and Papers, Volume XVIII*, 385–86.

3. Ibid., 159.

4. Sykes, *Orde*, 149.

5. Note of J.S. Bennett, 16 December 1938, CO 733/379/3. Emphasis in original.

6. Ayles to Downie, 19 October 1938, CO 733/372/16. The British Commonwealth Peace Federation was established in 1932. Its leadership was comprised of British MPs, who "aimed to unite the empire for world peace and progress, to press commonwealth governments to initiate and pursue policies that would make for international co-operation and peace." See: Jones (ed.), *Britain and Palestine, 1914–1948*, 147.

7. "Palestine: Lebanese attitude and views of Mr. Daniel Oliver," 5 September 1938, FO 371/21880.

8. Ayles to Downie, 19 October 1938, CO 733/372/16.

9. Bowden, "Politics," 161–62.

10. HC to CS, 4 August 1938, CO 733/371/6.

11. "Memorandum regarding a gendarmerie or a semi-military force for Palestine, General Staff Force H.Q., Jerusalem, August, 1939," CO 733/371/6.

12. See Bennett's handwritten note of October–November 1938 in CO 733/371/6. Emphasis in original.

13. Ibid.

14. "Personal impressions of the night of Friday, 20th August, 1938, and the morning of Saturday, 21st August, 1938," JEM, GB165-0161, Box 61, File 3, MECA.

15. "Shot Palestine official," 26 August 1938, *Times of London*.

16. "British official shot," 25 August 1938, *Times of London*.

17. Hughes, "Assassination," 8.

18. Letter of 9 September 1938, in IWM 88/8/1. The original letter is dated 9 September 1939, but its contents make clear that this was an error.

19. Hughes, "From Law and Order," 18; Keith-Roach, *Pasha of Jerusalem*, 194–95.

20. HC to CS, 5 September 1938, CO 733/367/1.

21. Ogden to Baggallay, "Police atrocities in Palestine," 8 September 1938, FO 371/21881.

22. HC to CS, 25 May 1938, CO 733/367/1.

23. Those members of the AHC who managed to elude the British after the outlawing of the Committee in October 1937 (and thereby avoid deportation) eventually settled in Beirut and Damascus. See: Porath, *Riots to Rebellion*, 242.

24. CID periodical appreciation summary no. 3/38, 28 May 1938, CO 733/359/10; Nafi, *Arabism, Islamism and the Palestine Question*, 314 (footnote 68).

25. Nimr, *The Arab Revolt of 1936–39*, Appendices E II and G.

26. Kabha, "The Courts of the Palestinian Arab revolt," 203.

27. Porath, *Riots to Rebellion*, 243–45.

28. Cohen, *Army of Shadows*, 127.

29. Ibid., 136.

30. "Extract from D.O. No. G.S.I. 27/1 dated 25.11.38, from H.Q. British Forces in Palestine & Transjordan," CO 733/379/3.

31. "Activities in Syria of the ex-Mufti and his associates," 27 May 1938, FO 371/21877.

32. HC to CS, 12 May 1938, FO 371/21877.

33. MacKereth to Baxter, 16 May 1938, FO 371/21876. The colonial secretary had made this claim before Parliament earlier in 1938.

34. "Palestine: Syrian press attitude," 7 May 1938, FO 371/21876.

35. "Palestine: Syrian press attitude," 13 May 1938, FO 371/21876.

36. "Report of the operations carried out by the British Forces in Palestine & Trans-Jordan, period 20th May to 31st July, 1938," pp. 2–3, WO 32/9497.

37. Kabha, "The Courts of the Palestinian Arab revolt," 209.

38. Porath, *Riots to Rebellion*, 248.

39. In at least some cases, Arab rebels wore uniforms that not only resembled those of the British, but actually *were* those of the British. *The Times* reported rebels' theft of police uniforms. See: "More Shooting in Palestine," 20 December 1937, *Times of London*. The CID noted another such case. See: CID periodical appreciation summary no. 14/36, 18 August 1936, ISA 1058/21–מ.

40. Keith-Roach, *Pasha of Jerusalem*, 196.

41. HC to CS, 24 October 1938, CO 733/366/4.

42. Ghandour, *Discourse on Domination*, 101.

43. Shepherd, *Ploughing Sand*, 204.

44. "Despatch on the operations carried out by the British Forces in Palestine & Trans-Jordan, Period 1st August to 31st October, 1938," p.7, WO 32/9498. The same incident is mentioned in Ibid.

45. Francis Costello, *The Irish Revolution and its Aftermath, 1916-1923*, 186–88.

46. Ibid., 202. Kevin O'Shiel would later become the attorney general of the Irish Free State.

47. "Despatch on the operations carried out by the British Forces in Palestine & Trans-Jordan, Period 1st August to 31st October, 1938," p. 8, WO 32/9498; "Insecurity in Palestine," 26 July 1938, *Times of London*.

48. Bowden, "Politics," 156.

49. Note by secretary of state beginning "You should read No. 15 before . . . ." 28 September 1938, CO 733/371/1.

50. Bushe to Lord Dufferin, 26 July 1938, CO 733/372/1.

51. Keith-Roach, *Pasha of Jerusalem*, 196.

52. Black, *Zionism and the Arabs*, 375.

53. Litvinoff and Klieman, *Letters and Papers, Volume XVIII*, 414–15.

54. Black, *Zionism and the Arabs*, 375–76.

55. "Five murdered in Palestine," 22 July 1938, *The Manchester Guardian*; "5 dead in Jewish settlement," 22 July 1938, *The Daily Telegraph*.

56. Litvinoff and Klieman, *Letters and Papers, Volume XVIII*, 422.

57. Ibid., 425–26.

58. Sykes, *Orde Wingate*, 162–65.

59. "Sabotage in Palestine," 25 August 1938, *Times of London*.

60. Shertok to Haining, 9 September 1938, CZA S25/4951.

61. P.T. 408, 14 September 1938, ISA 4159/9–מ; HC to CS, 24 October 1938, CO 733/366/4.

62. District Commissioner's Offices, Southern District, Jaffa, 8 October 1938, "Monthly Report for the month of September, 1938," CO 733/372/18; Bowden, "Politics," 162; HC to CS, 24 October 1938, CO 733/366/4.

63. No. S/39/38, 10 October 1938, CO 733/372/18; Porath, *Riots to Rebellion*, 238.

64. HC to CS, 24 October 1938, CO 733/366/4.

65. Humphrey Ernest Bowman, 21 September 1938, GB165-0034, Box 5, MECA.

66. Shertok to Moody, 5 September 1938, CZA S25/4951.

67. Burr, 22 September 1938, IWM 88/8/1.

68. Townshend, "The First Intifada: Rebellion in Palestine 1936–39."

69. Interview with Professor Mustafa Kabha, 22 April 2012, The Open University, Raanana, Israel.

70. Horne, *A Job Well Done*, 225.

71. Swedenburg, *Memories of Revolt*, 135.

72. CZA S25/7906.

73. CZA S25/4405.

74. "Despatch on the operations carried out by the British Forces in Palestine & Trans-Jordan, Period 1st August to 31st October 1938," 30 November 1938, WO 32/9498.

75. HC to CS, 2 September 1938, FO 371/21863.

76. Ghandour, *Discourse*, 99–100.

77. "Problems of Palestine," 16 September 1938, *Times of London*.

78. Major C. F. Tod to H. F. Downie, 9 September 1938, CO 733/366/4.

79. Lachman, "Arab Rebellion," 82.

80. Marlowe, *Rebellion in Palestine*, 226.

81. Porath, *Riots to Rebellion*, 249.

82. Rose, *Baffy*, 101.

83. Litvinoff and Klieman, *Letters and Papers, Volume XVIII*, 455.

84. Black, *Zionism and the Arabs*, 388.

85. Shepherd, *Ploughing Sand*, 209–210.

86. Porath, *Riots to Rebellion*, 265–66.

87. Ibid., 249.

88. Swedenburg, *Memories of Revolt*, 116.

89. Porath, *Riots to Rebellion*, 249.

90. "Confidential: From the Headquarters of the Arab Revolution in Palestine," Undated, JEM, GB165–0161, Box 61, File 3, MECA; Nimr, *The Arab Revolt of 1936–39*, Appendix E II.

91. Hughes, "Palestinian collaboration with the British," 20.

92. Ghandour, *Discourse*, 95.

93. I have chosen to translate the Arabic *al-Lajna al-Markaziyya lil-Jihad* as "the Central War Committee" rather than the more literal "Central Committee for Jihad" because of the potentially misleading overtones that attach to the term "jihad" in contemporary political discourse. The movement for Palestinian independence in the 1930s, while certainly shot through with the religious sensibilities of its constituents, was not comparable to contemporary "jihadi" groups in any uncomplicated way. The Arabic root of the term "jihad" is *j-h-d*, which connotes "struggle." In the political context of 1930s Palestine—and given the self-conception of the rebels fighting the British, with their uniforms and systems of rank—I believe "war" is the most faithful translation of "jihad" with respect to the "committee" in question. For an analysis of the multiple connotations of "jihad" from the time of Muhammad down to the twenty-first century, see: John Esposito, *Terror in the Name of Islam*, 26–70.

94. 'Allush, *al-Muqawama al-'arabiyya*, 126; Darwaza, *Mudhakkirat Muhammad 'Izzat Darwaza*, 113–14; Porath, *Riots to Rebellion*, 243–44.

95. "Developments in the camp of the gangs," 21 September 1938, HA 281/105.

96. Porath, *Riots to Rebellion*, 245.

97. Nimr, *The Arab Revolt of 1936–39*, Appendix G.

98. Ibid., 216; Porath, *Riots to Rebellion*, 246–47.

99. Ibid., 131–32; Porath, *Riots to Rebellion*, 247.

100. Zu'aytir, *Yawmiyyat*, 452–53.

101. Porath, *Riots to Rebellion*, 245–47.

102. Anderson, *From Petition to Confrontation*, 1,032.

103. Tilly, "War Making and State Making as Organized Crime," 174.

104. Ghandour, *Discourse*, 98.

CHAPTER SEVEN

1. HC to CS, 24 October 1938, CO 733/366/4.

2. CZA S25/9156.

3. HC to CS, 24 October 1938, CO 733/366/4.

4. A Picture of Palestine, 5 October 1938, *Times of London*.

5. "Palestine," 8 October 1938, *New Statesman and Nation*.

6. Marlowe, *Rebellion in Palestine*, 203–205; Bethell, *Palestine Triangle*, 46–47; Norris, "Repression and Rebellion," 30.

7. Bethell, *Palestine Triangle*, 46–47; Cohen, *Palestine: Retreat from the Mandate*, 71–72.

8. H.P.305 (Cipher) 4/10, GOC to WO, undated, CO 733/372/8; "Minutes of a ministerial meeting held at the War Office at 5 P.M. on Friday, 7th October, 1938," CO 733/372/8; "Secretary of State's interview with a Deputation of the Palestine Parliamentary Committee on Tuesday, 18th October, at 4 p.m.," CO 733/366/4.

9. Situation in Palestine, 20 October 1938, FO 371/21864.

10. "MINUTES of a Meeting of Ministers held at the Treasury, S.W.1., at 10 A.M. on Thursday, 13th October, 1938," CO 733/372/8.

11. "Minutes of a ministerial meeting held at the War Office," 7 October 1938, CO 733/372/8.

12. Military Operations in Palestine, 12 October 1938, FO 371/21864.

13. "MINUTES of a Meeting of Ministers held at the Treasury, S.W.1., at 10 A.M. on Thursday, 13th October, 1938," CO 733/372/8.

14. "Minutes of a ministerial meeting held at the War Office at 5 P.M. on Friday, 7th October, 1938," CO 733/372/8.

15. "MINUTES of a Meeting of Ministers held at the Treasury, S.W.1., at 10 A.M. on Thursday, 13th October, 1938," CO 733/372/8.

16. "Military Operations in Palestine," 12 October 1938, FO 371/21864. Emphasis in original.

17. "NOTE" from Attorney General Alan Rose, 19 September 1938, CO 733/372/8.

18. HC to CS, 7 September 1938, FO 371/21881.

19. "Despatch on the operations carried out by the British Forces in Palestine & Trans-Jordan. Period 1st August to 31st October, 1938," Force H.Q. Jerusalem, 30 November 1938, WO 32/9498.

20. Yasin, *al-Thawra al-ʿArabiyya*, 187.

21. Zuʿaytir, *Yaymiyyat*, 447.

22. *Sefer Toldot ha-Haganah*, Vol. 2, 774; HC to CS, 24 October 1938, CO 733/366/4.

23. Ibid., 774–75.

24. Shepherd, *Ploughing Sand*, 210–211; Gelber, *Sorshe ha-Havatzelet*, 231–32.

25. Zuʿaytir, *Yaymiyyat*, 509.

26. Lachman, "Arab Rebellion," 83.

27. See, for examples: "Tiberias Lessons," 7 October 1938, *Palestine Review*, in JEM, GB165–0161, Box 61, File 4, MECA; "New Palestine Conference" and "Disorders in Palestine," 6 October 1938, *Times of London*.

28. Jewish Agency to chief secretary, 6 October 1938, CZA S25/4951.

29. Segev, *One Palestine*, 414. Segev gives the figure of eleven children killed. According to an early Jewish Agency report, the victims were ten children, six men, and three women. See: Jewish Agency to chief secretary, 6 October 1938, CZA S25/4951.

30. "Extract from House of Commons Debates," 24 November 1938, pp. 1992–1993, FO 371/21871.

31. Sheffer, "Appeasement," 391.

32. "4th Meeting: Saturday, 8th October, 3 P.M.," FO 371/21864.

33. Ibid.

34. "Extract from House of Commons Debates," 24 November 1938, pp. 1992–1993, FO 371/21871.

35. "Extract from Cabinet Conclusions 57 (38) 30th November 1938," FO 371/21867.

36. A. Andrawus to HC, 26 October 1938, CO 733/371/4.

37. HC to CS, 1 December 1938, CO 733/371/4. A British court did indeed convict the four policemen involved in the murder. Three of the convictions were overturned on appeal, however, and the sentence of the fourth man was reduced.

38. "W.H.S. to J.G.M., General Situation," 12 November 1938, JEM, GB165–0161, Box 61, File 4, MECA.

39. Goodman, "British Press Control," 708, 713.

40. Zuʿaytir, *Watha'iq al-haraka*, 487. The editor yielded the high ground only a few sentences later when he extolled the "mujahideen" for attacking a Jewish bus in Acre, killing eight passengers and injuring five others. The point regarding British censorship was nevertheless valid.

41. "Despatch on the operations carried out by the British Forces in Palestine & Trans-Jordan, period 1st November, 1938 to 31st March, 1939," Force H.Q., Jerusalem, 24 April 1939, WO 32/9499; Papers of G. J. Morton CPM BEM KPM, PP/MCR/390, IWM; "My dear Bishop . . . ." 17 October 1938, JEM, GB165–0161, Box 61, File 4, MECA.

42. "Note on Operations in Palestine since 31st October, 1938," WO 106/2018A. Norris specifies, "By 1939 over 9,000 Arab detainees were being held in Palestinian prisons and detention centres, some ten times the figure of 1937." See: Norris, "Repression," 40.

43. Bowden, "Politics," 168.

44. Interview with Charles Ernest Packer, IWM 4493.

45. British Constable Sydney Burr, IWM 88/8/1.

46. "Extracts from a letter received from an English friend in Palestine dated 9.16.38," FO 371/21881.

47. Papers of G. J. Morton CPM BEM KPM, PP/MCR/290, IWM: "[4 November 1938] 1830: 1 child shot dead, 2 children, 1 man wounded by military whilst attempting to pass through cordon in darkness"; "[4 November 1938] . . . 5 p.m. to Silet el [illegible] to check village—4 children shot (one dead) by troops."

48. Numerous dismissive accounts of German news stories detailing British atrocities in Palestine appeared in the British press. Several are contained in CO 733/371/2.

49. "German critics of Britain," 21 October 1938, *Times of London*.

50. "Palestine," 3 December 1938, *New Statesman and Nation.*

51. Palestine and Syria, 14 January 1939, *New Statesman and Nation.*

52. "Don't Blame the Palestine Police, But—," 10 December 1938, *News Chronicle* (CO 733/371/2).

53. Ibid. GOC Haining made the same point in a classified report in December 1938. See: "Hostile propaganda in Palestine. Its origin and progress in 1938," 1 December 1938, pp. 9–10, FO 371/21869.

54. "Extract from District Commissioner, Southern District's Monthly Report for the month of November, 1938," CO 733/372/18.

55. "Address by the bishop and discussion at the council meeting on 6.12.38.," JEM, GB165–0161, Box 61, File 4, MECA.

56. Miller, "The other side of the coin," 198–228.

57. Dawson to Ormsby-Gore, 25 March 1938, CO 733/370/8. Newton's memoirs do indicate that she was hostile to Zionism on theological grounds, raising the suspicion among some that she was an anti-semite. Isaiah Friedman claims that Newton was spotted distributing copies of *The Protocols of the Elders of Zion* to Arab notables on one occasion. Friedman's source for the claim is p. 214 of Kisch's *Palestine Diary,* which actually paints a less sinister portrait: "At Haifa it had been arranged that Kalvarisky should fetch the guests from Miss Newton's, and when he arrived he found her in the act of showing them a copy of the *Protocols of Zion.*" It appears that Newton was seen with a single copy of the *Protocols,* not engaged in the more overtly promotional act of distributing multiple copies of the notorious forgery. See: Newton, *Fifty Years in Palestine,* 326; Friedman, *British Pan-Arab Policy, 1915–1922,* 366.

58. See: Newton's 20 March 1938 letter to Col. Newcombe, JEM, GB165-0161, Box 65, File 4, MECA; Newton to Pirie-Gordon, 12 March 1938, CO 733/370/8; the bishop's 25 February 1938 letter to the chief secretary, his letters of 6 April 1938 to Colonial Secretary Ormsby-Gore and of 26 February 1938 to the archbishop of Canterbury, and D. W. Irving's notes of the bishop's 26 February 1938 interview with the chief secretary, all in JEM, GB165-0161, Box 61, Files 1–2, MECA.

59. See: Newton's 6 March 1938 letter to the bishop; the bishop's 26 February 1938 letters to the archbishop of Canterbury; Newton's 22 February 1938 report on the village of Ikzim [*sic*]; the bishop's 18 February 1938 report to the district commissioner of Jerusalem. All are in JEM, GB165-0161, Box 61, Files 1–2, MECA.

60. See: Newton to Pirie-Gordon, 12 March 1938, CO 733/370/8; the bishop's 26 February 1938 letters to the archbishop of Canterbury, in JEM, GB165-0161, Box 61, Files 1–2, MECA.

61. D. W. Irving's notes of the bishop's 26 February 1938 interview with the chief secretary, JEM, GB165–0161, Box 61, Files 1–2, MECA.

62. Bishop in Jerusalem to chief secretary, 25 February 1938, JEM, GB165–0161, Box 61, File 3, MECA.

63. "Order under Regulation 15 of the Emergency Regulations, 1936, as amended by the Defence (Amendment) Regulations (No.19), 1938," 4 October

1938, CO 733/372/11; "NOTE. Miss F. E. Newton," 27 September 1938, CO 733/372/11.

64. Letter to bishop from representative of the archbishop of Canterbury, 3 December 1938, JEM, GB165–0161, Box 61, File 4, MECA.

65. Bishop in Jerusalem to Archdeacon Stewart, 29 November 1938, JEM, GB165–0161, Box 61, File 4, MECA.

66. Ibid.

67. Archdeacon Stewart to bishop in Jerusalem, 10 January 1939, JEM, GB165–0161, Box 62, File 1, MECA.

68. Letter to bishop from representative of the archbishop of Canterbury, 20 January 1939, JEM, GB165–0161, Box 62, File 1, MECA.

69. Dufferin to bishop, 13 January 1939, JEM, GB165–0161, Box 62, File 1, MECA.

70. "The Bishop to the Archdeacon," 12 January 1939, JEM, GB165–0161, Box 62, File 1, MECA.

71. Bishop in Jerusalem to the archbishop of Canterbury, 8 March 1939, JEM, GB165–0161, Box 62, File 1, MECA.

72. CAB 104/8; Klieman, "Divisiveness," 441; Cohen, *Palestine: Retreat from the Mandate*, 72–73.

73. Zu'aytir, *Yawmiyyat*, 515; Weizmann, *Trial and Error*, 406; Ruppin, *Memoirs*, 297; Teveth, *Ben-Gurion and the Palestinian Arabs*, 191–92; Black, *Zionism and the Arabs*, 394; Haim, *Abandonment*, 136–37.

74. "Notes for C.I.G.S.—February 1939," WO 216/111.

75. High commissioner's narrative of events for 7 February–9 March 1939, 24 March 1939, p.10, CO 733/398/2.

76. HC to CS, 7 September 1938, FO 371/21881.

77. "Notes for C.I.G.S.—February 1939," WO 216/111.

78. Bowden, "Politics," 171–72.

79. High commissioner's narrative of events for 7 February–9 March 1939, 24 March 1939, CO 733/398/2.

80. Papers of G. J. Morton CPM BEM KPM, PP/MCR/390, IWM.

81. David W. Irving to the bishop in Jerusalem, 28 February 1939, JEM, GB165–0161, Box 62, File 1, MECA.

82. British Constable Sydney Burr, IWM 88/8/1.

83. High commissioner's narrative of events for 7 February–9 March 1939, 24 March 1939, CO 733/398/2.

84. CO 733/398/2.

85. Unsigned letter from missionary beginning "My wife and I . . . ." 5 May 1939, JEM, GB165–0161, Box 62, File 1, MECA.

86. Swedenburg, *Memories of Revolt*, 107. 'Ali Husayn Baytam's list indicated that the massacre had occurred in April 1938, but his subsequent conversation with Swedenburg and Nimr made clear that the events to which he referred were those of February 1939.

87. Ibid., 109.

CHAPTER EIGHT

1. Kabha, *The Palestine Press*, 215–16.
2. Report quoted in Gelber, *Sorshe ha-Havatzelet*, 233.
3. Kabha, "The courts of the Palestinian Arab revolt," 209.
4. Cohen, *Army of Shadows*, 152–53. It was Irshid who would ultimately furnish the British with the intelligence needed to locate and kill one of the top rebel commanders, ʿAbd al-Rahim al-Hajj Muhammad, in March 1939.
5. Ibid., 153; Porath, *Riots to Rebellion*, 256.
6. Rose, *Baffy*, 119–120.
7. Black, *Zionism and the Arabs*, 391.
8. HC to CS, 20 January 1939, FO 371/23220.
9. HC to CS, 19 November 1938 and 29 November 1938, CO 733/386/22.
10. HC to CS, 23 December 1938, FO 371/23219. Matthew Hughes's account of this episode makes painfully clear the accuracy of the CID's assessment. See Hughes, "Palestinian Collaboration," 16–18.
11. "Despatch on the operations carried out by the British Forces in Palestine & Trans-Jordan, period 1st November, 1938 to 31st March, 1939," 24 April 1939, pp. 2–3, CO 733/404/2.
12. "Notes for C.I.G.S.—February 1939," WO 216/111.
13. "War on terrorists in Palestine," 23 January 1939, *Times of London*.
14. Black, *Zionism and the Arabs*, 391.
15. Ibid., 392; Rose, *Baffy*, 119.
16. Porath, *Riots to Rebellion*, 252–53.
17. Kabha, *Thawrat 1936 al-kubra*, 67.
18. Danin, *Teʿudot u-demuyot*, 3.
19. Parsons, *The Commander*, 138.
20. Hughes, "Palestinian Collaboration," 6–8.
21. Danin, *Teʿudot u-demuyot*, 90; Anderson, *From Petition to Confrontation*, 783.
22. Cohen, *Army of Shadows*, 150.
23. Quoted in Hughes, "Palestinian Collaboration," 19.
24. Kabha and Serhan, *Sijill al-qada wa-al-thuwwar wa-al-mutatawwiʿin*, 87.
25. Gelber, *Sorshe ha-Havatzelet*, 233.
26. Yasin, *al-Thawra al-ʿArabiyya*, 212.
27. HC to CS, 12 January 1939, FO 371/23220.
28. "My dear Bill . . . ." 1 January 1939, WO 216/111.
29. GOC to WO, 8 April 1939, CO 733/404/2.
30. Morton, *Just the Job*, 95.
31. Kabha, "The courts of the Palestinian Arab revolt," 205.
32. Regarding the British assessment of ʿAbd al-Rahim al-Hajj Muhammad, see: "Hostile propaganda in Palestine," p.3, FO 371/21869; Horne, *A Job Well Done*, 224–25; Morton, *Just the Job*, 65.

33. Kabha, "The courts of the Palestinian Arab revolt," 205. Regarding the British assessment of 'Abd al-Rahim al-Hajj Muhammad, see: "Hostile propaganda in Palestine," p.3, FO 371/21869; Horne, *A Job Well Done*, 224–25.

34. See, for examples: HC to CS, summary of events for 9 November–15 December 1938, 29 December 1938, CO 733/398/2, pp. 25–26; HC to CS, summary of events for 15–29 December 1938, 16 January 1939, CO 733/398/2, p. 8; "Troops Surprise Rebel Court," 31 October 1938, *Times of London*; "Gang Leaders in Palestine," 27 March 1939, *Times of London*; HC to CS, 19 April 1939, CO 733/398/2.

35. Kabha and Serhan, *Silsilat Dirasat al-tarikh al-shafawi li-Filastin, Vol. 1*, 52.

36. Cohen, *Army of Shadows*, 152–53.

37. Porath, *Riots to Rebellion*, 247.

38. "Hostile propaganda in Palestine," p. 3, FO 371/21869; Papers of G.J. Morton CPM BEM KPM, PP/MCR/390, IWM.

39. Kabha and Serhan, *Sijill al-qada wa-al-thuwwar wa-al-mutatawwi'in*, 75.

40. Unsigned letter from missionary beginning "My wife and I . . .," 5 May 1939, JEM, GB165–0161, Box 62, File 1, MECA.

41. Zu'aytir, *Yawmiyyat*, 588.

42. Ibid., 604–605.

43. Pearlman, *Violence*, 49.

44. Norris, "Repression and Rebellion," 26–27.

45. "Despatch on the operations carried out by the British Forces in Palestine & Trans-Jordan, period 1st November, 1938 to 31st March, 1939," 24 April 1939, CO 733/404/2.

46. CS to HC, 24 February 1939, CO 733/371/6.

47. Hurewitz, *The Struggle for Palestine*, 99–100.

48. Lesch, *Arab Politics*, 125.

49. "Palestine Conferences: informal discussion with Arab and Jewish delegates," 27 February 1939, FO 371/23225.

50. Ibid.

51. Ibid.

52. Statistical Abstract of Palestine, 1939, ISA.

53. Michael Bar-Zohar (trans. Len Ortzen), *The Armed Prophet: A Biography of Ben Gurion* (London: Arthur Barker, 1967), 64; Bar-Zohar, *Ben-Gurion*, 94–96.

54. Cohen, *Palestine: Retreat from the Mandate*, 76–77.

55. Bar-Zohar, *The Armed Prophet*, 64.

56. Ibid.

57. Lesch, *Arab Politics*, 152–53.

58. "Palestine Conferences: meeting with Jewish Agency Delegation: Secretary's notes of the 4th meeting with the Jewish Agency Delegation held on 13th February," 15 March 1939, FO 371/23228.

59. High commissioner's narrative of events for 7 February–9 March 1939, 24 March 1939, p.7, CO 733/398/2.

60. Teveth, *Ben-Gurion and the Palestinian Arabs*, 193. My emphasis.

61. "Palestine Conferences . . . 13th February," 15 March 1939, FO 371/23228.

62. Rose, *Baffy*, 122–23.

63. Cohen, *Palestine: Retreat from the Mandate*, 76.

64. Rose, *Gentile Zionists*, 184.

65. Ben-Gurion, *Letters to Paula*, 229.

66. "Palestine Conferences: informal discussion with Arab and Jewish delegates," 27 February 1939, FO 371/23225.

67. Ibid.

68. Rose, *Gentile Zionists*, 183.

69. Ibid., 184, 198 (footnote 22); Haim, *Abandonment*, 138.

70. Cohen, *Palestine: Retreat from the Mandate*, 76–78.

71. Bethel, *Palestine Triangle*, 62–63.

72. Ibid., 55–56.

73. Ben Gurion, *Letters to Paula*, 236–37.

74. Bethel, *Palestine Triangle*, 67. The words quoted are Bethel's.

75. Litvinoff and Rose, *Letters and Papers, Volume XIX*, 45.

76. Ibid., 67.

77. Summary of events for 10 March–8 July 1939, 21 July 1939, p. 5, CO 733/398/3.

78. Bar-Zohar, *The Armed Prophet*, 65.

79. Ben Gurion, *Letters to Paula*, 236.

80. The Irgun had its origins in the "Haganah B," an offshoot of the original Haganah. The Haganah B was established by non-socialist Zionists who resented the ascendancy within the Haganah of Mapai and Histradrut members. Members of Betar—the party of revisionist leader Ze'ev Jabotinsky—dominated the Haganah B. But an agreement reached between the Haganah and Haganah B in 1936 alienated many Betaris, who consequently set up their own underground military organization, the Irgun. The Irgun and Betar were, nevertheless, not the same entity. The Irgun's commitment to violence and radical-right nationalism more generally was opposed by Jabotinksy, who, while fond of promoting a "psychology of shooting," nevertheless drew back from what he regarded as excessive militarism. See: Shapiro, *The Road to Power: Herut Party in Israel*, 49, 53–54.

81. "Reprisals in Palestine," 28 February 1939, *Times of London*; Haim, *Abandonment*, 145.

82. British Constable Sydney Burr, IWM 88/8/1.

83. Boyd, "Hebrew-language," 108.

84. No. 373/2/G/S, 13 June 1939, CO 733/398/3.

85. Black, *Zionism and the Arabs*, 399–400.

86. Cabinet Conclusions (Extract), No. 10 (39), 8 March 1939, FO 371/23229.

87. Summary of events for 9 November–15 December 1938, 29 December 1938, CO 733/398/2.

88. HC to CS, 2 June 1939, CO 733/398/3.

89. CZA S25/7654.

90. Executive committee of Magen David Adom to inspector general of police, 19 May 1939, CZA S25/7654.

91. "Complaint against British constables," 21 May 1939, CZA S25/7654.

92. British Constable Sydney Burr, IWM 88/8/1.

93. Montgomery to DCIGS, 6 January 1939, WO 216/111. Emphasis in original.

94. HC to CS, 8 February 1939, CO 733/371/6.

95. Professor Rushbrook Williams (Colonial Office) to Mr. Bowen, "Dissemination of authentic news regarding Palestine," 25 May 1939 and 6 June 1939, FO 395/654.

96. Ibid.

97. "Alleged atrocities of British troops in Palestine," 17 June 1939, FO 371/23237.

98. See, for example: "Despatch on the operations carried out by the British forces in Palestine & Trans-Jordan. Period 1st November, 1938 to 31st March, 1939," 24 April 1939, CO 733/404/2.

99. "Newsreel showing scenes in Palestine," 22 March 1939, FO 395/653.

100. "Palestine: German press comments," 15 June 1939, FO 371/23237.

101. HC to CS, 17 May 1939, FO 371/23237; Copy of letter to bishop from doctor (unsigned, but almost certainly Dr. Elliot Forster), 25 May 1939, JEM, GB165–0161, Box 62, File 1, MECA; May 1939 entries of the diary of Dr. Elliot Forster, JEM, GB165-0109, MECA.

102. Diary of Dr. Elliot Forster, 14 May 1939, JEM, GB165-0109, MECA.

103. See the May 1939 entries in Ibid.

104. CZA S25/9156.

105. "Palestine Arab Higher Committee's Statement in answer to the White Paper," 30 May 1939, FO 371/23237.

106. Ibid.

107. Ibid.

108. Porath, *Riots to Rebellion*, 291.

109. Ibid.

110. Ibid., 291–92; Mattar, *The Mufti of Jerusalem*, 84.

111. Cohen, *Palestine: Retreat from the Mandate*, 64.

112. HC to CS, 9 June 1939, CO 733/398/3.

113. HC to CS, 28 June 1939, CO 733/398/3.

114. HC to CS, 12 July 1939, CO 733/398/3.

115. HC to CS, 18 July 1939, CO 733/398/3.

116. Raghib Nashashibi to HC, 11 August 1939, FO 371/23240.

CONCLUSION

1. Morris, *Righteous Victims*, 342.

BIBLIOGRAPHY

ARCHIVAL SOURCES

Central Zionist Archives, Jerusalem
Haganah Archives, Tel Aviv
Imperial War Museum, London
Israel State Archives, Jerusalem
Middle East Centre, Oxford
National Archives of the United Kingdom, London

BOOKS, ARTICLES, AND UNPUBLISHED MANUSCRIPTS

Abboushi, W. F. "The Road to Rebellion: Arab Palestine in the 1930s." *Journal of Palestine Studies* 6:3 (1977): 23–46.

Abu Gharbiyya, Bahjat. *Fi khidamm al-nidal al-'arabi al-Filastini: mudhakkirat al-munadil Bahjat Abu Gharbiyya, 1916–1949.* Beirut, 1993.

'Allush, Naji. *al-Muqawama al-'arabiyya fi Filastin, 1917–1948.* Beirut, 1967.

Anderson, Benedict. *Imagined Communities.* London, 2006.

Anderson, Charles W. *From Petition to Confrontation: The Palestinian National Movement and the Rise of Mass Politics, 1929–1939.* n.p., 2013.

Anghie, Antony. *Imperialism, Sovereignty, and the Making of International Law.* New York, 2007.

Anglim, Simon. *Orde Wingate and the British Army, 1922–1944.* New York, 2010.

Arnon-Ohanna, Yuval. "The Bands in the Palestinian Arab Revolt, 1936–1939: Structure and Organization." *Asian and African Studies* 15 (1981): 229–247.

Baffy: The Diaries of Blanche Dugdale, 1936–1947, edited by N. A. Rose. London, 1973.

Bar-Zohar, Michael. *The Armed Prophet: A Biography of Ben Gurion.* Translated by Len Ortzen. London, 1967.

———. *Ben-Gurion: A Biography.* Translated by Peretz Kidron. New York, 1978.

Barker, James. "Policing Palestine." *History Today* (2008). <http://www.historytoday .com/james-barker/policing-palestine>

Barr, James. *A Line in the Sand: The Anglo-French Struggle for the Middle East, 1914–1948.* New York, 2012.

Bartels, Elizabeth. *Policing Politics: Crime and Conflict in British Mandate Palestine (1920–1948).* n.p., 2004.

Bauer, Yehuda. "From Cooperation to Resistance: The Haganah 1938–1946." *Middle Eastern Studies* 2:3 (1966): 182–210.

Beinin, Joel. *Workers and Peasants in the Modern Middle East.* New York, 2001.

Ben Gurion, David. *Letters to Paula.* London, 1971 [1968].

Bennet, Geoffrey. "Legislative Responses to Terrorism: A View from Britain." *Penn State Law Review* 109:4 (2004–2005): 947–966.

Bethell, Nicholas. *The Palestine Triangle: The struggle between the British, the Jews and the Arabs 1935–48.* London, 1979.

Biger, Gideon. *An Empire in the Holy Land: Historical Geography of the British Administration in Palestine 1917–1929.* New York, 1994.

Black, Ian. *Zionism and the Arabs, 1936–1939.* New York, 1986.

Bowden, Tom. *The Breakdown of Public Security: The Case of Ireland 1916–1921 and Palestine 1936–1939.* London, 1977.

———. "The Politics of the Arab Rebellion in Palestine, 1936–39." *Middle Eastern Studies* 11:2 (1975): 147–74.

Boyd, Douglas A. "Hebrew-language clandestine radio broadcasting during the British Palestine mandate." *Journal of Radio Studies* 6:1 (1999): 101–115.

Britain and Palestine, 1914–1948: Archival Sources for the History of the British Mandate. Edited by Philip Jones. Oxford, 1979.

Brown, Mark. "Colonial History and Theories of the Present: Some Reflections upon Penal History and Theory." In *Crime and Empire, 1840–1940: Criminal Justice in Local and Global Context,* edited by Barry Godfrey and Graeme Dunstall, 76–91. Portland, OR, 2005.

Burstein, Moshé. *Self-Government of the Jews in Palestine since 1900.* New York, 1934.

Cahill, Richard Andrew. "The Image of 'Black and Tans' in late Mandate Palestine." *Jerusalem Quarterly* (Winter 2009/10): 43–51.

———. "'Going Beserk': 'Black and Tans' in Palestine." *Jerusalem Quarterly* 38 (2009): 64.

Cannadine, David. *Ornamentalism: How the British Saw Their Empire.* Oxford, 2001.

Chatterjee, Partha. *Nationalist Thought and the Colonial World: A Derivative Discourse.* Minneapolis, MN, 1993 [1986].

Chomsky, Noam. *Middle East Illusions.* Lanham, MD, 2004.

Cohen, Hillel. *Army of Shadows: Palestinian Collaboration with Zionism, 1917–1948.* Berkeley, 2008.

Cohen, Michael J. *Palestine: Retreat from the Mandate.* London, 1978.

———. "Sir Arthur Wauchope, the Army, and the Rebellion in Palestine, 1936." *Middle Eastern Studies* 9:1 (January 1973): 19–34.

Costello, Frank. *The Irish Revolution and its Aftermath, 1916–1923: Years of Revolt.* Dublin, 2003.

Courtney, Roger. *Palestine Policeman: An Account of Eighteen Dramatic Months in the Palestine Police Force during the Great Jew-Arab Troubles.* London, 1939.

Danin, ʿEzra (with Yaʿakov Shimʿoni). *Teʿudot u-demuyot mi-ginze ha-kenufyot ha-ʿArviyot bi-meʾoraʾot 1936–1939.* Jerusalem, 1981.

Darwaza, Muhammad ʿIzzat. *Hawla al-haraka al-ʿarabiyya al-haditha: tarikh wa-mudhakkirat wa-taʿliqat, Vol. 3.* Sidon, Lebanon, 1951.

———. *Mudhakkirat Muhammad ʿIzzat Darwaza, 1305 H-1404 H/1887 M-1984 M: sijill hafil bi-masirat al-haraka al-ʿarabiyya wa-al-qadiya al-filastiniyya khilala qarn min al-zaman.* Beirut, 1993.

Dodge, Toby. *Inventing Iraq: The Failure of Nation Building and a History Denied.* New York, 2003.

Duff, Douglas Valder. *Palestine Picture.* London, 1936.

Eshed, Haggai. *Reuven Shiloah, The Man Behind the Mossad: Secret Diplomacy in the Creation of Israel.* London, 1997 [1988].

Esposito, John. *Terror in the Name of Islam.* New York, 2002.

Evans, Julie. "Colonialism and the Rule of Law: The Case of South Australia." In *Crime and Empire 1840–1940: Criminal Justice in Local and Global Context,* edited by Barry Godfrey and Graeme Dunstall, 57–75. Portland, OR, 2005.

Fergusson, Bernard. *The Trumpet in the Hall, 1930–1958.* London, 1970.

Foucault, Michel. *Discipline and Punish: The Birth of the Prison.* Translated by Alan Sheridan. New York, 1977.

———. *The History of Sexuality, Volume 1: An Introduction.* Translated by Robert Hurley. New York, 1978.

———. *Power/Knowledge: Selected interviews and other writings,* edited by Colin Gordon. New York, 1980.

French, David. *The British Way in Counter-Insurgency, 1945–1967.* Oxford, 2011.

Friedman, Isaiah. *British Pan-Arab Policy, 1915–1922: A Critical Appraisal.* London, 2010.

Gelber, Yoav. *Sorshe ha-Havatzelet: ha-Modiʿin ba-Yishuv, 1918–1947, Vol. 1.* Tel Aviv, 1992.

Gellner, Ernest. *Nations and Nationalism.* Ithaca, NY, 1983.

Ghandour, Zeina B. *A Discourse on Domination in Mandate Palestine: Imperialism, Property and Insurgency.* New York, 2010.

Goodman, Giora. "British Press Control in Palestine during the Arab Revolt, 1936–39." *The Journal of Imperial and Commonwealth History* 43:4 (2015): 699–720.

Habas, Bracha. *Sefer Meʾoraʾot TRZ"V.* Tel Aviv, 1936.

al-Hafiz, Muhammad Mutiʿ and Nizar Abaza, *Tarikh ʿulamaʾ Dimashq fi al-qarn al-rabiʿ ʿashar al-hijri.* Damascus, 1986.

Haim, Yehoyada. *Abandonment of Illusions: Zionists Political Attitudes Toward Palestinian Arab Nationalism, 1936–1939.* Boulder, CO, 1983.

Harris, Jose. *Private Lives, Public Spirit: Britain, 1870–1914.* London, 1993.

Hobsbawm, Eric. *Bandits*. New York, 2000.

Horne, Edward. *A Job Well Done (Being a history of the Palestine Police Force 1920–1948)*. Essex, UK, 1982.

Hughes, Matthew. "Assassination in Jerusalem: Bahjat Abu Gharbiyya and Sami Al Ansari's Shooting of British Assistant Superintendent Alan Sigrist 12th June 1936." *Jerusalem Quarterly* 44 (2010): 5–13.

———. "From Law and Order to Pacification: Britain's Suppression of the Arab Revolt in Palestine, 1936–39." *Journal of Palestine Studies* 39:2 (2010): 6–22.

———. "Palestinian Collaboration with the British: The Peace Bands and the Arab Revolt in Palestine, 1936–9," *Journal of Contemporary History* 0:0 (2015): 1–25.

Hurewitz, J. C. *The Struggle for Palestine*. New York, 1976.

Hussain, Nasser. *The Jurisprudence of Emergency: Colonialism and the Rule of Law*. Ann Arbor, Mich., 2003.

al-Hut, Bayan Nuwayhid. *al-Qiyadat wa-al-mu'assasat al-siyasiyyah fi Filastin, 1917–1948*. Beirut, 1981.

Imray, Colin. *Policeman in Palestine: Memories of the early years*. Devon, England, 1995.

Jacobson, David C. "Writing and Rewriting the Zionist National Narrative: Responses to the Arab Revolt of 1936–1939 in kibbutz Passover haggadot." *Journal of Modern Jewish Studies* 6:1 (2007): 1–20.

Jankowski, J. P. "The Palestinian Arab Revolt of 1936–1939." *The Muslim World* 63 (1973): 220–233.

Jeffries, Sir Charles. *The Colonial Police*. London, 1952.

Jenkins, Brian. "1867 All Over Again? Insurgency and Terrorism in a Liberal State." In *Enemies of Humanity: The Nineteenth-Century War on Terrorism*, edited by Isaac Land, 81–97. New York, 2008.

———. *Fenian Problem: Insurgency and Terrorism in an Liberal State, 1858–1874*. London, 2008.

Kabha, Mustafa. "The Courts of the Palestinian Arab revolt, 1936–39." In *Untold Histories of the Middle East: Recovering voices from the 19th and 20th centuries*, edited by Amy Singer, Christoph K. Neumann and Selçuk Akşin Somel, 197–213. London, 2011.

———. "The Palestinian Press and the General Strike, April–October 1936: *Filastin* as a Case Study." *Middle Eastern Studies* 39:1 (2003): 169–189.

———. *The Palestinian Press as Shaper of Public Opinion, 1929–1939: Writing up a Storm*. London, 2007.

———. *Thawrat 1936 al-kubra: dawafi'uha wa-in'ikasatuha*. Jerusalem, 1988.

Kabha, Mustafa and N. Serhan. *Silsilat Dirasat al-tarikh al-shafawi li-Filastin, Vol. 1: 'Abd al-Rahim al-Hajj Muhammad, al-qa'id al-'amm li-Thawrat 1936–1939*. Qastal Cultural Center, 2000.

———. *Silsilat Dirasat al-tarikh al-shafawi li-Filastin, Vol. 4: Sijill al-qada wa-al-thuwwar wa-al-mutatawwi'in li-thawrat 1936–1939*, Kafr Qara', 2009.

Kalkas, Barbara. "The Revolt of 1936: A Chronicle of Events." In *The Transformation of Palestine: Essays on the Origin and Development of the Arab-Israeli Conflict*, edited by Ibrahim Abu-Lughod, 237–274. Evanston, IL, 1971.

Kanafani, Ghassan. *The 1936–39 Revolt in Palestine.* New York, 1972.

Kayyali, 'Abd al-Wahhab. *Palestine: A Modern History.* London, 1978.

———. *Watha'iq al-muqawama al-Filastiniyya al-'Arabiyya.* Beirut, 1968.

Kedourie, Elie. *Islam in the Modern World, and other studies.* London, 1980.

Keith-Roach, Edward. *Pasha of Jerusalem.* London, 1994.

Kelly, Matthew Kraig. "The Revolt of 1936: A Revision." *Journal of Palestine Studies* 44:2 (2015): 28–42.

Kerkkanen, Ari. "A Struggle Between Different Approaches as Response to the Arab Revolt in 1936," *Instituto Universitário Militar* 4:1 (2016): 69–88.

Khalidi, Rashid. *Palestinian Identity: The Construction of Modern National Consciousness.* New York, 1997.

Kimmerling, Baruch and Joel Migdal. *Palestinians: The Making of a People.* New York, 1993.

Kirkbride, Sir Alec Seath. *A Crackle of Thorns: Experiences in the Middle East.* London, 1956.

Klieman, Aaron S. "The Divisiveness of Palestine: Foreign Office versus Colonial Office on the Issue of Partition, 1937." *The Historical Journal* 22:2 (1979): 423–441.

Kolinsky, Martin. *Law, Order and Riots in Mandatory Palestine, 1928–35.* London, 1993.

Kroizer, Gad. "From Dowbiggin to Tegart: revolutionary change in the colonial police in Palestine during the 1930s." *The Journal of Imperial and Commonwealth History* 32:2 (2004): 115–133.

Lachman, Shai. "Arab Rebellion and Terrorism in Palestine 1929–39: The Case of Sheikh 'Izz al-Din al-Qassam and his Movement." In *Zionism and Arabism in Palestine and Israel,* edited by Elie Kedourie and Sylvia G. Haim, 52–88. London, 1982.

Lesch, Ann Mosely. *Arab Politics in Palestine, 1917–1939: The Frustration of a Nationalist Movement.* Ithaca, NY, 1979.

The Letters and Papers of Chaim Weizmann, Volume XVIII, Series A, January 1937–December 1938, edited by Barnet Litvinoff and Aaron Klieman. Jerusalem, 1979.

The Letters and Papers of Chaim Weizmann, Volume XIX, Series A, January 1939–June 1940, edited by Barnet Litvinoff and Norman A. Rose. New Brunswick, NJ, 1979.

Lockman, Zachary. *Comrades and Enemies: Arab and Jewish Workers in Palestine, 1906–1948.* Berkeley, 1996.

Mann, Michael. *Incoherent Empire.* London, 2003.

———. *The Sources of Social Power Volume 1: A History of Power from the Beginning to A.D. 1760.* Cambridge, UK, 1986.

Marlowe, John. *Rebellion in Palestine.* London, 1946.

Martin, Amy E. *Alter-nations: Nationalisms, Terror, and the State in Nineteenth-Century Britain and Ireland.* Columbus, OH, 2012.

Masalha, Nur. *Expulsion of the Palestinians: The Concept of 'Transfer' in Zionist Political Thought, 1882–1948.* Washington, D.C., 1992.

Matthews, Weldon C. *Confronting an Empire, Constructing a Nation: Arab Nationalists and Popular Politics in Mandate Palestine.* London, 2006.

Mattar, Philip. *The Mufti of Jerusalem: Al-Hajj Amin al-Husayni and the Palestinian National Movement*. New York, 1988.

———. *Encyclopedia of the Palestinians*. New York, 2005.

McCoy, Alfred W. *A Question of Torture*. New York, 2006.

McNay, Lois. *Foucault: A Critical Introduction*. New York, 1994.

McTague, John J. *British Policy in Palestine, 1917–1922*. Lanham, MD: University Press of America, 1938.

Meiton, Fredrik. "Electrifying Jaffa: Boundary-Work and the Origins of the Arab-Israeli Conflict." *Past & Present* (2016): gtw002.

Miller, Rory. "The other side of the coin: Arab propaganda and the battle against Zionism in London, 1937–48." *Israel Affairs* 5:4 (1999): 198–228.

Morris, Benny. "Revisiting the Palestinian exodus of 1948." In *The War for Palestine: Rewriting the History of 1948*, edited by Eugene L. Rogan and Avi Shlaim, 37–59. Cambridge, UK, 2001.

———. *Righteous Victims: A History of the Zionist-Arab Conflict, 1881–2001*. New York, 2001.

Morton, Geoffrey J. *Just the Job: Some Experiences of a Colonial Policeman*. London, 1957.

Mosley, Leonard. *Gideon Goes to War*. London, 1955.

Nadan, Amos. *The Palestinian Peasant Economy under the Mandate: A Story of Colonial Bungling*. Cambridge, MA, 2006.

Nafi, Basheer M. *Arabism, Islamism and the Palestine Question, 1908–1941: A Political History*. Reading, UK, 1998.

Nimr, Sonia. *The Arab Revolt of 1936–39 in Palestine: A Study Based on Oral Sources*. n.p. 1990.

Newsinger, John. "Hearts and Minds: The Myth and Reality of British Counterinsurgency." *International Socialism* 148 (2015).

Newton, Frances E. *Fifty Years in Palestine*. London, 1948.

Norris, Jacob. *Land of Progress: Palestine in the Age of Colonial Development, 1905–1948*. Oxford, 2013.

———. "Repression and Rebellion: Britain's Response to the Arab Revolt in Palestine of 1936–39." In *The Journal of Imperial and Commonwealth History* 36:1 (2008): 25–45.

The Origins of Criminology: A Reader, edited by Nicole H. Rafter. New York, 2009.

Palestine Royal Commission Report (London: His Majesty's Stationary Office, 1937), <http://unispal.un.org/pdfs/Cmd5479.pdf>

Parsons, Laila. *The Commander: Fawzi al-Qawuqji and the Fight for Arab Independence, 1914–1948*. New York, 2016.

———. "Soldiering for Arab Nationalism: Fawzi al-Qawuqji in Palestine." *Journal of Palestine Studies* 36:4 (2007): 33–48.

Pearlman, Wendy. *Violence, Nonviolence, and the Palestinian National Movement*. New York, 2011.

Peatling, G. K. "The Savage Wars of Peace: Wars against Terrorism in Nineteenth-Century Ireland and India." In *Enemies of Humanity: The Nineteenth-Century War on Terrorism*, edited by Isaac Land, 159–180. New York, 2008.

Porath, Yehoshua. *The Emergence of the Palestine-Arab National Movement, 1918–1929, Volume 1*. Ann Arbor, MI, 1974.

———. *The Palestinian Arab National Movement: From Riots to Rebellion (Volume Two, 1929–1939)*. London, 1977.

al-Qawuqji, Fawzi. *Filastin fi mudhakkirat al-Qawuqji, Vol. 2*. Prepared by Khayriyya Qasimiyya. Beirut, 1975.

Rabinow, Paul. *French Modern: Norms and Forms of the Social Environment*. Chicago, 1995 [1989].

Ransom, John S. *Foucault's Discipline: The Politics of Subjectivity*. Durham, NC, 1997.

Rose, N. A. *The Gentile Zionists: A Study in Anglo-Zionist Diplomacy, 1929–1939*. London, 1973.

Ruppin, Arthur. *Memoirs, Diaries, Letters*. London, 1971.

Sabbagh, Karl. *Palestine: A Personal History*. London, 2006.

al-Sakakini, Khalil. *Kadha ana ya dunya*, edited by Hala al-Sakakini. Jerusalem, 1955.

Schmitt, Carl. *Political Theology: Four Chapters on the Concept of Sovereignty*. Chicago, 1985 [1922].

Sefer Toldot ha-Haganah, Vol. 2. World Zionist Organization, 1963.

Segev, Tom. *One Palestine, Complete: Jews and Arabs Under the British Mandate*. New York, 2000.

Shafir, Gershon. *Land, Labor and the Origins of the Israeli-Palestinian Conflict, 1882–1914*. Berkeley, 1996.

Shamir, Ronen. *The Colonies of Law: Colonialism, Zionism, and Law in Early Mandate Palestine*. Cambridge, UK, 2000.

Shapiro, Yonathan. *The Road to Power: Herut Party in Israel*. New York, 1991.

Sheffer, Gabriel. "Appeasement and the Problem of Palestine." *International Journal of Middle East Studies* 11:3 (1980): 377–399.

Shepherd, Naomi. *Ploughing Sand: British Rule in Palestine, 1917–1948*. London, 1999.

Sherman, A. J. *Mandate Days: British Lives in Palestine, 1918–1948*. London, 1997.

Simson, H. J. *British Rule in Palestine and the Arab Rebellion of 1936–1937*. Charlottesville, VA, 1977 [1938].

Sinanoglou, Penny. "British plans for the partition of Palestine." *The Historical Journal* 52:1 (2009): 131–152.

Sinclair, Georgina. "'Get into a Crack Force and earn £20 a Month and all found . . .': The Influence of the Palestine Police upon Colonial Policing, 1922–1948." *European Review of History–Revue européene d'Histoire* 13:1 (2006): 49–65.

Smith, Charles. "Communal conflict and insurrection in Palestine, 1936–48." In *Policing and decolonisation: politics, nationalism, and the police, 1917–65*, edited by David M. Anderson and David Killingray, 62–83. New York, 1992.

Sufian, Sandy. "Anatomy of the 1936 Revolt: Images of the Body in Political Cartoons of Mandatory Palestine." *Journal of Palestine Studies* 37:2 (2008): 23–42.

Summary of the Report of the Palestine Royal Commission, <http://domino.un.org/unispal.nsf/0/08e38a718201458b052565700072b358?OpenDocument>

Swedenburg, Ted. *Memories of Revolt: The 1936–1939 Rebellion and the Palestinian National Past.* Minneapolis, MN, 1995.

———. "The Role of the Palestinian Peasantry in the Great Revolt (1936–1939)." In *The Modern Middle East: A Reader,* edited by Albert Hourani, Philip S. Khoury, and Mary C. Wilson, 467–502. Berkeley, 1993.

Sykes, Christopher. *Orde Wingate: A Biography.* Cleveland, OH, 1959.

Tamari, Salim. "Najati Sidqi (1905–79): The Enigmatic Jerusalem Bolshevik." *Journal of Palestine Studies* 32:2 (2003): 79–94.

Teveth, Shabtai. *Ben-Gurion and the Palestinian Arabs: From Peace to War.* New York, 1985.

Hodgkin: Letters from Palestine 1932–36, edited by E. C. Hodgkin. London, 1986.

Thomas, Martin. *Empires of Intelligence: Security Services and Colonial Disorder after 1914.* Berkeley, 2008.

Tilly, Charles. "War Making and State Making as Organized Crime." In *Bringing the State Back In,* edited by Peter Evans, Dietrich Rueschemeyer, and Theda Skocpol, 169–187. Cambridge, UK, 1985.

Townshend, Charles. "The Defence of Palestine: Insurrection and Public Security, 1936–1939." *English Historical Review* 103 (1988): 917–949.

Townshend, Charles. "The First Intifada: Rebellion in Palestine 1936–39." *History Today* 39:7 (1989). <http://www.historytoday.com/charles-townshed/first-intifada-rebellion-palestine-1936–39>.

———. "Martial Law: Legal and Administrative Problems of Civil Emergency in Britain and the Empire, 1800–1940." *The Historical Journal* 25:1 (1982): 167–195.

Verdery, Richard N. "Arab 'Disturbances' and the Commissions of Inquiry." In *The Transformation of Palestine: Essays on the Origin and Development of the Arab-Israeli Conflict,* edited by Ibrahim Abu-Lughod, 275–303. Evanston, IL, 1971.

Wagner, Steven. *British Intelligence and Policy in the Palestine Mandate, 1919–1939.* n.p., 2014.

Waines, David. "The Failure of the Nationalist Resistance." In *The Transformation of Palestine: Essays on the Origin and Development of the Arab-Israeli Conflict,* edited by Ibrahim Abu-Lughod, 207–235. Evanston, IL, 1971.

Weizmann, Chaim. *Trial and Error.* Berlin, 1966.

Wheatley, Natasha. "Mandatory Interpretation: Legal Hermeneutics and the New International Order in Arab and Jewish Petitions to the League of Nations." *Past & Present* 227:1 (2015): 205–248.

Wiener, Martin J. *Reconstructing the Criminal: Culture, Law, and Policy in England, 1830–1914.* New York, 1994.

Williams, Raymond. *Marxism and Literature.* Oxford, 1977.

Winder, Alex. "Abu Jilda, anti-imperial antihero: banditry and popular rebellion in Palestine." In *The Routledge Handbook of the History of the Middle East Man-*

dates, edited by Cyrus Schayegh and Andrew Arsan, 308–320. London and New York, 2015.

Wuthnow, Robert. *Communities of Discourse: Ideology and Social Structure in the Reformation, the Enlightenment, and European Socialism*. Cambridge, MA, 1989.

Yasin, Subhi. *al-Thawra al-ʿArabiyya al-kubra (fi Filastin), 1936–39*. Cairo, 1959.

Zuʿaytir, Akram. *Wathaʾiq al-haraka al-wataniyya al-Filastiniyya, 1918–1939*. Beirut, 1979.

———. *Yawmiyyat Akram Zuʿaytir: al-haraka al-wataniyya al-Filastiniyya, 1935–1939*. Beirut, 1980.

INDEX

Arabic, 112, 119, 134, 150, 201, 221; newspapers in Palestine, 25, 95; sources on the revolt, 5, 27, 159
al-'Armit, Salih, 51–52
Arnon-Ohanna, Yuval, 201
archbishop of Canterbury, 151
archdeacon in Jerusalem, 26–27, 32, 151–52
Arslan, Shakib, 50
assassination(s), 47, 128, 211, 214; AHC condemnations of, 95; connections to the mufti, 71, 100, 211; of British officials, 51, 108–12, 118–19, 126, 180; of rebels, 159–60
Association of Sephardi Jews, 198
'Attiyeh, Shaykh, 213

Baggallay, Lacy, 125, 127, 143
Bal'a, 1, 3, 33, 78
Balfour Declaration, 13, 16, 19, 141, 164; Arab protests against, 14, 24, 49, 190, 195; British reversal on, 161, 181
"bandits," 45, 58, 61, 74, 84, 89, 96, 119, 121, 145–46, 169, 175; designation in British press, 39, 44, 61; designation in British intelligence, 55, 71, 77–78, 87, 115, 131, 204, 206, 216; in Palestinian folklore, 50–53
Barker, James, 53
Barukh, Naftali, 18
al-Bassa, 126–27
Battershill, William, 105, 108–109, 117–18
Bauer, Yehuda, 97
Baxter, Charles, 116, 143, 163
Baytam, 'Ali Husayn, 154, 225
BBC, 119
Beersheba, 24, 112, 133, 144, 161
Beirut, 128, 219
Ben Gurion, David, 132, 197; private view of the Arab leadership, 38, 44; relations with the British, 36, 54, 65, 99, 168–71; at the St. James Conference, 163–67; testimony before the Peel Commission, 95; thinking on "transfer" of the Arabs out of Palestine, 103
Ben Gurion, Paula, 54, 165
Benjamin, Walter, 53
Bennett, J.S., 125–26
Ben Zvi, Yitzhak, 41, 170, 197

Betar, 228
Bethlehem, 8, 133
Bevan, Aneurin, 110–11
Bird, Robert, 27, 39
bishop in Jerusalem, 26, 119, 122, 150, 153, 159
Black, Ian, 43
Black and Tans, 53–54, 120
Blumberg, William, 58–59
Bowden, Tom, 30, 131, 148
Bowman, Humphrey, 38–39, 65, 78, 133
Boyd, E.B., 65
"brigands," 39, 61, 89, 129, 131
British: brutality, 4–5, 26–29, 32, 41, 54–55, 76, 84, 97, 119, 127, 147, 152, 217; causal implication in the revolt, 6–7, 29–34, 55–56, 62, 97–98, 137–39, 160, 173, 177, 182–84, 194–96; criminalization of Palestinian nationalism, 7, 15–17, 20, 35–36, 39–40, 43–45, 50–58, 64–87, 93–95, 105–8, 110–18, 126, 144, 153, 175, 178–84, 215–16; policy in Palestine, 1–4, 14, 17, 25, 28, 30–31, 36, 41–43, 48–50, 58, 71–72, 85, 93–94, 104–23, 152, 161–62, 167–90, 196, 215; press on Palestine, 40, 58, 63, 66, 70, 74, 89, 95, 107, 111, 122, 148, 181, 223; security forces, 1, 5, 24–27, 39, 83, 97, 139, 148, 159, 175, 195
British Commonwealth Peace Federation, 125
Brodetsky, Selig, 94
Bureau of the Arab Revolt in Palestine, 138–39
Burr, Sydney, 118–119, 122, 126, 148, 153, 168, 171

Cairo, 20, 22
Central Committee of the Arab Revolt, 173
Central War Committee, 138–39, 158–59, 221
Chamberlain, Neville, 116, 142, 211
Churchill, Winston, 53–54, 65, 205
civil disobedience, 20, 24–25, 31, 36, 38, 43
Cohen, Michael J., 30, 32
collective punishment, 15, 17, 32, 105
Collective Responsibility Ordinance (1924), 17

Colonial Office, 43, 107, 118, 125, 131, 143, 172; awareness of complaints against security forces, 42, 57, 120–21, 123, 147, 152, 154; involvement in martial law controversy, 79–82; published statements of policy, 71; Middle East Department of, 113; relations with the Foreign Office, 113–14, 116; view on the Arab leadership, 94, 100,

commissions of inquiry (British), 39, 172

Council of Jewish Women's Organizations, 63, 66, 68

counterinsurgency. *See* insurgents

courts: British mandatory, 1–2, 15–59, 33–34, 42, 51, 79–81, 94, 119, 133, 136, 143, 207, 223; military, 143; rebel, 3, 53, 128–34, 136, 155, 158–61, 179, 182

Courtney, Roger, 51, 201

Cranbourne, Lord, 83

crime: Criminal Investigation Department (CID, Palestine Police), 15, 41, 52, 55, 70, 74, 77, 135, 156, 189, 219; Criminal Law (Seditious Offences) Ordinance, 20; crimino-national (discourse), 2, 4, 6–7, 14, 35, 49, 58, 60, 62, 74, 85, 117, 157, 167, 170, 173, 177–85, 215; criminology, 4, 6, 73–75, 106, 117, 182, 184; Prevention of Crime ordinance (1933), 15

Cyprus, 32, 162

Daily Mail, 61, 65

Damascus, 20, 108, 213; British consul in, 100, 115, 127–28, 157; Central War Committee headquarters in, 138, 145, 158–59

Darwaza, Muhammad ʿIzzat, 32, 108, 138, 157

Davar, 78, 88

Dayr Ghassaneh, 138–140

democracy, 164, 183

demography, 102, 153, 192

de Rothschild, James, 54

detention, 32, 48, 56, 105–6, 223

De Valera, Eamon, 146

Dicey, Albert Venn, 80

Dickens, Charles, 73

Dickson-Poynder, John Poynder (Baron Islington), 61

al-Difaʿ, 24, 27, 57

Dill, John, 71, 86–90, 100–101, 114, 121; view on the first phase of the revolt, 30–32, 40–41; view on martial law, 79–80, 82–83,

diplomacy, 55, 152, 161, 163, 201, 214; of Arab states, 65; failure of Arab Palestinian, 14, 22, 200

Dodge, Toby, 196

Dome of the Rock, 134–35

Dowbiggin, Herbert, 15

Doyle, Arthur Conan, 73

Druze, 157, 160

Duff, Douglas V., 26–28, 84

Dufferin, Lord, 131, 146, 152

Dugdale, Blanche "Baffy," 61, 83, 124, 137, 156, 164–65

eastern department (Foreign Office), 104, 113, 115, 143, 163, 187

economic: strategies in British colonial thinking, 16, 161–162; conditions in Arab and Jewish communities, 48, 89, 137, 149, 190, 209

Egypt, 143, 146, 162–63, 165; Anglo-Egyptian Treaty, 162; as revolutionary exemplar, 14, 20, 23, 189

electricity, 16, 157

elites, 4, 22, 99, 197

emergency regulations, 122, 183

enemy, 121, 189; British definition of in Palestine, 72

Epstein, Eliyahu, 119

Europe, 75–76, 115, 140; Jewish emigration from, 16, 21, 167; looming war in, 116, 142, 167, 181

exchange: of populations in Peel Report, 102–4

expatriates: British in Palestine, 119–21

expulsion, 102, 132, 176

extortion, 137

extremism, 21, 24, 50, 61, 105, 169, 201

fellahin, 57, 78, 114

Fenians, 74, 184

Filastin, 25, 57–58, 100, 110

First Rural Arab Congress, 23

First World War, 2, 18–19, 72, 128

food, 70, 149, 172; British destruction of during searches, 25, 41, 57, 123
Foot, Sir Hugh, 32
foreign fighters, 78
Force Headquarters (RAF), 15
Foreign Office, 83, 100, 125, 163; and criminological framing of the rebellion, 113, 180–81, 187; knowledge of British atrocities, 127, 172; view on martial law, 143; view on partition, 93, 114, 116
Forster, Elliot, 173
Foucault, Michel, 190–91
French: mandate for Syria, 14, 20, 35, 160, 189
French, David, 189
Friedman, Isaiah, 224

Galilee, 107, 127, 141, 152–53, 156, 180, 200; importance of in Peel Report, 101–3, 112, 124, 133
Gandhi, Mahatma, 25
"gangs," 29, 145–46, 157; designation in British intelligence, 45, 52, 70, 74, 78, 87–88, 120–21, 127–30, 144, 152–53, 158, 161, 187; designation in the British press, 39–40, 133; designation in Zionist sources, 23–24, 47, 49–50, 63, 67–68, 76, 89, 111, 135, 169, 200
Gaza, 8, 24, 28, 39, 110, 114
Gelber, Yoav, 30
Gellner, Ernest, 2
gendarmerie, 53, 218
general officer commanding (GOC). See Dill, John; Haining, Robert; Wavell, Archibald
Germany, 172
Ghandour, Zeina, 115, 138, 140
Ghazi (king of Iraq), 85, 96, 110
Ghoury, E.A., 40
Goodman, Giora, 148
Graham Brown, George Francis, 119, 150
Grattan-Bushe, H., 79–80, 131, 146
Graves, Philip, 87
Gurney, Henry, 208

Haaretz, 95
ha-Boker, 89
Hadashot Aharonot, 89

hagadot, 67
Haganah, 3, 41, 66, 78, 97, 120, 124, 168, 198, 228
Haifa, 57, 102, 118, 128, 133, 171, 173, 200, 202, 211; Anglican missionaries in, 123, 150, 153, 159, 224; British strategic calculations concerning, 162; revisionist bombing in, 132
Haim, Yehoyada, 30
Haining, Robert, 80, 114, 124–25, 133, 135, 156–61, 170–71, 174, 224
Halhoul, 172–73
Hall, John Hathorn, 18
al-Haram al-Sharif, 109
havlagah, 66–68, 89, 131
Headquarters of the Arab Revolt in Palestine, 127–28, 137
Hebrew, 29, 69, 90
Hebron, 8, 18, 88, 126, 130, 144, 156, 172–73
high commissioner. See Wauchope, Arthur and MacMichael, Harold
Histadrut (General Federation of Labor), 36, 66, 168
histories of the Great Revolt, 3–4, 50, 180
Hitler, Adolf, 96, 116, 142, 181, 210
Hobsbawm, Eric, 206, 216
Hodgkin, Thomas, 28, 112–13
Horne, Edward, 134
House of Commons, 54, 58, 61, 64, 145–47
Hughes, Matthew, 29, 126, 137, 194, 202
al-Husayni family, 22; Amin, 22, 64, 96, 99, 103, 108–10, 118, 127–29, 132, 136, 138, 157, 162, 175, 200, 214; Jamal, 138; Musa Kazim, 100
al-Husayni-al-Nashashibi rivalry, 95, 99
Hussain, Nasser, 53, 85
al-Hut, Bayan, 109

"I" section (Royal Air Force), 15
Ibn Sa'ud, 28, 85, 87
Ijzim, 123
illegality, 43, 51, 54, 101, 106, 198; (supposed) of the 1936 strike, 20, 24, 35, 44, 46, 178; (Arab claim of) regarding Jewish immigration, 23; (debate concerning) British actions in Palestine, 40, 51, 58, 84, 82, 114, 143, 167,

Namier, Lewis, 65
al-Nashashibi family, 99–100, 137, 155–57, 162, 174, 182; Raghib, 95, 99–100, 103, 118, 175; Fakhri, 156–57
National Arab Committee, 64
national committees, 76, 180, 194; British outlawing of, 38, 104, 108, 137; and rebel violence, 24, 31, 195
National Defence party, 103
National Military Organization (*ha-Irgun ha-Tsva'i ha-Le'umi*), 66, 168, 228
nationalism. *See* Arab; British; Palestinian
Nazareth, 28, 86, 107, 111–12, 132
Nazis, 21, 61, 112, 148, 210
Nebi Musa disturbances, 14
Negev, 114
New Statesman and Nation, 59, 89, 98, 112, 142, 148
newspapers: Arab, 51, 57–58, 110, 119, 126–28, 148, 154, 192, 214; British, 122, 135, 154, 172, 213; Jewish, 43, 57–58, 83
Newton, Frances, 150–55, 224
Nimr, Sonia, 139, 154, 199–200, 225
nonviolence, 13–14, 24–25, 31, 36, 39, 44. *See also* peaceful protest
Norris, Jacob, 16, 30, 160

Ogden, Frank, 127
Old City of Jerusalem, 11, 18, 27, 37, 96, 144, 173
Oliver, Daniel, 125
Orientalism, 65, 74
Ormsby-Gore, William, 43, 71, 87, 93–94, 99, 119, 124; assessment of the strike, 48; awareness of British atrocities, 28; relations with Zionist leadership, 65; testimony in Parliament, 106, 110–11, 123, 219; thinking on martial law, 81–83
Orts, Pierre, 102
Ottomans, 18, 99

Palestine: British mandate for, 14, 16, 60, 188; British strategic calculations regarding, 161–62; police, 5, 15, 29, 30–31, 51–54, 84, 120, 125, 127–28, 134, 147, 171; proposal to partition. *See* Peel Commission
Palestine Arab Party, 40

Palestine Martial Law (Defence) Order in Council, 86, 94
Palestine Post, 43, 63, 84, 111
Palestine Railway, 133
Palestine Royal Commission, 93. *See* Peel Commission
Palestinian: art, 201; nationalism, 3, 6–7, 13–17, 35–39, 50, 67, 75–76, 96, 105, 115, 133, 178;
Great Revolt, 2–4, 11–12, 109, 177, 182–83, 185; parastate, 124–40, 158; political imagination, 50–53; national memory, 50; rebels, 2–3, 75, 121, 131, 138, 179, 213; villagers, 126, 148
Pan-Arabism, 24
Pan-Islamism, 50
Parkinson, Cosmo, 99, 107
Parliament, 106, 110, 113, 123, 219; Zionist efforts to influence, 38, 54, 64, 142–43
"peace bands," 155–59, 175, 182
peaceful protest, 2, 4, 14, 21, 24–25, 44, 50, 105. *See also* nonviolence
Pearlman, Wendy, 160
peasants, 4, 17, 55, 154, 202, 216. *See also fellahin*
Peatling, G.K., 74
Peel Commission, 93–123; Arab and Jewish witnesses before, 95; Lord Peel, 84, 97 partition proposal of, 93, 97–105, 112–18, 124, 129, 142, 145–46, 211–15
Peirse, R.E.C., 4–5, 28–31, 41–42, 45, 88
Permanent Mandates Commission. *See* League of Nations
Petah Tikvah, 11–12
Petrie, David, 15
Plumer, Herbert, 17
Poale-Tsiyon, 66, 197
police posts, 77, 98, 114, 133. *See also* punitive posts
police stations, 12, 133, 144, 153
Porath, Yehoshua, 110, 114, 139, 213; and "no repression" thesis, 4, 30; on the rebel courts, 129–30; on rebel criminality, 50, 137–38, 200; on rebel uniforms, 52
press, 38, 94–95, 154–55; Arab press in Palestine, 18, 22, 24, 31, 41, 57, 110, 192; Arab press outside of Palestine, 128, 131; British, 40, 58, 63, 66, 70, 74, 89, 95,

Made in the USA
Las Vegas, NV
23 November 2021